Family or Freedom

FAMILY
OR
FREEDOM

People of Color
in the Antebellum South

Emily West

UNIVERSITY PRESS OF KENTUCKY

Scholarly publisher for the Commonwealth,
serving Bellarmine University, Berea College, Centre College of Kentucky, Eastern
Kentucky University, The Filson Historical Society, Georgetown College, Kentucky
Historical Society, Kentucky State University, Morehead State University, Murray State
University, Northern Kentucky University, Transylvania University, University of
Kentucky, University of Louisville, and Western Kentucky University.
All rights reserved.

Editorial and Sales Offices: The University Press of Kentucky
663 South Limestone Street, Lexington, Kentucky 40508–4008
www.kentuckypress.com

16 15 14 13 12   5 4 3 2 1

Library of Congress Cataloging-in-Publication Data

West, Emily, 1971-
  Family or freedom : people of color in the antebellum South / Emily West.
      p. cm. — (New directions in southern history)
  Includes bibliographical references and index.
  ISBN 978-0-8131-3692-9 (hardcover : alk. paper) —
  ISBN 978-0-8131-3693-6 (epub) — ISBN 978-0-8131-4085-8 (pdf)
  1. Free blacks—Southern States—History—19th century. 2. Free blacks—Legal
status, laws, etc.—Southern States—History—19th century. 3. Free blacks—Family
relationships—Southern States—History—19th century. 4. Slaves—Legal status, laws,
etc.—Southern States—History—19th century. 5. Slaves—Family relationships—
Southern States—History—19th century. 6. Slavery—Southern States—History—19th
century. 7. Slavery—Law and legislation—Southern States—History—19th century.
I. Title.
  E449.W512 2012
  306.3'620975—dc23   2012029590

Manufactured in the United States of America.

 Member of the Association of
                      American University Presses

For Conor and Dominic

CONTENTS

Introduction   1

1. Presumed Enslaved: Free People of Color and the Law in the Southern States   21

2. Free People of Color and Residency Requests   53

3. "Traditional" Motivations and White Perspectives on Voluntary Enslavement   75

4. Free People of Color and the Enslaved   93

5. Expulsion, Enslavement, and Ties across the Color Line   123

Conclusion   153

Acknowledgments   157

Notes   161

Bibliography   203

Index   221

INTRODUCTION

In 1859 a twenty-eight-year-old free black woman named Jane Moore requested of the Sixth District Court of New Orleans that she be enslaved. Explaining in her petition how she was emancipated in Cincinnati, Ohio, in 1855, prior to her move to New Orleans in 1856, Jane Moore did not wish to remain free:

> By virtue of an act of the legislature approved March 1859, permitting free persons of African descent to select their masters and become slaves for life, she is . . . thereof willing to select and has selected Elias Wolf as a fit and [able?] person to become her said master for life in accordance with the aforesaid act. . . . [The] petitioner shows that this application is her real and voluntary intent and purpose to become the slave of the said Elias Wolf and that she is acting according to her own dictates and in accordance of the provisions of the aforesaid act in selecting Elias Wolf as her master to possess her as his slave for life without the persuasion of any other third person. Wherefore petitioner prays for due and legal publication of this application as required by law, and that she said Elias Wolf, her decided master, be cited to appear and answer this petition and that after due and legal proceeding . . . that your petitioner be decreed a slave for life and the property of Elias Wolf for the costs of suit and all general relief.

The "real" writer of this petition (perhaps Elias Wolf himself) was obviously familiar with both the etiquette of legalistic prose and recent changes in Louisiana law that permitted "voluntary" enslavement.[1] Jane Moore's only input was to sign the document with an "X." Notice of her request was then posted outside the courthouse for the requisite thirty

1

days, after which Jane Moore became Elias Wolf's slave. Wolf was described in the 1860 census as a "clothier." A married man, he had no children and apparently no other slaves. So why might he want to possess Jane Moore as chattel? Was he intimately attached to her? Might Jane Moore have had her own reasons for seeking enslavement to Elias Wolf? Did pecuniary, rather than personal, considerations assume priority in this petition? Like many of the petitions considered here, more questions are raised than can be answered. But explanatory clues can nevertheless be found. Elias Wolf was required only to pay for the "costs of proceedings," so in acquiring an adult female under the age of thirty, he probably anticipated considerable financial gain, if not intimate liaisons, with the newly enslaved Jane Moore.[2]

The "right" of free people of color to enter bondage in the antebellum South was both extraordinary and contradictory.[3] With the free black population standing at just over a quarter of a million in 1860, surviving records indicate that fewer than two hundred of these individuals attempted to make use of the legal provisions to allow them to enter slavery. But these petitioners—when viewed in the context of moves to expel or enslave all free people of color by state legislatures in the 1850s—throw into sharp focus the desperate ways free blacks and the enslaved fought to maintain their family formations in a climate of increasing adversity. Placing their families first, enslavement petitioners offer illuminating insights into marital and other familial ties across the slave-free divide, economic conditions and the impact of legislation upon free people of color, relationships across the color line, and the broader proslavery defense in the Old South.

HISTORIOGRAPHICAL CONTEXT

This book integrates free people of color into broader historical narratives. While other historians have written about free blacks (particularly more prominent individuals and families) in considerable depth and within broad geographical contexts, little attention has been granted to their relationships with enslaved people outside the major cities of the South and particularly within their affective communities.[4] Earlier historians of antebellum free people of color have regarded enslavement petitioners as elderly and impoverished, as claimed by Ira Berlin. John Hope Franklin saw such enslavement as a last resort for desperate individuals seeking a way out of specific legal difficulties.[5] But the motivations behind enslavement (and residency) requests were more complex than Franklin and Berlin recognized. These petitions reveal the ways that free people of color prioritized their families at any cost and were bound to the enslaved through affective and community ties, and that free black women may have been exploited by white men into becoming enslaved concubines. These conclusions are at odds with some of the earlier explanations for voluntary enslavement.[6]

More recent historians have hinted at the complexity of motivations behind enslavement requests without recourse to any in-depth analysis, and most works devote no more than a few pages to issues of expulsion and enslavement.[7] Other historians have examined both phenomena within the narrower geographical context of individual states. In her book *Becoming Free, Remaining Free*, Judith Kelleher Schafer devotes considerable time and attention to several enslavement requests in New Orleans.[8] She quite rightly regards voluntary enslavement as the "culmination of the 'positive good' theory of slavery—that people of African descent lived happily as slaves and found freedom inconvenient or miserable."[9] Free blacks' requests for enslavement, Schafer argues, can also be framed in terms of individual action to maintain affective ties: "What we do know is that to some free persons of color, at least a form of slavery, if not real enslavement, proved a viable and acceptable alternative to leaving family, friends, community, and property. In these instances, free people of color used the law that allowed them to enslave themselves to resist expulsion and exile from their homes. In doing so, they made the great sacrifice of their freedom for their homes and families."[10] In a similar vein, William Link, in *Roots of Secession*, briefly describes "the strange phenomenon" of voluntary enslavement in Virginia, although, like Schafer, he is wary of offering explanatory motivations from a free black perspective. Link writes that following the passing of legislation facilitating voluntary enslavement in 1856, "unknown numbers of free blacks relinquished their freedom under the terms of this act, and their motives remain obscure. But the insecurity of freedom and the pressures of a hostile white society were crucial considerations."[11]

Unlike prior research, which explored expulsion and enslavement within the context of individual state histories, this book paints with a broader brush in considering the two phenomena across the whole of the South, with the aim of giving a sense of the direction in which legislation was traveling and also to show how free blacks responded to a changing legal climate. In her brilliant analysis of enslaved women and the law in the post-revolutionary Carolinas, Laura Edwards stresses the significance of local courts and local control within a legal framework. Enslaved women, she argues, "had a direct relationship to the state, a position that enabled them to shape the legal process, without experiencing liberation." These women "acted as if they thought they were included within the legal system."[12] And there are parallels here with free blacks' enslavement requests. Despite lacking formal legal citizenship, these people could still, somewhat paradoxically, use the law in their attempts to change their legal status and to move yet further into positions of subordination and oppression.[13] Likewise, Ariela Gross persuasively argues that legal trial narratives should be read as "performances," and this notion also has great relevance for enslavement and residency petitions. Public notions of honor and dishonor shaped the antebellum legal context, and petitioners typically sought to appeal to white lawmakers by performing to expected racial identities. The common discourses expressed within the often poignant petitions therefore reveal much about what Gross terms "the legal determination of race," "local contestation and negotiation over racial identity," and the "moral" understanding of enslavement where white slaveholders argued, as François Furstenberg has noted, that those held in bondage "deserved" it.[14]

Research by Edwards and Gross contributes to a growing body of scholarship on slavery and the law that has bridged a gap between the previously distinct fields of legal history and social history. Their research also helps fill a historical gap in the "middle grounds between black and white."[15] But the relationship between free people of color and the southern legal system has been relatively neglected. This is surprising, considering its significance. As Ira Berlin perceptively observed, the origins of post-emancipation racial institutions such as the black codes, sharecropping, and segregation can be found not in slavery but in antebellum legislation about free people of color.[16]

FREE PEOPLE OF COLOR AND THE MOTIVATIONS BEHIND ENSLAVEMENT AND RESIDENCY REQUESTS

Traditional liberal ideologies of slavery support the notion that "choosing" enslavement is and was conceptually impossible. Since slavery is a condition based upon compulsion and coercion, the very notion of "voluntary" enslavement is problematic, as it involves a contradiction in the notion of liberty. One cannot, according to this logic, "select" or "choose" enslavement. So the idea of "voluntary" slavery has tended to concern the minds of philosophers, economists, and economic historians, especially in relation to human rights, and has been rather neglected by social historians interested in the lives of enslavement petitioners themselves.[17] Perhaps because of their scarcity, too, those who "chose" bondage have received scant historiographical attention and their own perspectives have not been at the center of any discussion of "voluntary" enslavement. Yet the "choice" enslavement petitioners made should be situated within the broader context of the very limited options available to them, all of which—as will be shown—were undesirable. Racial discrimination and poverty imposed constraints on free blacks' "choices."

Social historians have been inclined to avoid "atypical" experiences precisely because the methodological nature of the discipline is concerned instead with representation and the majority. Yet, in thinking beyond this paradigm and in analyzing the discourses and performances within the petitions themselves—their stock phrases and repeated vocabularies—the more intimate experiences of free people of color and the enslaved in the late antebellum era are revealed. Moreover, the petitions also illustrate some of the ways issues of consent and enslavement were framed and debated by white southerners during a highly uncertain era.

"Voluntary" slavery existed in some ancient societies and in Africa, Asia, premodern Europe, and South America.[18] This type of bondage was often seen as a means of escaping financial difficulties, and sometimes it involved the sale of children as well as adults. So there are some parallels with the nineteenth-century petitioners in the antebellum South and across time and space: "voluntary" slavery was a "choice" only in the sense that it was a decision made by the very desperate.[19] However, the reasons antebellum free people of color sought enslavement were much more varied than has hitherto been recognized. While requesting slavery was indeed a drastic act, the petitioners were ultimately trying to raise their quality of life in personal and material senses.

Economically, petitioners sometimes envisaged enslavement as a means of improving their material quality of life. Most free blacks were poor and unskilled. How to secure subsistence was a problem, therefore, they shared with other impoverished workers across time and space.[20] Entering bondage might, for some, have offered a respite from the relentless toil of seeking and performing menial labor to support themselves and their families. And while antebellum black notions of "family" are sometimes elusive, free black petitioners placed their families first by prioritizing their ties of affection above everything else, even their liberty. For free black southerners living under racial oppression, "liberty" was a rather abstract concept anyway.

Terms such as "kinship" and "family" remain malleable, but it is clear that both held strong resonance for free people of color in terms of their notions of "home" and "belonging." Frederick Cooper, Thomas C. Holt, and Rebecca J. Scott have considered the ways the antithesis of enslavement in African societies was not "'freedom' qua autonomy but rather 'belonging,'" although they acknowledge both concepts were contested across time and space.[21] But freedom itself could be isolating for antebellum free people of color, especially when the threat of expulsion made likely familial separations across the free-slave divide. Families that crossed the line from slavery to freedom have been rather overlooked by historians, with the notable exception of John Wess Grant, who developed the concept of "stranded" families, where black households consisting of enslaved and free members in antebellum Richmond undermined the efforts of the American Colonization Society because of their strong kin ties across the slave-free divide.[22] Kinship and broader affective communities among free people of color and the enslaved ensured ties of affection— be they between husbands and wives, parents and children, siblings, or others—and were of paramount importance to enslaved and free black families, as well as to those "stranded" in between. And for enslavement petitioners families came first, above their desire for freedom.

More broadly, black southerners conceptualized bondage and freedom as opposite ends of a whole spectrum of racial exploitation rather than polar opposites per se, and this idea of a continuum, rather than polar opposites, has recently gained credence among historians, especially those interested in post-emancipation societies where, despite new citizenship, ambiguities of status remained.[23] Black conceptualizations of race were hence at odds with those constructed by antebellum white southerners following the American Revolution, for whom black people, whether slave or free, belonged to the same inferior "race." For white southerners, "race" was understood to represent biological difference, and this was utilized in their attempts to "resolve the contradiction between slavery and liberty" and to rationalize the enslavement of blacks.[24] But, as argued by François Furstenberg, so long as there existed free black southerners, the correlation "between freedom, virtue, and whiteness, on the one hand, and slavery, sin, and blackness on the other" was not exact, especially as some free blacks were deemed by whites as "worthy" of freedom.[25]

Voluntary enslavement thus grew in popularity for white southerners over the course of the nineteenth century as their concerns about the existence of free people of color in their states grew ever larger. Free people upset whites' idealized notions of "moral" slavery based on innate biological difference where all blacks were enslaved and all whites were free. Moreover, by opposing traditional liberal ideologies of enslavement, pro-slavery ideologues convinced themselves that the "selection" of bondage by black people need not be a conceptual impossibility; indeed it could instead be seen as a "moral duty" of responsible and "caring" whites. Questioning the logic that "liberty" was, by definition, a good thing for "inferior" peoples, slaveholders were able to convince themselves that the institution provided the enslaved with masters "who protected them against a much worse fate."[26] Slavery, they contended, was a "recurring and justifiable feature of well-ordered societies from ancient times to the present."[27] "If the status of slavery is right, and best for the African," proclaimed one southern ideologue, "then of course the status of the free negro is the worst; and it is the duty of those under whose care and control this class is to do [that] which is best to promote their welfare—which is, to enslave them."[28]

Enslavement and residency petitions, therefore, have to be located within the context of oppressive measures by southern states designed to push free people of color out of the South or into bondage. Those who petitioned for slavery did not necessarily believe that life in slavery would be better than freedom, but in the face of limited "choices" for those whose personal and economic relationships were under threat, enslavement might have been grudgingly accepted as the lesser of two evils. And because southern states debated and passed laws on the expulsion and enslavement of free blacks, there arose a chilling climate of fear among free people of color, a fear factor that was serious enough for some to choose to relinquish their liberty in the face of adversity.[29] Lying behind many of the enslavement and residency petitions, then, was legislative action, be it real or threatened, and this is supported by the clustering of petitions around the time of relevant legal debates. A minority of free people of color saw bondage as preferable to being driven away from their families, homes, and communities, while others appeared to have been willing to wait and see what changes time might bring, gambling that remaining still would be the right decision in the long run.[30]

But those who made the momentous decision to ask for bondage lost a lot. Free black people who became slaves could no longer testify in court or enter legal contracts. They could not own or inherit property. Children born to enslaved women were, of course, enslaved themselves and could be sold away. When accused of criminal acts, the enslaved had to stand trial in special tribunals. Slaves were forbidden from owning guns or weapons and had to have a pass to leave their place of residence. They lived under the threat of sale or mortgage.[31] These enormous liabilities had to be weighed against any perceived benefits of enslavement, be they economic or tied to the maintenance of loving personal relationships.

Legislative action and legal debate, however, do not fully explain the motivations of the free blacks who asked for residency or enslavement, some of whom were not even aware of any political discussions among white men at the upper echelons of society. Discourses within the petitions themselves instead reveal motivations for enslavement and residency operating at a more personal, individualistic, and emotional level. The petitions offer insights into the nature of often elusive kinship ties that bound free and enslaved people of color together within homes, families, and communities. They show how free blacks relied on their own initiative in appealing to the perceived benevolent worldview of slaveholders though the language employed in enslavement and residency requests. The petitions reveal that free people of color placed primary significance on survival in terms of their emotional attachments and their economic livelihoods, and that free blacks wanted to remain still rather than to be moved. Finally, enslavement and residency petitions reveal the callousness of white southerners in their attempts to trick, cajole, or otherwise persuade free people of color that bondage was better than freedom.

The petitions are also testament to the "agency" or initiative of free black men and women in the late antebellum period. I use the term with caution, mindful of Walter Johnson's call for historians to move beyond "agency" and to instead separate "activity" from "resistance." Indeed, enslavement petitioners provide a prime case in point of individuals enacting the former if not the latter.[32] In a different context—that of enslaved freedom suits—Edlie L. Wong has recently stressed the complexities behind the term "agency," arguing for a reconsideration of: "the meaning of liberal agency and the circumscribed forms of action available to slaves within the system of chattel slavery. . . . [L]egal stories offer a much more complex understanding of the countervailing forces that structured the agency and lives of those who sought from the state legal recognition of their personhood."[33]

Wong's convincing points are also applicable to the free people of color who submitted enslavement petitions. "Freedom" and "slavery" initially appear oppositional, but the practical ramifications and implications for black people living as slaves or free are actually rather similar. All blacks in the antebellum South resided under a system of race-based oppression. To change from slave to free or from free to slave required initiative and action from black people who acted individualistically or in the immediate interests of their beloved families.[34] And another parallel can be drawn between the enslavement petitioners and the actions of freedpeople in the emancipation era. Writing comparatively about post-emancipation societies, Rebecca J. Scott has emphasized: "the complexity of the former slaves' initiatives in the context of the constraints placed upon them. . . . [S]lave emancipation was neither a transcendent liberation nor a complete swindle, but rather an occasion for reshaping—within limits—social, economic, and political relationships."[35] Enslavement petitions provide an example, albeit a more marginal one, of such a reshaping as free black people used their own initiative within a broader regime of racial oppression to question their own "meanings of freedom" and its practical relevance to their everyday lives.

Of course, antebellum free people of color who considered their lives to be under threat had options other than enslavement to consider. But all tended to involve movement away from beloved homes and communities, and some free blacks merely wanted to be still. Some free people of color left the South for Canada or the northern states.[36] Others departed for Haiti and Mexico, while some partook in the colonization movement to Liberia. The experiences of the latter are considered later in relation to those who wanted to return back from Africa.[37] The minority of free people of color across the South who petitioned for residency or enslavement were those who wanted to stay somewhere rather than go somewhere.

The broad geographical context adopted here facilitates the interpretation of regional differences (where they exist), despite the obvious limitations imposed by a lack of surviving documentation. Legislative debates over expulsion and enslavement are used in conjunction with enslavement petitions and residency requests to offer broad conclusions about the changing nature of the slave regime in the 1850s, while still remaining mindful of the complexities of the petitions themselves. The historian Ruth Bogin wrote: "Petitions, although used by all levels of American society, give us the voice of people who seldom if ever pro-

claimed their social goals and political opinions in other written forms."
But in the case of mid-nineteenth-century enslavement petitions, power
relationships within a context of racial oppression mean that voluntary
slavery requests have to be read with a more cynical eye.[38] Edmund Morgan
cleverly referred to petitioning as an "act of ventriloquism," and free blacks
were very much at risk of being tricked, exploited, or cajoled into requesting enslavement by white men desirous of increasing their chattel.[39]

The histories of slavery and race relations in the antebellum South are
littered with unfortunate paradoxes. Enslaved women were "freed" from
some of the arduous burdens of domesticity and patriarchy, yet they labored on relatively equal terms with their menfolk precisely because of
the regime's oppression. Likewise, enslaved couples were able—before
many in white society—to enter wedlock for reasons of romance rather
than of the more mundane property and pragmatism, but these spousal
relationships were party to permanent destruction at the whims of slave
owners at any time. In terms of the distinction between slavery and freedom, it is also paradoxical that the actions of the enslavement petitioners
were illustrative of free black initiative in the face of limited choices.

But it remains true that these men and women displayed considerable initiative and bravery in seeking recourse to the law in an attempt
to improve their quality of life. While contemporary liberal philosophers
questioned whether people could technically actually ask for the removal
of their liberty, the paradox philosophers identified only in the abstract
manifests itself in reality through the actions of black enslavement petitioners in the antebellum southern states. Franz Kafka later picked up the
concept of voluntary slavery, writing in The Trial, "It is often better to be in
chains than to be free."[40] Indeed, there was something Kafkaesque about
the complicated bureaucracies created by southern legislatures in their
attempts to legislate on the enslavement and expulsion of free blacks.

The actions of the petitioners for enslavement and residency are also
paradoxical in a broader sense: despite their numerical atypicality, the petitioners convey the common human response in times of stress or crisis
of turning inward toward one's familial and community support networks. Requesting residency or enslavement was an individualistic rather
than collective response to oppression from people who were nonethe-
less placing their families first. Despite lacking formal citizenship and
legal equality, free people of color were still able to use the apparatus of
law to try to change their status when they felt under threat.[41]

While historians are now moving toward a fuller exploration of the inability of enslaved people (and families that crossed the line from slave to free) to resist the regime, family—however malleable that word is—remained antebellum blacks' only hope for a modicum of privacy, love, and intimacy in the place they called home. Free and enslaved black people were also prepared to fight for family whatever the cost and against all odds.[42] Because the distinction between slavery and freedom held less relevance for black people than for white, free people of color and the enslaved sought practical, relational solutions to the threat of familial separations that are out of a "normal" narrative of slavery and freedom as polar opposites. Family was a first priority. Material concerns about economic survival were of secondary importance but still vital for impoverished people seeking a subsistence standard of living. Slaves and free people of color were individuals who lived in a complicated, nuanced world, and the end of "high revisionism" means it is now time to ask and answer the difficult questions about their lives, including why some free blacks might have requested bondage.

That black men, as well as women, were prepared to seek refuge in their families; prioritize their loved ones; and seek the support of parents, spouses, children, or other members of their affective communities has not received the historical attention it deserves. Prior research has exaggerated the distinction between black women—allegedly tied to their families through their childbearing and rearing—and black men, who were themselves allegedly at greater liberty to partake in geographical mobility. But both men and women wanted to remain at the heart of their kin networks and simply be still. Free people of color did not want to leave their homes and communities in enforced migration any more than Cherokees wished to join the Trail of Tears or than the enslaved wished to be "sold down the river." Family was paramount regardless of gender because both men and women had kin whom they dearly loved. Family also assumed priority regardless of people's legal status because rising racial oppression in the nineteenth century rendered "freedom" increasingly meaningless. While African American women were arguably the first females in America to work an exploitative "double day," everyday domestic lives within these women's homes can also be characterized as comforting refuges from a hostile wider world, despite the arduous and repetitive nature of the domestic labor involved.

African American history has often been written in a rather celebratory tone in which resistance to oppression triumphs in a grand narrative arc. But the reality of everyday life for people in the past can best be characterized in terms of multiple historical narratives that do not fit neat, linear frameworks. In her innovative work on rape and sexual power in early America, Sharon Block argues convincingly for use of a multiplicity of approaches and sources in the writing of history, "even if the results provide a messier story then we may prefer."[43] Block's work has inspired this research into free blacks in the antebellum South; my findings are similarly complex, hard to decipher, and reliant on limited surviving primary sources. This book also investigates the lives of free people of color in the late antebellum era from a variety of different perspectives, both black and white. Stephanie Camp's work has also been influential. Lamenting the lack of evidence for exploring the emotional lives of enslaved women, Camp argued persuasively for the use of imagination and speculation in historical writing: "As we work with our written evidence—whether it remains in shards or in linear feet—we can also employ the imagination, closely reading our documents in their context and speculating about their meanings."[44] This work also embraces speculation as a means of enhancing knowledge about private pasts.

The views of proslavery white southern polemicists about free blacks are easy to trace, because prominent white southern writers left written documentation and hence have been the subject of considerable historical research. But the voices of free people of color, of enslaved people with whom free blacks had relationships, and of poorer whites on the fringes of the slaveholding class are harder to find. This book, therefore, necessarily combines a number of techniques and approaches. To trace the laws relating to free blacks that were passed by southern legislatures in the 1850s and before, it includes a brief foray into legal history. It undertakes a textual analysis of enslavement petitions and residency requests, contextualized by supplementary research into relevant census schedules, and I sometimes hypothesize about why free people of color seeking bondage considered—or were cajoled into—taking such a desperate step. I also use quantitative techniques to build a picture of the number of surviving enslavement petitions in the antebellum South and to explore the black and white motivations that lie behind enslavement and residency requests. Because the ratio between surviving enslavement and residency petitions and those actually written is unknown, the end result may be—to use Sharon Block's term—rather "messy." But I hope I have shed invaluable light on the lives and emotions of some free black southerners in the latter days of slavery and the ways their emotions, their feelings, were "raced, classed and gendered."[45]

So although this project was not explicitly conceptualized in terms of gender, without women it would be only half a book. Gender has now been integrated into broad historical narratives, including this work. There were important similarities and differences in the lives of free black men and women in the late antebellum era, and the enslavement petitions have proven especially revealing here. While gender profiles were relatively equal, the motivations and implications of enslavement could be very different for men and for women. For men, enslavement was mostly an individualistic pursuit, with the legal implications affecting only themselves. But for women, especially those in states that allowed for the enslavement of free black children, the consequences and ramifications of enslavement were different. Black women also lived in a world where there was more fluidity between slavery and freedom because "more women than men crossed over from slavery to freedom."[46] And the free black men and women who sought residency and enslavement through the law were characterized by their courage, ingenuity, and strength.

THE REQUESTS FOR ENSLAVEMENT AND RESIDENCY

All surviving enslavement petitions I found have been quantified, and census evidence has been used in conjunction with the petitions to establish the socioeconomic profiles of petitioners and their potential owners.[47] The research into enslavement petitions is also contextualized through some comparative analysis of residency requests by free people of color in the antebellum South. Although they date mostly from an earlier time period, there are considerable parallels between the enslavement and residency petitions when viewed from both black and white perspectives. Enslavement petitions were researched in relevant archives of the southern states and through the Race and Slavery Petitions Project at the University of North Carolina, Greensboro.[48] Founded in 1991, the project aims to collate and publish all surviving legislative and county court petitions concerning race and slavery from the 1770s to the 1860s.[49] Although Arkansas, the District of Columbia, Kentucky, and Maryland have no surviving legislative petitions at all, some county court enslavement requests for Arkansas were found within the archives themselves.[50]

The petitions collated for the North Carolina project address a myriad of issues—including manumission, colonization, laws governing slaves, racial mixing, and military service—and the range of themes is reflected in the wide range of people who wrote petitions: black and white, slaveholder and non-slaveholder, women and men.[51] The project contains many of the enslavement and residency requests (made to county courts and state legislatures) included here; others were located in secondary sources (where possible, these were then traced back to the original source), within southern archives, and in contemporary newspapers. The number of enslavement and residency requests that survived through the Civil War, its aftermath, and through the twentieth century is unknown, and those included here represent a bare minimum of the number of people who sought legal recourse in their bids to remain in their home states or become chattel. That five enslavement requests were cited in contemporary newspapers but could not be found in southern archives is also a cause of concern. These examples may have been written for proslavery propaganda purposes, an issue explored in chapter 3.[52] But the relative scarcity of enslavement requests does not mean the phenomena can be dismissed as irrelevant, and there may well be more petitions for voluntary slavery lurking within local county courthouses.

The number of petitions found was so small that any sort of quantitative analysis had to be approached with caution. Nevertheless, some of the major findings are presented in tabular form, beginning with a representation of states for which there are surviving enslavement and residency petitions made to county courts or state legislatures:

There were 143 petitions for enslavement and 38 for residency (181

Table I.1: Enslavement and residency requests by state

State	Enslavement	Residency	Total
Alabama	16	3	19
Arkansas	8	0	8
Delaware	3	0	3
Florida	5	0	5
Georgia	3	0	3
Louisiana	13	0	13
Mississippi	14	13	27
North Carolina	27	0	27
South Carolina	8	1	9
Tennessee	4	1	5
Texas	7	11	18
Virginia	35	9	44
TOTAL	**143**	**38**	**181**

in total). Where an individual petitioned more than once, which happened in only a handful of cases, the request was counted only once, for the purposes of collation, but these multiple petitions are considered in more detail within individual chapters. Additionally, there were 7 petitions for indentured servitude rather than slavery; these are included for the purpose of comparison about possible free black motivations. Of the requests for indentured servitude, 2 were from Maryland, while the others were from Delaware, Florida, Louisiana, North Carolina, and South Carolina. Also included are a further 9 petitions, all of which were made by groups of whites and related to enslavement, expulsion, or colonization in a broader sense. Thus, the total number of petitions used was 197, and of these, 115 were made to state legislatures, and 70 to county courts. All information for the remaining 12 was obtained from secondary sources (5 of which cited newspapers as a primary source), and no other information could be found.

Men made up the majority of the petitioners, though the gender profiles were fairly equal overall. Women did not shy away from using their initiative to seek recourse to the law, and males and females perceived the entering of bondage in rather different ways. For free black men, the desire for enslavement was mostly an individual pursuit of, for example, those who were married to enslaved women and who had slave children. However, some of the female enslavement petitioners had to decide whether they wanted bondage for their offspring as well as themselves. Others petitioned on behalf of their entire families, but, as it was for the individual petitioners, a desire to remain with beloved kin at any cost seems to have been the primary motivation. Enslavement petitioners often felt under threat of expulsion and wanted to stay with beloved families in their homes and communities. The enslavement and residency petitions break down according to gender, as shown in table I.2.

Table I.2: Enslavement and residency requests by gender

Petitions	Men	Women	Families	Total
Enslavement	76 (53)	56 (39)*	11(8)	143 (100)
Residency	22 (58)	8 (21)	8 (21)	38 (100)
TOTAL	**98 (54)**	**64 (35)**	**19 (11)**	**181 (100)**

Notes: Percentages given in parentheses.
* Of these women, twelve included their children under the age of eighteen in their enslavement requests, an issue considered in more detail in chapters 4 and 5.

The outcomes of enslavement and residency requests are considered on an individual basis. Frustratingly, in the vast majority of cases any outcomes either remain unknown or the decision was postponed. Sometimes petitions were referred to committees; at other times, "approved" or "rejected" was scrawled across the bottom of a petition.[53] But these committees apparently either failed to meet or they failed to report and record their findings. Only 39 enslavement requests were granted, and 10 were rejected or dismissed. Only 1 residency request was approved (Esther Barland), and 2 were rejected (Lucy Boomer and Narcissa Daniels). A relative lack of surviving evidence about whether enslavement petitioners had previously been held in bondage was also disappointing. In only 10 petitions for bondage could an individual be identified as seeking reenslavement, and, significantly, only *one* person asked to be enslaved to a former owner (Emily Hooper). A mere 10 enslavement petitioners sought ownership by women: of these, 8 were female and 2 were male. The other 133 requested that they belong to men.

The ages of enslavement petitioners was collated (there was very little information given on the ages of those seeking residency, so they have not been included in table I.3). Numbers involved were small, since sometimes the petition noted only that the free person of color was "over the age of twenty-one." Children included in enslavement requests, whether in conjunction with their mothers or as part of a broader family group, are not included below but are considered on an individual basis within later chapters. These findings contradict those of Ira Berlin, who suggested that the majority of enslavement petitioners were "paupers decrepit with age."[54] Instead, a majority of petitioners were young adults

Table I.3: Enslavement requests by age

Age	Men	Women	Total
10–19	0	4	4
20–29	8	17	25
30–39	6	1	7
40–49	4	2	6
50–59	1	1	2
60–69	1	0	1
70 and above	2	0	2
TOTAL	**22**	**25**	**47**

of childbearing age, for whom the prioritization of familial relationships was paramount. That so many petitioners were in their twenties is also testament to their value to white slaveholders. Moreover, that there was an even higher proportion of women in their teens and twenties hints at interracial relationships between free black women and white men. Of the adult petitioners, the age profiles appear in table I.3.

The earliest petitions for enslavement came from 1795, the latest was dated 1864, and several had no date at all. The decades in which enslavement and residency petitions were submitted have been summarized in table I.4. The patterns here are unsurprising. Most petitions are clustered around the time of legislation on expulsion or enslavement, with requests for the latter concentrated in the late 1850s and early 1860s.

Table I.4: Enslavement and residency requests by decade

Decade	Enslavement (percentage)	Residency (percentage)	Total (percentage)
1810s and earlier	4 (3)	5 (21)	6 (4)
1820s	0 (0)	3 (12)	3 (2)
1830s	2 (2)	11 (46)	13 (8)
1840s	0 (0)	1 (4)	1 (1)
1850s	50 (38)	4 (17)	54 (36)
1860s	76 (57)	0 (0)	76 (49)
TOTAL	**132 (100)**	**24 (100)**	**156 (100)**
No date	11 (8)	14 (58)	25 (16)

At the very heart of this book lie free people of color's possible motivations for enslavement and residency, the explanations behind such drastic acts. The motivations explained within petitions were divided into several broad categories, as shown in table I.5. These results show free black petitioners' clear desire to remain with their families at any cost. The contentious issue of interracial relationships is considered more fully in chapter 5, while other themes, including proslavery propaganda cropping up within the requests, and white people cajoling free people of color into making their petitions, are also analyzed in more detail within individual chapters. The petitioners' feelings and emotions were often difficult to measure and were sometimes hard to decipher from the rather legalistic prose within the petitions themselves. Table I.5 includes some petitioners who were counted more than once. They might, for

Table I.5: Motivations for enslavement and residency

Motivation	Enslavement (percentage)	Residency (percentage)	Total (percentage)
Love of family	38 (39)	11 (65)	49 (43)
Possible interracial relationship	27 (28)	1 (6)	28 (24)
Slavery "better"	11 (11)	0 (0)	11 (10)
Fear of leaving or does not want to leave	9 (9)	3 (17)	12 (11)
Court costs	5 (5)	0 (0)	5 (4)
Age or poor health	4 (4)	1 (6)	5 (4)
Poverty or debt	4 (4)	1 (6)	5 (4)
TOTAL	**98 (100)**	**17 (100)**	**115 (100)**

example, have cited their love for their family *and* the poverty they faced as explanations for their requests. But other petitions gave no explanation for the request for residency or enslavement; these, therefore, raise more questions than they answer, especially where the decision of the assembly or court was unknown.

Because free people of color in the 1850s requested enslavement for a variety of reasons, they posed problems for state legislatures that attempted to formulate laws to facilitate voluntary bondage. A relative absence of state laws meant enslavement requests were often dealt with individually and that, as John Hope Franklin noted, "one is inclined to believe that the influence of the prospective master or the sponsor of the bill had a great deal to do with its passage."[55] In states such as North Carolina, where a general law providing for the enslavement of free people of color was never enacted, he argues, slavery petitions were sometimes regarded unfavorably "because the Senate looked forward to the enactment of a general law which would make unnecessary the consideration of individual cases."[56] However, the onset of war meant that such a law was never passed.

The authorship of enslavement and residency petitions is also a difficult issue. Mostly the amanuenses remain unknown. In some petitions, free blacks marked their documents with an "X," sometimes in the presence of "independent" witnesses.[57] While the majority of free people of color who sought enslavement or residency were illiterate, the real writers of their petitions do not reveal their names. This adds a further layer of complexity to the idea of the petitions as performance; the performer is unknown. There were only six cases where a request for residency or slavery was explicitly written by someone other than the petitioner. One of these concerned three men returning from Liberia. The others were written by prospective owners.[58] These cases raise more suspicions than others about the real motivations of those "choosing" bondage. However, census records provide valuable additional information about potential owners, especially where sexual relationships between free women of color and white men were suspected. The ages of those involved, coupled with the marital status of potential owners, offer tantalizing clues about whether intimate relationships were at play. Sometimes, too, enslavement or residency requests had attached affidavits or supporting documents by community members or justices of the peace vouching for the petitioners' claims, suggesting some white support networks were behind moves to enslave free blacks.[59]

OVERVIEW OF CHAPTERS

Chapter 1 sets the context by detailing the various laws and restrictions imposed on southern free people of color over the course of the antebellum era, particularly during the 1850s, when moves to expel or enslave free blacks reached a crescendo. Subsequent chapters analyze enslavement and residency petitions within an increasingly hostile climate. Chapter 2 explores free people of color's residency requests. Although most of these were submitted prior to the 1850s (when the majority of enslavement requests were written), there are striking parallels in the motivations behind both residency and enslavement petitions. Traditional motivations for enslavement from the perspective of both proslavery ideologues and earlier historians form the basis of the third chapter, which also shows how less wealthy whites were anxious to buy their way into the slaveholding class through the acquisition of free people of color. Free blacks had every right to be increasingly fearful of being tricked, forced, or cajoled into enslavement by the late 1850s.

Chapters 4 and 5 consider expulsion and enslavement from the perspective of free people of color themselves. Drawing upon emotions and the importance of familial and community ties, chapter 4 illustrates how free blacks who submitted enslavement petitions were often enmeshed in spousal or other affective relationships that crossed the boundary between slavery and freedom. These people placed their families before

their legal status. Chapter 5 continues this emphasis upon personal relationships by offering hypotheses about why apparently single women
might request bondage. The conclusion suggests a reconceptualization of
the meanings of slavery, freedom, and the significance of affective relationships under a system of racial oppression.

1

Presumed Enslaved

Free People of Color and the Law
in the Southern States

A free person of color, over twenty years of age, may voluntarily sell him or herself into slavery. In all such cases the sale must be made openly at a regular term of the Inferior Court of the county, where the Justices of said court shall privately examine such free persons of color to satisfy themselves of his or her free consent. A record shall be made of such sale in the minutes of said term and also in the book of registry of free persons of color in said county.

—*The Code of the State of Georgia, 1863*

The ground taken by those who opposed the selling of those negroes, seems to us altogether untenable. We are opposed to giving free negroes a residence in any and every Slaveholding state, believing as we do, that their presence in slave communities is hurtful to the good order of society, and fraught with great danger. . . . We confess that we were not a little surprised upon reading the council proceedings, to find one member styling this law "monstrous." We can't see for the life of us how anyone understanding full the great principle that underlies our system of involuntary servitude, can discover any monstrosity in subjecting a negro to slavery of a white man.

—Editorial from the *Atlanta Daily Intelligencer,*
9 January 1860.

Although Georgia was the last southern state legally to enable voluntary enslavement, the issue had been a controversial one, debated for some time within the state legislature. This *Daily Intelligencer* editorial exemplifies how responses to humanitarian complaints about the exploitation of free blacks' enslavement were couched in proslavery rhetoric. Indeed, supporters of the act regarded the movement of free people of color into a system of bondage as a deed of benevolence. Voluntary enslavement legislation thus represented the culmination of a proslavery rhetoric that assumed slavery was a positive good. It also facilitated the shift toward an idealized biracial South of black slaves and free white people, and demands for a South based upon this kind of racial separation had been growing in strength for some time.

The concerns of proslavery advocates about the status of different "races" and how they might be separated date back to the earliest days of American history, when the first ships brought enslaved Africans to help build a new society. Free people of color existed in the South either through slave owners' emancipations or because they were born liberated by virtue of having free black mothers. This followed a precedent set in Virginia in 1662 when lawmakers decreed all enslaved children should follow their mothers' status, a decision that was to have enormous implications for the evolving system of slavery because owners thereafter had vested interests in encouraging their enslaved women to procreate. This law overlooked interracial liaisons between white women and black men and assumed such relationships involved only black enslaved women and white men. A later act of 1691 excluded the enslaved from legal marriage and forbid interracial wedlock.[1]

Despite these early efforts to separate black from white and slave from free, a combination of manumissions and intimate relationships among black men and white women who then bore children contributed to the doubling of the South's free black population between 1820 and 1860, which numbered 260,000 on the eve of war.[2] These free people caused growing concerns among whites who enacted increasingly hostile legislation against them, culminating in the expulsion and enslavement debates and legislation of the late 1850s. Antebellum southern lawmakers strove to create a binary division between black slaves and free whites. Yet white men's sexual interference with enslaved women made this black-white distinction impossible to achieve, despite complex legislation on how one defined a person as being of "mixed race."[3] Southern states also sought to limit the numbers of free people of color within their borders, primarily by seeking to prevent further migration of free blacks into their states. They also legislated to restrict emancipations; set up complicated systems of registration, taxation, and guardianship; and attempted to send free blacks "back" to Africa through colonization initiatives. Taken to its logical conclusion, such legislation meant that free people of color had nowhere to go by the 1850s, when southern states debated and passed exclusion and enslavement laws.

This chapter will first contextualize the ever-more restrictive legislation toward free people of color enacted prior to the 1850s. It will then consider those laws debated and passed during this decade and the early 1860s and suggest broader implications of their severity. Comparing legislative action across the South, despite somewhat imbalanced surviving evidence and different degrees of legislation against free blacks, reveals the motivations behind expulsion and enslavement laws. Moreover, while the coming of war meant some laws were never enacted or enforced, debates over expulsion and enslavement offer a stark reminder of the direction in which the American South was traveling—toward the enslavement of all free people of color. The perspectives of free blacks toward expulsion and enslavement form the basis of this book, which does not aim to provide a comprehensive political history of enslavement and expulsion debates. But it is no coincidence that many of their petitions for enslavement, whether addressed to state legislatures or county courts, were made in the late 1850s and early 1860s, when laws enabling both voluntary enslavement and the expulsion of free blacks from their states were being debated.

THE COMPLEXITIES OF COLOR IN THE OLD SOUTH

Proslavery advocates regarded as paradoxical the very existence of free people of color in southern states, and it was a popular perception that free blacks were "problematic." Whites feared free people of color would entice their slaves into a state of discontent or even outright rebellion, but the reality was that, with the exception of a small, urban "mulatto elite," most free blacks were impoverished agricultural laborers eking out a subsistence living, some of whom worked alongside slaves. And this labor was needed. Some white members of society valued the economic input of free people of color through their work and taxation. Others saw free blacks as providing a "positive example" to the enslaved, especially when they owned property and were economically self-sufficient.[4]

Such conflicting attitudes, coupled with some humanitarian concerns about enslaving free people of color, delayed the implementation of expulsion and enslavement laws.[5] In the 1860s, the Civil War also drew a firm line under attempts to enslave and expel as white attentions were diverted toward the more pressing war effort. An instinct to enslave was, therefore, a reflection of both a sense of insecurity about the future of the institution coupled with the apparently contradictory but equally valid feelings of self-confidence expressed by proslavery ideologues. In a climate of growing sectional tensions, whites increasingly categorized free blacks in terms of race and, subsequently, enslavement. Furthermore, because of their racism, white southerners did not perceive freedom to be in the best interests of people of color. Enslavement was therefore a "kindly" act of benevolence. As George Fitzhugh wrote in 1851: "Humanity, self-interest [and] consistency all require that we should enslave the free negro."[6]

As proslavery ideology grew more sophisticated over the course of the antebellum era, free blacks increasingly contradicted the notion of bondage as a positive good. Demands to enslave them were therefore put forward on various grounds. One argument claimed that since slavery was morally a good thing, a failure to impose bondage on free blacks would be wrong in the eyes of God. Indeed, the very idea of free people of color seemed increasingly illogical to some whites. Most southerners saw enslavement "as the logical outgrowth of slavery and a final solution to their frustrating inability to make free Negroes conform to the logic of white racial thought. Besides, if slavery was benevolent and freedom a tyranny for the Negro, the truly moral man would want to help the free Negro find happiness."[7] In a context where George Fitzhugh could memorably proclaim: "A free negro! Why, the very term seems an absurdity," it is not surprising that some legislatures embraced the possibility of enslaving or excluding free blacks.[8] Pseudo-scientific concerns about the alleged "inferiority" of people of African descent also contributed to the development of a more hostile climate for them in the 1850s when ideologues such as Samuel Cartwright popularized the idea of lifelong bondage as a natural solution to "the negro problem."[9]

Enslavement would also have practical benefits. There would be no free blacks to assist runaways, the supply of labor would be enlarged, and new slaves could be sold to poor whites, helpfully defusing potential class conflict.[10] The opportunities for race-based insurrection and rebellion would also be diminished. It is not surprising that legislation against free people of color often came in flurries following a crisis or panic in southern race relations. For example, Denmark Vesey's 1822 plot alarmed many white southerners about the possibility of slave-free political relations among blacks. Likewise, many whites deemed an outrage the 1829 publication of David Walker's *Appeal*.[11] In 1831, the Nat Turner rebellion also contributed to the notion that free people of color were somehow dangerous; even though they "had little to do with that or with any other rebellion, whites directed their ire at that hapless segment of the population."[12]

When the future of southern states grew more and more uncertain, suspicions about the mere existence of free blacks rose, with some arguing that they could never truly be integrated into existing social and economic systems. So ideas about enslavement and expulsion within legislatures were often linked, and both initiatives gained momentum following the 1857 *Dred Scott v. Sandford* Supreme Court case. Free blacks had been excluded from American citizenship (and hence legal marriage) under the terms of the 1790 Naturalization Act because they were not "free white persons." Dred Scott, himself born enslaved, brought this thorny issue to the forefront of political debate; he argued for his freedom because he lived in territories where slavery was illegal. But in decreeing that "once free no longer meant always free," the Supreme Court placed the weight of the law behind proslavery forces.[13] Its judges also explained that Dred Scott was automatically excluded from citizenship because of his color, thus boosting white southern confidence about moving toward expulsion and/or enslavement. These initiatives had new vigor.[14]

Also important in terms of shifting the racial climate toward a favoring of the enslavement and expulsion of free blacks was the panic caused by John Brown's 1859 raid on Harpers Ferry, increasing sectional tensions and anticipation about what laws *other* southern legislatures were passing.[15] For many southern states, permitting voluntary enslavement was an easier option than expulsion. It shifted the onus onto freedpeople and so quelled some humanitarian doubts whites held about enforced bondage.[16] So, more states facilitated voluntary bondage than expulsion in the late 1850s, although the two measures were often considered together, with voluntary slavery sometimes suggested as a suitable alternative for free blacks who were unwilling to leave. Racial fears about "problematic" free blacks were also quelled by southern states having already legislated against the movement of free people of color into their borders.

Table 1.1: Enslavement and explusion legislation in the antebellum South

State	Statehood	Free people of color as a percentage of total black population of 1860	Legislation on voluntary enslavement
Delaware	1787	91.7	None
Georgia	1788	0.8	1863
Maryland	1788	49.1	1860
South Carolina	1788	2.4	1859
Virginia	1788	10.6	1856
North Carolina	1789	8.4	None
Kentucky	1792	4.5	None
Tennessee	1796	2.6	1858
Louisiana	1812	5.3	1859
Mississippi	1817	0.2	None
Alabama	1819	0.6	1860
Missouri	1821	3.0	None
Arkansas	1836	0.1	None*
Florida	1845	1.5	1858
Texas	1845	0.2	1858

Source: These figures are taken from Peter Kolchin, *American Slavery, 1619–1877* (New York: Penguin, 1993), 241.
Note: * Arkansas did, however, have enforced explusion from January 1860.

Between 1856 and the outbreak of the Civil War, legislative provision was made for the voluntary enslavement of free blacks in seven states: Alabama, Florida, Louisiana, Maryland, Tennessee, Texas, and Virginia. South Carolina and Georgia approved of it by means of special acts of the legislature in individual cases, and the issue was also debated elsewhere.[17] This evidence is presented in table 1.1. Of the five states that did not legislate on voluntary slavery, four were in the Upper South (Delaware, Kentucky, Missouri, and North Carolina). Only Mississippi was in the Deep South. But of these, only Delaware's free black population stood at over 10 percent of the total number of free people of color. There was no correlation between the relative size of the free black population and legislative action on enslavement, nor was there a link between the geographic location of states and the desire to legislate. In states such as North Carolina, voluntary slavery was debated even though it did not pass into law. Essentially, all southern states were moving toward the enslavement of their free people of color.

RESTRICTIVE LEGISLATION BEFORE THE 1850S

Adopting a longer-run approach to assess legislation directed against free blacks on a state-by-state basis provides a broader context in which to situate the expulsion and enslavement debates of the 1850s and early 1860s. The residency petitions submitted by free blacks are considered in chapter 2. Arkansas forbade any free person of color from immigrating to or settling in the state after March 1843. Moreover, individuals could be fined up to five hundred dollars, should they "employ, harbor, or conceal, any negro or mulatto acting as a free person."[18] The wording here is significant. The legislature referred to black people "acting" free, thus implicitly suggesting bondage to be their natural status. Moreover, free people of color living in the state before 1843 also found their freedoms curtailed. All free blacks had to present to their county courts certificates of freedom and "proof" via the testimony of "competent witnesses" ("white people" might well have been inserted here) that they had settled in Arkansas prior to March 1843. Many free people of color would have been unable to provide such evidence. And the repression continued: free blacks deemed eligible for residency had to enter into a bond with the State and obtain a certificate from a court clerk confirming that they were permitted to live there. Failure to comply resulted in a fine of up to two hundred dollars, or being "hired out by the sheriff" to cover the fine's costs.[19] In this chilling climate, it is not surprising that some free people of color chose to leave Arkansas, as the legislature indeed hoped they would. Others simply ignored these increasingly bureaucratic and cumbersome local laws. A further minority chose to fight for the right to remain with beloved families in their homes and communities by formally requesting residency or enslavement.

Arkansas seemed unable to enforce the restrictive laws it imposed upon free people of color, and the state relaxed its 1843 laws two years later. From 1845 onward, citizens were permitted to bring in "any free negro or negroes, or mulatto or mulattoes, as a servant or servants," provided they remained in the citizen's service and stayed no more than three months. Those wishing to remain after this point were subject to the provisions of the original 1843 act.[20] Perhaps as a result of difficulties related to law enforcement, Arkansas then shifted its concerns toward free blacks already there. By the early 1850s slaves, free blacks, and "mulattoes" were all banned from working "in any retail grocery, dram shop, or other place where vinous or ardent spirits are sold in less quantities than one quart."[21] Specific fears about insurrection combined with more general concerns about free blacks' autonomy lay behind this legislation, which similarly operated at local levels. From the 1830s onward, the Little Rock City Council required its free people of color to file certificates confirming their freedom, and by the 1840s the city also imposed restrictions on free blacks' ownership of weapons and their socializing with the enslaved.[22]

Excluding free people of color from entering their states in the first place was the easiest and most common way southern lawmakers rather myopically sought to alleviate the perceived "problem" of free blacks. As early as 1811, Delaware prohibited free people of color "not now residing in this state" from entering. Punishments for breaking this law operated on a scale that included an initial fine but also sale into temporary servitude "as shall be sufficient for payment of said fine and costs together with the charges of imprisonment and sale." White people could also be fined for bringing free blacks into the state, while free people of color already there had to provide certificates "of fair conduct and character signed by at least one Justice of the Peace of the county, town or place where such negro or mulatto has resided for one year immediately preceding his or her coming into this state."[23] Floridian "free negroes" brought into the territory from 1832 onward were, from 1842, similarly liable to be sold unless they left the territory. They also faced sale if they reentered Florida.[24] Southern lawmakers created complex systems of certification to confirm residential eligibility, but they also legislated on the enforced servitude of free people of color some forty years before the 1850s' voluntary slavery legislation.

Acts passed in Georgia subjected free people of color in the city of Savannah and other towns to similar regulations and laws as those imposed on the enslaved from 1807 onward.[25] From 1818 free blacks in the state also had to undergo an annual registration process, with failure to prove one's freedom resulting in sale as a slave. This harsh act was, however, later overturned and replaced with banishment from Georgia or a fine.[26] In 1845, the state senate thundered that it, and it alone, should decide on the issue of free black citizenship: "The question whether free negroes should be considered in the light of citizens or not, is one that the constitution fixes, and the States may determine for themselves—one too, which the State authorities long since have determined."[27] And the pattern in Louisiana was much the same. From the 1840s onward, restrictions were imposed upon free blacks who wished to enter the state, in a climate of rising white concerns about their presence.[28] Mindful of the practical problems of enforcement, southern states ideally wished to permit the entry of no free blacks at all.

Mississippi consolidated its laws relating to "slaves, free negroes and mulattoes" in 1822 through a lengthy act that fell into eighty-six parts. Lawmakers wished to leave no stone unturned in their treatment of free blacks. For example, owners who permitted free people of color (or slaves they did not own) onto their plantations for more than four hours with no pass were liable to be fined ten dollars. Interaction between slaves and free blacks was seen as very dangerous indeed, but the imposition of such restrictions militated against the development of intimate personal relations much more than it facilitated insurrectionary plots.[29] However, Mississippi implicitly acknowledged the existence of spousal relationships among slaves and free people of color. Where enslaved women were married to free men, masters could sue for recovery if their bondwomen left the state with their spouses.[30] That this law spoke to enslaved women and free black men and not vice versa is revealing. Mississippi slaveholders had every reason to encourage their bondwomen to procreate, regardless of their husbands' status. Enslaved women produced valuable children, but enslaved men did not.

Like other states, Mississippi attempted to blend rather idealized laws with evolving custom and practice. For example, an 1822 law on emancipations decreed slaves would only be freed through last will and testaments that were verified by two "credible witnesses."[31] Southern states wanted enslaved and free people of color to be treated—at least in a legal sense—as one and the same. By categorizing all black people in one group, the Mississippi legislature thus implicitly attempted to assert that a color line (rather than one between slave and free) was the significant boundary.[32] For example, "any negro or mulatto, bond or free" would suffer "up to thirty-nine strokes of the lash," except in cases of assault, for using abusive language or "lifting their hand" to a white person. It was also deemed illegal for a "free negro or mulatto" to enter the state, and those found in Mississippi contrary to law (the state was obviously expecting its new law to be broken) were given only thirty days to leave. During this period, free blacks caught living illegally in Mississippi had also to provide security of five hundred dollars, agree to "keep the peace, and be of good behavior."[33]

That poor and impoverished free people of color would be able to pay such a large amount of money to remain in their homes was extremely unlikely. So the legislators again assumed their laws would be broken. Free blacks who were unable to provide such security faced twenty days of jail before being sold into bondage to the highest bidder. Money raised was then to be deposited with the relevant county treasury. Mississippi was thus prepared to enforce free blacks into slavery as early as 1822, and even those with residency rights found their lives increasingly circumscribed. Free blacks already living legally in the state had to "be registered and numbered in a book for that purpose . . . and the age, name, sex, color and stature of such free negro and mulatto, together with any visible mark or scar on his or her face, head or hands, and by what last will and testament, or instrument in writing, he or she was emancipated, in the manner provide by this act; or that such free negro or mulatto was born free." The Mississippi legislature also cruelly insisted that all free people of color partaking in this procedure of cumbersome bureaucracy, against their wills, had to pay costs of one dollar.[34]

And the list of restrictive legislations imposed on free people of color went on: free blacks were only allowed to work upon production of their "certificates of freedom." Their right to labor should also be updated every three years by register of the county's orphans' court. Wary of fraud, Mississippi lawmakers also decreed that new certificates could not be issued until the old ones were destroyed. Free blacks could be jailed, and later enslaved, for failure to present their certificates upon request. The detailed Mississippi legislation of 1822 confirms that a proslavery ideology based on the notion that people of color were "problematic" predated the Nat Turner rebellion by at least a decade.[35] The new laws were also testament to the growing importance of paper certification as a defining component of racial difference. By the late nineteenth-century, the American government was attempting to impose a similar system of certification upon Asian Americans.[36]

Mississippi passed a whole new raft of laws in the 1840s, when efforts to deport free people of color at this time became known as "the Inquisition."[37] The new laws also suggest that those implemented a generation earlier had proven unsuccessful. In 1842, for example, the State declared all justices of the peace were authorized at the request of "any freeholder of this county" to bring before local courts "any free negro or mulatto unlawfully within this state." Those subjected to this action had to provide security of one hundred dollars and declare "that he or she will be of good behavior while in this state." A failure to comply could result in imprisonment and sale in a similar way to that outlined in the legislation of 1822. Mississippi also attempted at this time to tighten up on emancipations. Freed people of color outside the state who had returned to Mississippi, perhaps to visit their loved ones, were liable to be "conveyed" to the county sheriff or constable for arrest. Local justices of the peace were authorized to inflict "up to thirty-nine lashes" and insist upon the free black's departure within twenty days. Those who failed to leave faced jail and sale as slaves.[38]

Emancipation by last will and testament was also outlawed in Mississippi by 1842. Instead, slaves were to be "distributed amongst the heirs at law of the testator . . . as if such testator had died intestate." Executors of last wills and testaments could request to manumit slaves for "meritorious services" but only through obtaining legislative approval on an individual basis.[39] Mississippi's 1842 legislation was therefore attempting to reinforce and reassert the state's laws affecting the lives of free blacks as well as tighten up existing legal loopholes. Fundamentally, all southern states were trying to create idealized biracial societies of free whites and enslaved blacks. For example, in 1845 Missouri revised its statutes so that free people of color had to obtain a license to live within the state, and they were also forbidden from entering Missouri. These residency licenses were granted only to a "certain class of persons" including those born free or emancipated within the state.[40]

South Carolina restricted manumissions and the immigration of free people of color in the 1820s and in the 1840s. But even before then, free blacks had to "assume the burden of proof" that they were not slaves.[41] In 1820, the state forbade manumission except by special act of the legislature, which decreed: "The great and rapid increase of free negroes and mulattoes in this state, by migration and emancipation, renders it expedient and necessary for the Legislature to restrain the emancipation of slaves, and to prevent free persons of color from entering into this State." Subsequently, in 1822 all free black people over the age of fifteen were required to have "respectable freeholders" as guardians, and free blacks who left the state were not allowed to return.[42] Any free person of color caught living in South Carolina illegally was forced to pay a fine and then leave. Failure to do so enabled sheriffs, like those in Mississippi, to sell the individuals concerned into a five-year period of servitude.[43] In 1841, the state imposed a blanket law that all slaves manumitted from that year onward had to leave South Carolina.[44]

Although Texas only entered the Union in 1845, the government of the preceding Republic had similar concerns about manumissions and the migration of free people of color into its borders. An 1836 ordinance was designed "to prevent the importation and emigration of Free Negroes and Mulattoes," and those flouting this rule could be "sold at public auction to the highest bidder." Proceeds from such sales were divided three ways. One third was awarded to the "apprehender" who caught the free black, while another proportion was used to pay for court and costs. The remainder was paid to the Texas treasury.[45] "Africans, the descendents of Africans, and Indians" within Texas were also excluded from citizenship. Yet at the same time, the Constitution of the Republic also declared, "No free person of African descent, either in whole or in part, shall be permitted to reside permanently in the Republic, without the consent of Congress."[46] This issue was apparently resolved in 1837: "That all free Africans or descendents of Africans who were residing within the republic of Texas at the date of the Declaration of Independence, and their natural issue, are hereby granted and allowed the privilege of remaining in any part of the republic as long as they choose, on the condition of performing all the duties required of them by law."[47]

Such "accommodating" attitudes, though, were short-lived, and in 1840 the government of the Republic was still deliberating on the status of free blacks *already within* Texas at the time of independence. For example, legislation of February of that year outlined how, within two years of the act, "all free persons of color who are now in this Republic, to move out of the same; and all those who shall be found here after that time, without the permission of Congress, shall be arrested and sold as provided in this Act." Texas's treatment of free people of color therefore changed from 1837 to 1840. Having initially been told they could remain in Texas, free blacks now found themselves forced to migrate. Moreover, free people of color caught illegally in Texas had to give bond of one thousand dollars to county judges or chief justices before leaving the Republic. If they failed to comply, like elsewhere, free blacks could be forced into a year of enslavement before their departure or else enforced bondage for life.[48]

Numerous Texas free blacks petitioned for exemption from such restrictive laws, even though the dithering Texas Congress introduced yet more uncertainty over free blacks' status in December 1840. This new legislation declared "all free persons of color, together with their families, who were residing in Texas on the day of the declaration of independence, are, and shall be exempt from the operation and provisions" of the February 1840 act.[49] These changing laws were inevitably more effective in theory than practice; free people of color continued to enter and leave

Texas as their lifestyles dictated. Nor is there any surviving evidence of any free black being forced to leave the Republic.[50] Many free people of color "quietly went their way" and either ignored (or were unaware of) the legislative debates over their status. This remained the case even after statehood in 1845, when it became illegal for free blacks to reside within Texas unless the legislature provided them specific relief.[51] In its earliest years, Texas displayed an unusual degree of leniency toward free people of color, reflecting its more malleable race relations and its uncertainty over its future. But such attitudes were short-lived, and Texas soon moved in the same direction as other southern states in attempting to create a biracial state of free whites and enslaved blacks.

Not surprisingly, Virginia stood at the forefront of restrictive legislation about free people of color. Manumission laws of 1782 permitted owners to free their slaves under certain conditions, but the nineteenth century witnessed changing attitudes. In 1806 lawmakers decreed that slaves given their freedom had to leave the state within one year or "relinquish their freedom" unless county officials permitted them to remain, although this law's effectiveness has been questioned.[52] New laws of 1819 and 1834 imposed further penalties on free people of color who remained in (or returned to) Virginia, but, as was the case in the Republic of Texas, "many" stayed illegally.[53] However, that some free people of color took to the law by asking to remain in Virginia conveys how seriously this threat was taken. Residency requests tended to be passed "with the support of sympathetic whites" who would vouch for the "worthiness" of free blacks, and it is no coincidence that free people of color who were granted residency possessed considerable economic value.[54]

Virginia also took the initiative in enacting new legislation designed to restrict the freedoms afforded both the enslaved and free people of color following the 1831 Nat Turner insurrection. Famous legislative debates of this year and 1832 moved forward proslavery defenses to a significant degree, and in 1832 there was a flurry of restrictive legislation, for example: "No slave, free negro or mulatto shall preach, or hold any meeting for religious purposes either day or night."[55] Up to "thirty-nine lashes" faced those caught breaking this law. Masters were permitted to take slaves and free blacks only "with them to religious worship conducted by a white minister." That same year, the legislature also decreed that "no free negro shall hereafter be capable of acquiring ownership, except by descent, to any slave other than his or her husband, wife and children." The legal status of free people of color was both paradoxical and confusing. Free blacks were denied legal marriage, as were the enslaved, but this legislation shows at least some implicit recognition that black people, whether in bondage or freedom, entered wedlock and formed lifelong stable partnerships.[56] Southern state legislators thus had to weld together their notions of an idealized biracial society with the everyday practices and norms of behavior among all people within state borders. But in the longer-term idealism beat reality. Free people of color were forbidden to enter Virginia from any other state "or foreign country" from 1834 onward, and from 1838 infants returning to the state could be bound out as apprentices until the age of twenty-one.[57] New legislation in 1848 decreed that any free black would "forfeit his right to freedom" and be sold as a slave if he remained in Virginia for more than one year following emancipation after the age of twenty-one.[58]

Free people of color were not immune to this evolving climate of hostility. Their enslavement and residency petitions convey from a free black perspective the broad spectrum of ways initiative was used for protest. And of immediate concern was the ability to remain with and provide for one's beloved families in the place called home. "Freedom" was a limited concept of limited value for a poor free person of color—perhaps married to someone enslaved and who labored on a plantation alongside slaves for minimal wage—whose mobility was curtailed, who was unable to partake in civic life, and who was denied citizenship and voting rights. It is not surprising that in petitioning for residency and enslavement some free people of color turned inward to their families, regardless of their status before the law, and these responses show that free blacks conceptualized slavery along a broad spectrum of exploitation. Free people of color did not make a sharp distinction between bondage and freedom, precisely because everyday life did not distinguish between the two.

Prior to the 1850s, then, all southern states imposed increasingly restrictive laws on free people of color as white men developed a sophisticated proslavery ideology to justify a racial separation based on white freedom and black bondage. This was true for states in the Deep South and in the Upper South, for net importers of the enslaved and for net exporters, for states with high percentages of free blacks and for those with low percentages. The one defining feature of hostile legislation against free blacks in the antebellum South is its uniformity across space: restrictive laws were also clustered around certain pivotal periods of time when white southerners felt under threat. Southern states were influenced both by each other and through a rising climate of racial fears bolstered by the blustering of proslavery ideologues. White legislators embraced the creation of complex and bureaucratic systems of registration and certification that are testament more to idealism than reality. These antebellum laws set the tone for the even harsher legislation to come.

ENSLAVEMENT AND EXPULSION LEGISLATION IN THE 1850s

A summary of states' rulings on enslavement and expulsion is detailed in table 1.1. Although not all southern states passed legislation on expulsion or enslavement, that most states seriously considered both conveys how very real the possibility of enforced enslavement actually was for free people of color in the late antebellum era. The direction of travel for all states was the same. Enslavement laws enacted by Alabama, Florida, Georgia, Louisiana, Maryland, South Carolina, Tennessee, Texas, and Virginia will first be considered. Thereafter, some of the debates over expulsion and enslavement in other states will be explored, and then the chapter will move to an investigation of the brutal exclusion law passed by Arkansas in 1860.

In February 1860, the General Assembly of Alabama permitted "free negroes to select masters and become slaves." Individuals wishing to become enslaved were instructed to apply in writing to the judge of the probate courts of the counties where they lived, "praying to become the slave of some white person of good moral character, residing permanently in the state." Alabama lawmakers also insisted that guardians be appointed for petitioners under the age of eighteen. Decision-making also rested with judges of probate, who had to be "convinced" that individual petitioners "filed the petition voluntarily and free from undue influence, and that the petitioner or petitioners really desire to surrender freedom and to become the slave or slaves of the person named in the petition." Judges also had to have "the proof of disinterested witnesses" in enslavement petitions, and potential owners were instructed to provide their written consent. Finally, Alabama lawmakers stated that any new slaves acquired under this ruling "shall not be sold under any legal process for the debts or liabilities of the master or mistress they have selected, or their heirs or distributees."[59]

The Alabama legislature thus attempted to avoid the exploitation of voluntary slaves by preventing new owners from acquiring new slaves purely to pay off their debts. But this left a significant legal loophole:

nowhere did the law forbid the sale of voluntary slaves for profit. Perhaps legislators did not want to acknowledge publicly that such sales took place. Indeed, the legislature's careful wording suggests policymakers genuinely believed the process of "selecting" bondage should be a voluntary one, in which "unfortunate" free blacks would be "relieved of freedom" by new benevolent masters. For example, at the same legislative session Tarleton Moss was permitted to become enslaved to Sidney J. Coleman of Pickens County. It was declared that should Coleman die, Moss could "choose another master" rather than simply be passed on to one of Coleman's descendants. Yet, no provision was made for the enforcement of this act by any individual.[60] The lawmakers' proslavery rhetoric was more important than the implementation of enslavement policies.

Florida considered both the expulsion and enslavement of free people of color, and although the governor vetoed the former in 1856, Florida newspapers often observed moves toward expulsion enacted by other states in generating publicity for the cause.[61] From 1856 onward, free blacks over twelve could be fined "not less than ten dollars" or face jail for being without a guardian.[62] Two years later, the state decided that all free people of color over fourteen years old were permitted to enter slavery voluntarily and that free black women could "select" bondage for their children under this age.[63] The lengthy act specified how individuals interested in enslavement had to file petitions with their county circuit courts, which then had to be signed by their judges of probate. Petitions then had to be posted "on the Court House door" for four weeks, after which the clerk of the court had to "issue a summons as well to the petitioner as to the proposed master or mistress, citing them to appear before the Court." All parties were then to be examined separately, "and if, upon such examination, the Judge shall be of opinion that said petitioner has made a judicious choice of a master or mistress . . . he shall grant the prayer of the petitioner."[64] Most legal processes by which free blacks sought enslavement were, then, broadly similar across the South. States wanted to convey the impression that they took such requests seriously and gave the legal process due time and consideration. Sharing a similar proslavery ideology, lawmakers across the South adopted a somewhat cautious approach to their enslavement legislation, as states influenced each other, gained confidence from one another, and utilized similarly worded laws.

The General Assembly of Georgia declared that from 1851 onward every free person of color in the state had to pay an annual tax of five dollars.[65] From 1854, free blacks could be fined one hundred dollars for "non-registry in terms of the law." Bryant Oxendine was unable to pay his fine in that year and was therefore hired out "under the Laws of this State, for a term of eighteen months . . . to John Montgomery."[66] Temporary servitude of this kind existed on the fuzzy borders between bondage and freedom. As was the case elsewhere in the South, as concerns about the very existence of free people of color grew, there was a parallel rise in restrictive legislation directed against free blacks. In December 1859, an act was passed "to prevent free persons of color . . . from being brought or coming into the State of Georgia." Moreover, "violation thereof, shall, on conviction of said violation, be sold as a slave or slaves, by the Sheriff of the county in which aid conviction shall be made." So moves toward the enslavement of free blacks existed prior to legislative action on voluntary bondage. One half of the proceeds of these sales went to the informer, the other to unspecified "county purposes." There was a real financial incentive for white people to catch free blacks living illegally in Georgia. And for every carrot there was a stick; the 1859 act dealt harshly with whites who aided or assisted free blacks entering the state, through the imposition of a fine "of not less than one thousand dollars" and imprisonment of "not less than twelve months."[67]

Georgia also went farther than many other states in forcing free people of color into bondage. As well as facing enslavement for living illegally in the state, the legislature also decreed "that any free person of color wandering or strolling about, or leading an idle, immoral or profligate course of life, shall be deemed and considered a Vagrant, and shall be indicted as such, as in other cases, and upon conviction, shall be punished by being sold into slavery, for any given time, in the discretion of the Judge of the Superior Court . . . such term of slavery shall not exceed two years, for the first offence, and upon conviction of the second offence, such free person of color so offending, shall be sold into perpetual slavery."[68]

Such sales had to be advertised by the sheriff "in some public gazette of the state . . . the rules and regulations which now govern Sheriff's sales of slaves, shall also govern sales of free persons of color." Sales of free blacks could only be made in cash, and "after deducting the cost of trial, jail fees, if any, and advertising, [money remaining] shall become part of the public school fund of the county where the free person of color convicted of vagrancy has been tried and condemned."[69] Georgia therefore imposed a "scale" of penalties before free people of color might eventually be forced into slavery, and the state also had prerequisites for the terms of sale itself. But the ambiguity of terms such as "strolling about," "idle," "immoral," and "profligate course of life" suggests immense scope for exploitation into bondage. Situated within the context of these gradual legislative measures toward the enslavement of free blacks, Georgia finally permitted voluntary bondage in 1863, the last state to do so.[70]

Louisiana prohibited any future emancipation of slaves in 1857, a move historians subsequently perceived as an "extraordinary legal right," and the status of free people of color, like that of those elsewhere in the South, was gradually eroded over the course of this decade.[71] For example, any new "religious, charitable, scientific or literary society composed of free people of color," all notably "respectable" activities, was outlawed in 1855, when the state also placed restrictions on free blacks entering Louisiana. By 1856, free people of color were banned from obtaining liquor licenses.[72] A whole raft of legislation in 1859 tackled the complex problems connected to New Orleans's status as a major port. Prohibiting the entry of free blacks was a practical impossibility, so the state instead created complex and bureaucratic systems of registration that drew upon legislation enacted against free people of color elsewhere in the South, especially laws passed in South Carolina, where Charleston was a major port.[73]

For example, free blacks who entered Louisiana via the state's waterways or by land were to be "lodged in the parish jail, and shall remain therein until the vessel, steamer, or other watercraft, on board which said free person of color arrived, shall be ready to leave port." Captains of vessels or masters were required to pay bond of five hundred dollars and supply a written affidavit confirming the free person of color "shall not be allowed to go on shore." They also had to pay forty cents every day toward the costs of free blacks' imprisonment. A failure to pay meant the free person of color involved had five days to leave Louisiana, or else be subjected to between three and twelve months imprisonment "at hard labor in the state penitentiary" before leaving the state. Those who subsequently returned could be imprisoned for a further five years.[74]

Imprisonment, rather than bondage, was the punishment of choice Louisiana legislators imposed on free blacks who illegally entered the state, and in this respect their policies were different from those imposed elsewhere. From a purely economic perspective, this was a missed opportunity for Louisiana to obtain more slaves, and the policy may have reflected humanitarian concerns about enforced moves into slavery. But voluntary enslavement was a less controversial issue for the lawmakers, and in March 1859, the state approved "to permit free persons of African descent to select their masters and become slaves for life." The law applied to people over twenty-one and was broadly similar in scope to the legislation passed elsewhere. Free people desiring enslavement had to select a master or mistress "willing to become their owner and then file . . . in the office of the Clerk of the District Court of the parish wherein such free person resides, a petition setting forth such desire, together with the name and place of residence of the person whom he or she shall have so selected as a master or owner." Potential slaves also needed to sign their petitions in the presence of two witnesses from the same parish (or mark the document with an "X"), before the petition was posted on the courthouse door for thirty days.[75]

Thereafter, the petitioner, prospective owner, and witnesses all had to appear before the open court, where the district judge had to examine all parties separately to ensure there was "no fraud or collusion between the parties, and that the proposed master or owner is of good repute, and that it is the real and voluntary intent and purpose of said free person to enslave him or herself for life." The district judge then had the power "to grant and decree in accordance with the prayer of the petitioner. . . . [S]aid free person of African descent shall be a slave for life . . . and subject to all the laws of this state regulating slaves; Provided, however, that the said slave shall not be liable to be sold for any debt contracted by the owner before the decree aforesaid."[76]

Louisiana and Alabama used similar wording in their voluntary slavery legislation, which seems deliberately designed to appear "benevolent." The states indicated a desire to protect the interests of vulnerable free people of color by protecting them from "exploitative" sales by careless owners who could not retain control of their own finances. But there was an important caveat in the Louisiana legislation, namely that people could not be sold for debts incurred *before the decree aforesaid*. So it was perfectly legal to sell newly enslaved people, should an owner fall into debt *after* he or she had acquired them. And this was a legislature that also permitted the enslavement of children. Ultimately, then, economic factors underscored voluntary enslavement legislation in Louisiana rather than "humanitarian" concerns. Any mother of children under the age of ten who obtained enslavement for herself also rendered her children the property of her new owner: "Children under ten years, of mothers thus enslaved, become slaves," but like adults, such children were exempt from sale—and also mortgage, execution, or seizure—for debts incurred prior to the enslavement.[77] The Louisiana legislation thus differed from Florida's on children's enslavement: while the latter state permitted mothers to choose whether their children might enter bondage, in Louisiana the process was cruelly automatic.

Maryland combined its restrictive legislation on emancipation and voluntary enslavement after considerable legislative debate.[78] An act of 10 March 1860 prohibited all further manumissions and allowed free blacks to "renounce their freedom" and become enslaved:

> No slaves shall henceforth be manumitted by deed or by last will and testament, nor shall the fact of a negro's going at large and acting as free or not being claimed by an owner, be considered as evidence of the execution heretofore of any deed or will manumitting the party or as a ground for presuming freedom; Provided, that this section shall not apply to such negroes as may have been heretofore manumitted by deed or by the last will and testament of a deceased person to become free at a period which has not arrived and who are now in service as slaves for a term of years.[79]

Reference to indentured servitude ("in service") refers to the somewhat different pattern of racial oppression in the Upper South, where such servitude was more common, and the line between slavery and freedom even more malleable. A second section of this act outlined the process for free blacks seeking slavery as follows:

> Any free negro above the age of eighteen years, may go before the circuit court for the County in which such free negro has resided for three years, next preceding such application or before the Superior Court of Baltimore City, if such negro has resided in said city, and after a full examination in open court by said court, so as to ascertain whether force, fraud, imposition or undue persuasion has been used to induce such application, and upon being perfectly satisfied by such examination, and by any other evidence, which the said court may think it proper to inquire, that such application has not been induced by force, fraud, imposition or undue persuasion, the said court may permit such

negro to select a master or mistress, and shall cause such order to be recorded in perpetual proof of the fact; if such negro shall be a female, her children if any under five years of age, shall be included in such order and become slaves, and those above five shall be bound out.[80]

Regional differences inevitably led to some variations in enslavement legislation, even though the laws passed across the South can be characterized in terms of their broad similarities. In Maryland, where temporary servitude or apprenticeship was more common, the legislature permitted enslavement alongside their mothers only for children under five because children were often bound out after that age. But no surviving voluntary enslavement petitions exist for Maryland. Free blacks in this state who utilized the law through the process of petitioning chose to seek apprenticeships instead. Despite living in the Upper South, Maryland's free people of color were not immune from the harsher racial climate of the 1850s. Throughout this decade, the state "gradually confined them within a bewildering profusion of legal restrictions," and after 1858 "they could be sold upon being convicted of crimes for which whites would be punished by imprisonment."[81]

South Carolinian legislators increasingly argued for expulsion or enslavement as the only options available to "solve" the perceived "problem" of free blacks within the state's borders, much like other southern legislatures.[82] Free people of color themselves therefore lived in an ever more hostile and contradictory world. For example, proslavery advocates rather bafflingly rationalized petitioning for enslavement as an "escape from freedom," with the latter increasingly perceived as an economic "burden" for "inferior" free blacks who were incapable of providing a subsistence standard of living.[83] And by 1859, the state was moving toward the adoption of even harsher legislation against free people of color; the legislature considered more than twenty restrictive bills, including enforced bondage (via being sold to the highest bidder) for those free people of color who did not leave the state by 1 March 1860 and failed to select an owner. The state also permitted voluntary enslavement through individual legislative act.[84] That no bills relating to expulsion or enforced enslavement were passed before the legislature adjourned and war began is rather a moot point. Like other southern states, South Carolina would have moved to implement such laws in the absence of conflict and continued to debate these controversial issues throughout the Civil War.[85]

Notably, the *Charleston Mercury* reported a proposed bill to render all free people of color in the state "slaves to all intents and purposes" from January 1862 onward.[86]

At a local level, historians Michael P. Johnson and James L. Roark have written extensively about the impact of the harsh racial climate of the 1850s upon the port city of Charleston's free black population. Authorities demanded proof of free status from 1860 onward, which had a particular impact upon Charleston's so-called brown elite, previously invulnerable to the changing legal context: "The nightmare of enslavement and the politics that lay behind it caused a profound change in the outlook of the city's leading free colored families. Their confidence in the security of their freedom was shattered, and they began to despair. . . . The enslavement crisis and secession forced the free colored elite to confront as never before the vulnerability of their freedom."[87] And the "brown elite" had every reason to be worried. Legislators such as Edward Moore of York District defined all free blacks as "trifling vagabonds [who] should be sold or compelled to leave the state." White involvement in free blacks' residency petitions shows that in the 1830s white people tended to differentiate between "deserving" and "undeserving" free blacks. But by the 1850s free people of color were increasingly viewed as an undesirable homogenous mass, unworthy of residency, who imbalanced the careful coexistence between free whites and enslaved blacks in southern society. Moreover, while none of these South Carolina bills proscribing free blacks were approved, they remained on the table even though the subsequent war meant they never were enacted.[88]

In March 1858, the Tennessee assembly passed a law "that described a process by which free blacks could voluntarily become slaves," and one year later the legislature, like that of South Carolina, debated a bill in which all free people of color in the state would be removed to Africa or face enslavement.[89] Tennessee's voluntary enslavement law applied to those over eighteen, and bondage was forbidden to those under that age.[90] Details of the legislative debates about enslavement and expulsion within Tennessee reveal the inherent contradictions at the heart of both issues, as well as the nervous tentativeness that characterized discussion. For example, William Ewing drew a distinction between "citizens" and "subjects," with the latter equally eligible for rights (if not true citizenship) under the law regardless of the Dred Scott case. Gustavus Memminger put forward similar arguments in the South Carolina House of Representatives. He proclaimed: "The free negro is a subject, and in all countries where the definition of subject is understood, he has his rights just as well as any other citizen. The citizen may vote, but the subject and every man is entitled to the protection of our laws."[91]

Memminger and Ewing both believed free people of color should have *some* entitlements in society. Ewing argued they should have "rights of life" and liberty as pronounced by the Constitution, adding: "I do not think . . . that a free man had a right to dispose of his freedom by his own voluntary act, any more than he had to dispose of his life. . . . Liberty is that thing with which he is endowed by his Creator, and being so endowed, he cannot, by his own act, dispose of it. All our constitutions and laws recognize the condition of slaves as one of *involuntary* servitude, and that word is always attached [italics in the original]."[92] Significantly, Ewing omitted the word "black" from his speech, selecting the term "free man" instead. Ewing also regarded "choosing" bondage as conceptually impossible, notwithstanding any practical benefits it might bring to slaves and masters. Liberty, like life itself, was a gift from God that could not be subjected to a change in status.

Ewing also presented a rigorous defense of "free negroes" already living in Tennessee. Their existence was "not to be feared," because their numbers stood at only around seven thousand and "we have more than twenty times that number of free white men within the confines of this state." Free blacks were also of economic benefit to slave owners: "In my opinion it prevents a violent antagonism between free and slave labor. The free negro performs many menial offices to which the white man of the South is peculiarly averse. They are our hack-men, draymen, our messengers and barbers; are always ready to do us many necessary services; if they are driven from the Southern States who will supply their place?"[93] In valuing the economic input of free blacks, William Ewing was not unusual, but in his views he had more in common with white people who supported residency petitions in the 1830s than with the late antebellum proslavery ideologues. These people saw expulsion and enslavement as easy solutions to the growing "problem" posed by southern free people of color, although across Tennessee there survive only three petitions from free blacks seeking bondage, suggesting black perceptions of enslavement there were very different.[94]

While Tennessee forbade the enslavement of children, Texas adopted the same age profile as Florida, whereby all free blacks over fourteen could enter bondage, and those younger could have it "selected" for them by their mothers.[95] In 1858, Texas and Florida also both passed their legislation on voluntary slavery. The Texas lawmakers declared it legal for "any free person of African descent, now in this state, or who may hereafter be within its limits, being over the age of fourteen years, to choose his or her master, and become a slave." However, there was also a restrictive clause: "Provided, said slave shall not be subject to forced sales for any debt incurred by, or judgment rendered against the chosen master prior to the period of enslavement."[96] Thus, sales in response to owners' debts again emerged as a restrictive clause in enslavement legislation. Like Louisiana and Alabama, Texas sought to outlaw the acquisition of slaves as collateral specifically to pay off previous debts, so legislators must have been anticipating some cajoling into bondage for this purpose. But again, the lawmakers enacted no legislation to prevent the sale of new slaves for debts accrued subsequent to their purchase. Moreover, despite the existence of laws designed to prevent free blacks from entering the state, in making reference to free people of color "who may hereafter be within [Texas]," legislators made it clear that they expected further migration of free blacks into their state.

The second part of the Texas act described in detail the processes by which free people of color could petition for enslavement via district courts. Potential owners had to be named, and petitions signed in the presence of two witnesses. Requests then had to be "posted at the court house door for four weeks," during which time petitioners and their proposed masters had to appear in court. The third part explained how each party had to separately be examined, to check for "fraud and collusion" and that "the proposed master is a person of good repute." The court then had the power "to grant the prayer of the petitioner; and from the entry of such decree, the property in said person of African descent, as a slave, shall vest in the person so chosen as master, and his rights and liabilities, and the condition of the petitioner shall in all respects be the same as though such petitioner had been born a slave to the master so chosen."[97] So Texas's procedure for becoming a slave was broadly similar to those of other states, and the wording employed by legislatures was remarkably similar across the South.

But Texas stood typically alone in that it was the only state for which legislation about the enslavement of free black orphans survives. These poor children were allowed to enter bondage: "In that case the next friend of such children shall have authority in their behalf, to proceed in the same manner to the selection of a master for them, as the mother might do under the provisions of this act." This rather ambiguous wording suggests any free black person caring for free children of color could seek enslavement for themselves and the children for whom they were responsible. This was a very flexible interpretation of voluntary enslavement, which left free black children with an increased risk of bondage. Texas also specified, as did Virginia, that all costs of voluntary enslavement proceedings "shall be paid by the master to whom the slave may be decreed."[98] Elsewhere in the South, details about payment for new slaves accrued voluntarily tended to be summarized within individual petitions themselves and were not specified in a more general way by legislatures.

In 1856, Virginia became the first state to formalize voluntary enslavement legislation, in keeping with the state's reputation as a torchbearer for laws on slavery. Other southern states looked to Virginia for leadership in the areas of expulsion and enslavement, and followed the state's legislative example. Before 1856 individual free people of color in Virginia could become enslaved, but only through "special" legislative act.[99] After 1856, the state proudly proclaimed that any free woman of color over the age of eighteen, and man over the age of twenty-one, could choose a master by court petition: "The value of the Negro shall be ascertained and the individual chosen as master shall pay into court one half of such valuation, and enter into bond, in such penalties the court may prescribe, with condition that the said Negro shall not become chargeable to any county or city. . . . [T]he condition of the petitioner shall in all respects be the same as though the Negro has been born a slave . . . the children of any such female free person of color previously born shall not be reduced to slavery."[100] Permitting women to choose bondage at a younger age than men meant that the supply of future slaves could be maximized through these women's enslaved offspring. However, there was also a nod toward humanitarianism in Virginia's exclusion of the enslavement of free black children, and this action was later replicated in Tennessee.[101] Perhaps in states where the legislatures felt more confident and secure about the future of the institution, they were willing to forbid the movement of free black children into bondage. Yet opinions could change, especially as sectional tensions increased. In 1861 the Virginia legislature amended its laws about "free negroes" who entered slavery while they had free children. Owners were required to "take the custody, control and service of such children as are free, until the females arrive at eighteen years and the males at twenty-one." Thereafter the former owners had to pay for their labor.[102] Virginia therefore imposed upon these free black children slavery in all but name. Moreover, by the ages at which free women and men could petition for their own enslavement, their "masters" might have cajoled them into requesting legal bondage.

Court costs in voluntary slavery cases had to be met by new owners and paid into the public treasury.[103] Like the procedures subsequently adopted in other states, then, the processes behind enslavement were very cumbersome and laborious. A free person of color had to file a petition in the circuit court of the county in which he or she lived and to name the person "he or she desires to select as an owner." Potential slaves and two independent witnesses had to sign petitions. After this, the petitions were displayed "at the front door of the court house for one month" before petitioners and potential owners were separately examined in court to ensure "that no injustice is done to the petitioner. . . . If upon examination, the court shall be satisfied that there is no fraud or collusion between the parties, and that there is no good reason to the contrary, the said court shall have the power to grant the prayer of the petitioner." The court also had to decide the value of the petitioner "as if he or she were a slave," and the potential master had to pay one half of this value and "enter into bond with approved security."[104] The prices involved in enslavement requests are considered in more detail in chapter 3, despite there being a relative scarcity of surviving evidence on such monetary exchanges. But, like all southern states, Virginia attempted to make the acquisition of free people of color as new slaves relatively inexpensive, facilitated by a system of bonds, thus opening up slave-ownership to a wider pool of potential masters.

Virginia also considered the enforced expulsion of free people of color throughout the 1850s, with the case being pushed most strongly by Democrat John Rutherfoord. However, expulsion bills failed in 1853 and 1858, largely on the economic grounds that free blacks provided much needed labor.[105] But nooses were tightening round the necks of free people of color in Virginia, all of whom (like those in Georgia), from 1853 onward, were forced to pay an annual tax of one dollar. At least one person was forced into bondage for failing to leave the state, and from 1858 all free blacks were forbidden from owning slaves except by descent. Two years later, free people of color convicted of crimes could be sold into bondage "at the discretion of the County Court."[106]

Whether states legislated on expulsion and enslavement (either enforced or voluntary) or not, all southern states were moving in the same direction by seriously considering excluding and enslaving free people of color. Regional differences between the states in terms of their voluntary slavery provisions were slight, even when variation in surviving evidence is taken into account. A relative lack of legislation within some southern states can be attributed to issues of timing and the impact of the Civil War rather than any deep-seated ideological opposition to expulsion and enslavement. But states of the South looked to each other for leadership and guidance, and this inevitably meant some states enacted harsher legislation than others prior to the outbreak of war. Some were still mulling over both issues as war broke out, while Arkansas took the lead in the culmination of pre–Civil War hostility toward free blacks, expelling all free people of color from its borders.

Like Arkansas, Delaware, Kentucky, Mississippi, Missouri, and North Carolina all failed to legislate on voluntary enslavement before the Civil War. Unlike Arkansas, these states also failed to legislate on the enforced expulsion of free blacks. But all implemented ever more hostile laws directed against free people of color as concerns about their presence grew. Even in the Upper South, Delaware passed in 1851 a raft of restrictive new legislation, decreeing: "The rapid increase of free negroes in this state is a great and growing evil, injurious and corrupting to the resident negroes and mulattoes, and the necessary consequence of our laws and geographical position; And Whereas, other states in 'the Union' which do not recognize the institution of slavery, have, by their constitutions and statutes, guarded against the evils of a large free negro population, it becomes the duty of the Legislature of Delaware, to pass such laws as will be practical in their bearing, and at least arrest the grievance now so generally felt." A new act "in relation to free negroes and slaves" therefore replaced the previous laws of 1811. For example, free blacks were not permitted to leave for more than sixty days or to assemble for political purposes.[107] In 1863, the amount of time for which free people of color could leave Delaware was reduced to only five days.[108] Laws of 1861 outlined how free blacks could be sold for indebtedness, although the term of servitude could not be for more than seven years. Buyers were also prohibited from selling free people of color out of the county without judicial approval, and it was made illegal to "bind away [a] free negroe or mulattoe child, to any other free negroe or mulattoe within this state."[109] There were, then, significant parallels between the laws governing free people of color in the Upper South and those imposed elsewhere.

Kentucky did not legislate on voluntary enslavement but prohibited all manumission and forbade free black immigration into the state in 1860.[110] Likewise, although Mississippi failed to enact legislation on voluntary enslavement, in 1860 the general assembly considered a law remanding *all* free people of color to slavery unless they left the state.[111] Missouri also attempted to order free blacks from its borders in the final session before the Civil War, but the state governor vetoed the move, as was the case for a similar initiative in Florida.[112] Enforced expulsion and the voluntary enslavement of free blacks were also debated by the North Carolina legislature. The Humphrey bill, which provided for the enslavement of those who refused to leave the state, was put before the assembly in late 1858 but postponed in February 1859, as some legislators expressed reservations about the harshness of enforced bondage.[113] But free people of color in North Carolina still submitted individual enslavement requests to the legislature and county courts. The absence of a state law, therefore, meant that voluntary enslavement was dependent on the initiative of individuals, either free people of color themselves or their potential owners. North Carolina "demurred on the proposition to eliminate its free negro problem" despite growing suspicions about free people of color's presence there.[114] Across the South, free white and black people were aware of voluntary enslavement initiatives regardless of whether their home states actually legislated on the issue or not.

EXPULSION IN ARKANSAS

Arkansas went further than all other southern states in its discriminatory treatment of free blacks. In February 1859 the state decreed that "there shall be no further emancipation of slaves in this state" and all deeds, wills, or other emancipating acts were "deemed a nullity."[115] The same year Arkansas also famously declared "no free negro or mulatto to reside in the State after January 1st 1860."[116] There are historical parallels between this legislation and the earlier removal of Native Americans westward on the Trail of Tears in the 1830s. Convinced that removal was in the best interests of all concerned, both black and white, late antebellum Arkansas policymakers felt the same way as the federal lawmakers who had deemed Native American removal the only viable option a generation earlier. The 1859 Expulsion Act, in twelve sections, made it illegal for any free person of color to remain in the state after January 1860 and outlined procedures for their expulsion. All responsibility for free black removal was placed with county sheriffs, who were granted the right to arrest and imprison any free person of color without warrant. After twenty days' notice "at five of the most public places in the County," captured free blacks were to be hired out to the highest bidder for twelve months. These bidders had to "give bond, with good and sufficient security . . . and furnish him with the usual amount of clothing that is usually given to hired slaves." Proceeds from these hirings went to the state school fund, and thereafter, the free person of color had thirty days to leave Arkansas.[117]

Hirers of free black people were also "required" to take children under seven, whom they were allowed to keep in their possession until the age of twenty-one. Thereafter, "such purchaser shall give such child, or children, each one suit of comfortable clothing and twenty-five dollars, and such child, or children, shall immediately depart beyond the limits of this state." The Arkansas legislature did not pause to question where these people might go, isolated and lonely, with but twenty-five dollars to their names. Instead, the state offered only one route by which free people of color might choose to stay within Arkansas: through enslavement. The 1859 laws outlined how "any free negro or mulatto" could remain by choosing a master or mistress, provided that the potential owner gave written consent.[118] This was amended in 1861 to include children's enslavement, and again, the state was harsh: "Such [new] master or mistress shall be required to take the minor child or children of such free negroe or mulatto."[119]

Historians have estimated that at the time of the expulsion ruling, there were only around seven hundred free people of color in Arkansas, most of whom chose to flee the state.[120] In his detailed case study, Billy D. Higgins illustrated how a free black community in Marion County diminished by 120, leaving only 8 individuals in the area. Oppressive laws rendered the free black population of Arkansas virtually extinct, but because the free people of color involved left no written sources, historians have been able only to hypothesize about their movements. Higgins wrote: "Their decision to go raises several questions. Was their departure forced by Marion County whites who suddenly bought into the passionate rhetoric of the 'fire-eaters'? Did the community travel to a common destination together, or did they leave individually, each seeking to find new beginnings in another place?"[121]

At the dawn of the 1860s, Arkansan free people of color found themselves in a truly desperate situation. Leaving the state collectively—in groups that included beloved family and community members—was certainly an option. But what about free blacks whose primary affective ties were to the enslaved? The eight surviving enslavement petitions from Arkansas, while representing a tiny minority of all free blacks, do reveal something of the heartbreaking dilemmas facing free people of color who found themselves in this place at this time. Some free people of color who remained chose simply to lie low, to be still and hope for better times ahead, but this was a risky strategy. County sheriffs caught at least three free blacks living illegally in Arkansas. All were forced into slavery, as detailed in chapter 4.[122] So, free people of color in Arkansas faced the stark and bewildering "choice" of expulsion or enslavement; enslavement requests from this state all make reference to free blacks' desire for residency. These were people who wanted to remain stationary, and they prioritized their homes, families, and communities in the place called home above their legal status.

Keeping a low profile may well have been the most sensible option for free people of color unwilling or unable to leave Arkansas. As the impact of war escalated, the expulsion act became increasingly hard to enforce, and so expulsion was suspended by lawmakers until January 1863: "All free negroes and mulattoes, now within the limits of this state, who are held in duress, or by operation of law, by and they are, hereby permitted to remain until the first day of January 1863, free and exempt from the operation of an act approved February 12th 1859, requiring all free negroes and mulattoes to leave the state, until that time."[123] Even in the bitter racial climate of Arkansas, the practical implications of military conflict assumed priority. County sheriffs were simply unable to seek out free people of color living illicitly within Arkansas's borders and then force them into bondage via a complicated and bureaucratic system. And, fortunately for the remaining free people of color awaiting a "better day," the Emancipation Proclamation and subsequent Union victory halted these moves toward a biracial system where all blacks were slaves and all whites were free.

From the early nineteenth century through to the eve of Civil War, southern states as a whole passed numerous restrictions on the lives of free blacks as concerns about their existence within the borders of the South grew. These restrictive laws are striking for their similarities across regions rather than their differences. The white men of state governments were certainly considered in their approach, and the laws they directed against free blacks were frequently cumbersome and bureaucratic. Legislation against free people of color was designed to cover all eventualities and prevent legal loopholes through which free blacks could slip unnoticed. And there are other parallels in the restrictive legislation against free blacks, especially the clustering of laws within a relatively short time period. Southern states influenced and inspired each other. They took confidence from one other as they all moved in the same direction: toward an "idealized" biracial system of free whites and enslaved blacks.

But it is questionable whether these laws directed against free people of color were effective and enforceable. Legislation was often framed in a way that suggests policymakers expected a failure to comply and remained unconvinced their policies could practically be implemented. The existence of residency and enslavement petitions submitted by free blacks for which no decisions were ever reached certainly suggests that some legislation was unworkable, especially once the South entered war with the North. Finally, that the southern states continued to formulate their laws individually represents a missed opportunity for the rather inward-looking proslavery legislators of the South; while states undoubtedly influenced each other, the creation of more "federal" laws for the governance of free blacks would have had a stronger impact. At the end of the day, the creation of a biracial system remained for white southern legislatures in the realm of idealism rather than a reflection of reality.

2

FREE PEOPLE OF COLOR AND RESIDENCY REQUESTS

Julius Dabney obtained his freedom from William McKay at some point during the antebellum era. Thereafter, he purchased his wife, Lucinda, and the couple subsequently had a child, Juliet Ann. But all was not well in the Dabney household, with both husband and wife worried about expulsion from their home in Virginia. So Julius and Lucinda decided to petition the legislature, asking for permission to remain in the state. In this request, Julius described how he and his wife "had flattered themselves that they and their infant should henceforth enjoy the blessings of liberty and the right of acquiring property in Virginia their native state, but your petitioners have been lately informed that by law, as soon as their deeds of emancipation shall be executed and recorded, they are required to leave the state of Virginia and if they do not they are subject to be sold as slaves."

The Dabneys did not indicate who told them about their legal expulsion, but their sentiments toward it were made perfectly clear: "That to leave Virginia, the only country known to your petitioners and be compelled to migrate to some other part of the world would to your petitioners be worse than their former condition." Enforced expulsion would also, Julius argued, negate "any benevolence and benefit intended your petitioners by their former masters . . . the only alternative by the law appears to be slavery on the one hand or migration to a strange country on the other, unless aid should be accorded by your honor."[1]

The choice facing the Dabneys was indeed stark, and their anguish is testament to the ties that bound free people of color to their families and communities in the place they called home where they believed they belonged.[2] Although Julius and Lucinda were required under Virginia law to leave within their nuclear family unit, with their infant child and with each other, their petition makes it clear that their affective ties transcended their nuclear household and extended more broadly into their local area. Quite understandably, the Dabneys both believed enslavement or expulsion left them little choice at all. Perhaps hinting at their fear of colonization—an enforced move "back" to Africa, Julius also described their reluctance to move somewhere else in "the world," a "strange country."

Seeking enslavement was not the only unfortunate choice facing free people of color under threat in the antebellum South, and prior to the 1850s, most free blacks seeking legal recourse via petitioning did so by submitting requests to remain in their home states. There were also a small number of legal requests to enter indentured servitude. However, unlike the enslavement requests, for which I have attempted to provide a comprehensive survey of all surviving petitions, for this part of the book I have collated all residency requests from the online version of the Race and Slavery Petitions Project. (A breakdown of these findings has been included in the tables of the introduction.)[3] There are significant parallels between the motivations of free black petitioners for residency and those for enslavement. Indeed, in many senses free people of color's residency requests were poignant forerunners to the enslavement petitions of the 1850s. Slavery and racial discrimination enforced movement, be it related to westward migration, travel between farms and plantations, the hunt for work, or the enforced sales and separations of people.[4] Free blacks who petitioned for residency or enslavement were often asking that they be able to remain still.

Residency petitions also reveal (like enslavement requests) how white and black perspectives toward expulsion differed. Many white people wrote residency petitions on behalf of free people of color, and they couched their words in terms of free blacks' economic worth. Some free blacks also adopted this language, recognizing that they needed to perform to expected modes of behavior in their residency petitions.[5] But other free people of color believed they held little economic value and framed their rather desperate residency requests as appeals to humanitarian compassion. Just as the enslavement petitions illustrate very different perspectives on underlying motivations among blacks and whites, so do those for residency.

As shown in the tables of the introduction, residency requests were skewed geographically, an issue apparently relating to rates of survival rather than to the actions of any particular state. Otherwise, one would expect more requests from Arkansas, the only state to pass (rather than merely debate) an expulsion order. A higher percentage of residency requests (when compared to those for enslavement) came from men and from family groupings. Finally, the residency petitions tended to be clustered within an earlier time frame. While the majority of enslavement requests were made in the 1850s, the 1810s and 1830s proved the most popular decades for submitting residency petitions. Despite the not insignificant difficulties involved in quantification and measuring the motivations behind residency and enslavement requests, what united both was the love for family expressed by free people of color, their desire to remain within their homes with beloved kin. The largest percentage of petitioners behind both enslavement and residency requests stressed this point above all others.

REQUESTS FOR INDENTURED SERVITUDE

There are surprisingly few surviving requests from free people of color who petitioned for indentured servitude, and it was rarer for a free black to ask for a period of indenture than for lifelong enslavement. In total, just seven requests for such indentured servitude were found. Because free people of color conceptualized bondage and freedom as a continuum rather than polar opposites, they would have undertaken processes of indenture much more informally. There was no need for free blacks to seek recourse from either state legislatures or county courts when they entered informal and flexible systems of servitude with white people. Consequently, there is little surviving written testimony about the labor free people of color performed for whites. More formal indenture was also more common in the Upper South, where the dividing line between slavery and freedom was traditionally more blurred and a system of guardianship was more common. For example, in 1837 Francis Jackson, a free black man, was sold in Newcastle County, Delaware, as "a servant to the highest bidder for the period of seven years."[6]

Other cases of indenture across the South include William Brown, who in 1818 bound himself to Daniel Ferguson of St. Landry Parish, Louisiana.[7] Later, in 1860, ten residents of Newberry District, South Carolina, requested the sale of a free woman of color who was in debt. Enforced enslavement was at the forefront of these white minds as a "punishment" for the woman—Justine Birdie—who was notably not seeking indenture for herself. Justine Birdie was apparently indebted for "medical services," and the petitioners noted the law "offers no compulsory process by which she can be made to labor." Significantly, they failed to mention that the law offered no such process for the compulsory servitude of white people either. Exhibiting typically defeminizing attitudes toward black womanhood, the petitioners urged the legislature to sell Justine so she could labor off her debt, she "being stout of body and having children that are large enough to assist her in her work." The petitioners therefore requested Justine be sold "for such time as would be sufficient to pay up all of her debts."[8]

David Bowser, of North Carolina, requested temporary indenture to John M. Baxter in 1861, though the length of service was not indicated. Like Justine Birdie, Bowser was in debt, and he would have perceived servitude as a way of escaping a payment that was impossible for him to make.[9] So his motivations were similar to those of some of the enslavement petitioners who saw bondage as a means of escaping financial difficulties. Where surviving evidence about black motivations is lacking, I have necessarily speculated about why some free people of color asked for temporary servitude while others requested enslavement. Because state legislatures were debating voluntary enslavement in the late antebellum period, it would have been a process with which the petitioners of this time were familiar, thus explaining why there are more petitions for slavery than indenture. Free black people were also likely to be cajoled into enslavement by white people, who no doubt preferred slaves for life to servants for a while. Many whites also had a relative distaste for the entire notion of temporary servitude, because it undermined the biracial system of free whites and enslaved blacks. That there survive more petitions for enslavement than for servitude is testament to the power of white people in cajoling free black people into the former rather than the latter within a context in which, in any case, few experiences of servitude went before the law.

RESIDENCY PETITIONS

Free people of color petitioned for legal residency because they had either entered a state illegally or they believed their current residency was under threat. Southern states considered increasingly restrictive laws designed to expel free blacks from their homes and communities. But free blacks wanted to be still, to remain with their loved ones in the places they called home. So free people of color asked—sometimes very formally, at other times in more desperate tones—to be allowed to stay. Residency petitions hence add considerable strength to the argument that free people of color prioritized their immediate families above all else, even when they offer little detail on the exact composition of kin networks. Moreover, in an increasingly hostile legal climate, black appeals to the compassion of white men of state government were likely to fail. Free people of color petitioning for residency therefore had to signal their appeal by "offering" something that differentiated them from the mass of "undesirable" free blacks. From a white perspective, free people of color living within the borders of their states was permissible for one reason above all others, and that reason was economic. When white people petitioned legislatures or courts requesting free blacks' residency, they frequently framed their requests in terms of the economic worth of free people of color. Residency requests were also more common in the earlier decades of the antebellum period, before voluntary enslavement was widely debated and accepted by state legislatures.

For example, in 1823 a slave owner named William Blake petitioned the legislature of Alabama asking that a man whom he had previously emancipated, named Jacob, be allowed to remain in the state rather than leave within twelve months. Blake had his own economic interests at heart. He posted a "good behavior" bond for one thousand dollars and confirmed that Jacob was a useful "machanick." However, he also testified to Jacob's own ties of affection in a way similar to many of the later enslavement petitioners—Jacob's family members were enslaved and could not be removed with him.[10] Secondary to economic concerns, Blake's emphasis on black familial ties across the free-slave divide was probably designed to highlight Jacob's "respectability" as a contented and able family man. Other white people—thirty-three total—petitioned the Mississippi legislature requesting that Esther Barland of Natchez be exempted from the rulings of an 1822 expulsion act. It had caused Esther "much anxiety," and she was "much grieved at the idea of being driven from the land of her home and friends to find shelter she knows not where." All these words—"land," "home," "friends"—held much resonance for her. But that the request was granted is perhaps testament to the rather different claims of the petitioners about her "industry": she was a productive and efficient worker.[11] Regardless of their legal status as slave or free, black people were all subjected to commodification in terms of their economic value.

So, residency requests framed in terms of humanitarian rather than economic grounds sometimes posed problems for legislators. The Tennessee legislature seemed unsure of how to proceed when executors of the estate of Edward Holmes from White County attempted to find a way around laws that excluded freed slaves from the state. The executors explained in an 1833 petition how Holmes had wished to emancipate "a certain negro woman named Lydia." Aged between forty and fifty, she had "been always a faithful, humble and obedient servant," but "owing to the existing statutory laws of the state they [the executors] are unable to effectuate his intention and wish in the emancipation of said slave without sending her beyond the limits of the State of Tennessee." Holmes's executors simply presented the issue as a problem for the legislature to solve, adding that Lydia was "desiring to remain with her children [and] would prefer a state of slavery to removal." So the petition is rather ambiguous. The executors did not explicitly ask for Lydia's enslavement, instead explaining her preferences, as well as those of Edward Holmes. Not surprisingly, the lawmakers reached no clear decision; they noted rather ambiguously that the request seemed "reasonable."[12] Lydia's motivations have to be speculated, but no doubt her desire to remain with her children (who perhaps remained enslaved to Holmes's descendants) assumed priority over her legal status. This petition, like some others, therefore falls between the two types of requests, for enslavement and for residency.

Much of the surviving evidence on residency petitions is from Texas. Through restrictive legislation on the residency of free people of color prior to 1845, the republic moved in the same direction as the rest of the South. But before statehood, at a time when states further east were driving free blacks further away from any notion of citizenship, free people of color and their supporters in Texas took advantage of a perceived malleability in race relations to request legal equality. Entering the Union after the development of a more systematic and detailed proslavery ideology, Texas lawmakers were chiefly concerned about immigration of free people of color into the state, and after the admission of Texas in 1845, it was technically illegal for free blacks to reside within the state unless the legislature provided them specific relief. Yet, as historian Andrew Forest Muir sensibly pointed out in the 1940s, "despite all this legislative thundering and executive evasion, those free negroes already living in Texas quietly went their way and disregarded both Congress and President."[13] This quiet majority aside, there were some free blacks who sought recourse to the law in an attempt to gain residency. Some petitioned on their own behalfs, while others had some white support.[14]

For example, Greenberry Logan was born enslaved but emigrated to Texas from Kentucky after being manumitted. He described in his 1837 residency petition how he had "been informed that the Constitution contains a clause which prohibits all free persons of color from coming to or remaining in the country, unless by the consent of Congress." Logan protested that he should be able to stay in Texas: he had fought in the Texas War for Independence, during which he severely wounded his arm. He had subsequently settled in Brazoria with his free-born black wife, Caroline, where they ran a boarding house and where he wanted to remain. Logan protested that he "had hoped that the zeal and patriotism evinced by him, in fighting for the liberty of his adopted country, and his willingness to shed blood in a cause so glorious, he might be allowed the privilege of spending the remainder of his days in quiet and peace." His eloquent petition was referred to a special committee, but no outcome was ever decided upon. Indeed, Greenberry Logan would have probably found his "quiet and peace," had he not alerted the authorities to his plight. However, he and his wife continued to live in Texas, so it seems he was not expelled. The couple appears in the 1860 census for Fort Bend, where Greenberry, or "Granbery," as he appears, worked as a blacksmith.[15]

Other Texas residency petitions are similar in scope to that submitted by Greenberry Logan. Nelson Kavanaugh petitioned twice in 1838. In the first, brief, petition he asked simply for residency and protection for any property acquired. But after this was rejected, he thought he should "perform" better. In his subsequent request, therefore, he sought more explicitly to appeal to proslavery ideology. Playing up to white expectations of racial subservience, he claimed to "always have been humble, honest and industrious." He was "no friend to the abolitionists."[16] Two petitions were also filed on behalf of Emanuel Carter in 1838. The first, allegedly written by Carter himself, asked for residency in Red River County "to enjoy, unmolested, the privileges of a citizen so far as to be protected by the laws of the country, and to hold land and other property in his own name." The second was submitted on Carter's behalf by twenty-six white residents of the county, who described the free black man as "industrious," "well disposed," and "honest." They supported his desire to remain in Texas with his property protected but did not allude to his request for citizenship, undoubtedly a more controversial issue than the economic benefits to Texas Emanuel Carter might bring.[17] Economic interests were paramount for whites.[18]

Somewhat curiously, three very similar petitions were submitted to the Texas legislature on behalf of a free black man named Edmund Carter, also of Red River County, who had emigrated there in 1837. This was two years later than Emanuel Carter's arrival, though both men hailed from Tennessee. Edmund Carter, like Emanuel before him, requested citizenship, land, and property rights, and two other supporting petitions (from forty-seven and fifty-five white residents of Red River County) somewhat surprisingly agreed Edmund Carter should be granted citizenship.[19] Although no other evidence survives, it can be assumed that Edmund Carter made a solid economic contribution within the county. Other free people of color who sought permission to remain in Texas in the late 1830s and early 1840s included William Goyens, whose supporters politely described how he had been "of great service to the country in our Indian difficulties." In contrast, Robert Thompson had no record of military heroism with which to appeal to Texas legislators, and there is a note of real desperation in his poignant residency request: "Although he did not fight in 1836 he contributed a valuable mare and rifle to the Army of Texas."[20]

While petitioners hoped military heroism would help them curry favor with white legislators, more common was their more generic plea of "respectability," which encompassed both free black petitioners' emotional attachments and their economic worthiness in the eyes of white supporters. More broadly, too, notions of black respectability existed within a paradigm of accepted racial inferiority that stressed black "difference" from the norm. For example, white citizens of Jefferson County used the phrase "peaceful and respectable" to describe Elisha Thomas and Joshua, Aaron, David, and William Ashworth, all of whom sought legally to remain in Texas.[21] But the legislature apparently ignored their requests, along with those of other Texas free people of color. This sense of uncertainty over free blacks' residency rights and their status under Texas law more generally opened up opportunities for free people of color to remain in Texas, prospects that did not always exist in other southern states.[22]

Texas's uniqueness notwithstanding, the framing of residency requests in terms of respectability was common across the South. An 1859 petition submitted by white citizens of Shieldsborough, Mississippi, requested that a total of twenty-seven free blacks be allowed to remain in the town as "useful members of the community." The petitioners protested that the bill "now before the legislature" would exclude from Mississippi "all free negroes and mulattoes without distinction."[23] Indeed, this issue of distinction was vital in differentiating between free blacks who were respectable and unrespectable, between the deserving and undeserving because only the respectable were deserving of the rights to live in their home states. Such notions explain the flurry of residency requests in the late 1850s and early 1860s. White people, who then petitioned for residency on their behalf, deemed certain free people of color "deserving." Employed within the petitions were common terminologies about respectability to describe free people of color, and the petitioners frequently emphasized words such as "deference" and "sobriety" and referred to free blacks' economic "industriousness" and "usefulness." Petitions white people submitted on behalf of free blacks were not, then, borne out of a sense of benevolence: the free people of color whom whites wanted to keep within their neighborhoods and communities had significant economic worth, with the majority being skilled or semi-skilled workers.

For example, in 1859 white citizens of Hinds County described a free black carpenter named Joseph Nelson as "sober and respectful in his deportment" when they requested he be allowed to remain in Mississippi.[24] A later residency petition allegedly written by Joseph Nelson himself also survives. Nelson's request illustrates that even after the debating of enslavement laws, some free people of color sought legally to remain in their states without recourse to bondage, although the latter course of action was less common. Joseph Nelson protested he had lived in Mississippi since his childhood and he now had an enslaved wife and children belonging to Judge A. Dabney of Raymond. Dabney himself possessed eight slaves, one of whom was an elderly man. Another was a woman of thirty-four, who must have been Nelson's wife. The remaining six were children, perhaps the offspring of Joseph Nelson and his wife.[25] Through his residency petition, Joseph Nelson prioritized his intimate familial relationships in a way similar to those who submitted enslavement requests as detailed in chapter 4. However, Nelson's white supporters framed his residency request rather differently, stressing his respectful, and no doubt deferential, "deportment."

That Joseph Nelson did not mention his own enslavement as a possible future course of action is also interesting. He may have hoped his residency request would be permitted and so was saving his possible enslavement as a last resort. Such a course of action supports the notion that free people of color perceived the distinction between bondage and freedom not as a clear line of delineation but as a whole spectrum of unequal relationships. Joseph Nelson considered himself to have at least some degree of bargaining power in what he was offering to the legislature. His request can be compared to that of William Lewis, who had requested permission of the Alabama legislature to remain in the state in 1839. Lewis conveyed how he had traveled into Alabama with his enslaved wife following the death of her owner (presumably the estate had been divided and she had been forced to move). Describing himself, notably, as a "carpenter and house joiner," thus a skilled laborer, William Lewis also stressed the stability of his marriage by commenting that he had been wed for more than a decade. Finally, if the legislature remained unimpressed with both his economic value and his "respectable" marriage, Lewis had one last card to play. Fully aware of his inferior position in society, he acted on expected racial etiquette, writing that he "always demeaned himself humbly."[26]

All residency requests, whether written explicitly by whites on behalf of free people of color or allegedly by free blacks themselves, were thus constructed around discourses of free blacks' respectability and economic value. A. L. Chevis of Hinds County, Mississippi, labored as a bricklayer and barber. According to the forty-four white supporters of his 1859 residency petition, Chevis always conducted himself "with honesty, sobriety and humbleness; never having, to our knowledge, indulged in any conduct calculated to render his residence here objectionable." Chevis's supporters therefore vouched for his respectability. But A. L. Chevis had, like Joseph Nelson and William Lewis, an enslaved wife and slave children (eight, in his case). Chevis's own urge to remain in Mississippi was therefore motivated by his desire to remain with his spouse and children in a family that straddled the hazy line between the enslaved and the free.[27] Other Mississippi residency petitions similarly reveal only the white motivations behind such residency requests. In Copiah County, residents acting on behalf of the carpenter John Hunter in 1859 described how he "universally deported himself in a humble and praiseworthy manner."[28] That same year saw three other petitions: "Green" was a planter's supply-man, and "sober, industrious and very useful," while

Hinds County blacksmith Edward Hill was described as "temperate, honest and industrious" in the way he ran his own business.[29] Finally, residents of Kemper County proudly described a carpenter known only as "Gillam" as being "of good character."[30]

Notions of free black respectability and usefulness therefore impinged on moves to create a biracial South where all free people of color were regarded as undesirables suitable only for expulsion or enslavement. The explicit distinction between "desirable" and "undesirable" free blacks hence conveys the malleability of racial constructions in the antebellum South, where racial oppression existed in many guises of varying severity. Indeed, some white petitioners were freely open about the divisions they created between different free blacks. There were certainly "vicious and evil disposed" free people of color in Mississippi, thundered residents of Adams County in 1859. But there were also free blacks who "have spent a life here free from reproval, or even the suspicions of improper conduct," and the petitioners urged the legislature to discriminate between the "loyal" and the "unworthy" in expelling free blacks from the state.[31] Moreover, an impressive military record could be used to curry favor with lawmakers in Mississippi as well as in Texas. In their residency petition submitted on his behalf, Warren County residents drew attention to the efforts of a sixty-three-year-old black man who fought in the War of 1812.[32]

Notions of respectability in residency petitions also have resonance for the conceptualization of "appropriate" gendered behavior. Free black women were often denied many of the trades available to men, so their residency requests tended to concentrate (as do some of their enslavement requests) upon maternal roles. For example, Agnes Earhart of Natchez requested to remain in Mississippi because she was the mother of many free children, all of whom were economically productive. But Earhart also posted a "good behaviour bond" on her own behalf.[33] Cleverly playing up to white expectations of "desirable" racial behavior, Agnes Earhart therefore cleverly framed her request in terms of economic viability and "respectability." Likewise, Ann Caldwell was born enslaved, but she obtained her freedom from Margaret Cameron, for whom Caldwell cared when she was confined with consumption. In 1859, she twice petitioned the Mississippi legislature for residency. She gave no information about her own affective ties but instead stressed her role as a "caring" nurse, a performance deliberately designed to appeal to notions of female domesticity. But, like Agnes Earhart, Ann Caldwell did not want to appear in any way "burdensome" and indicated she could give a behavior bond. Moreover, Caldwell was not "chargeable to the state or any county in which she may be permitted to reside."[34] She was an economically independent woman.

In Texas, Zelia Husk and her daughter, Emily, were the subjects of two petitions, in 1840 and 1841. White citizens of Harris County argued Husk should be allowed to remain in the republic and continue to work as a washerwoman. Emphasizing her economic value, the petitioners proudly declared "that she is a good and industrious woman peaceably earning her own livelihood, and that she has not the means of removing with her child beyond the limits of the Republic." In a later petition, which she allegedly wrote herself, Husk noted that she had always conducted herself in an "obedient and respectful" manner.[35] These three free black women—Agnes Earhart, Ann Caldwell, and Zelia Husk—were all victims of a double standard. Racial discrimination ensured that, unlike white women, they were not expected to be dependent on men, or burdens on their states. All had to work outside their homes to make certain a subsistence standard of living for themselves and their families, and such labor typically defeminized black women in the eyes of white southern society. But these proud, hard-working women turned their economic value to their own advantage by framing their residency requests in ways that emphasized their economic independence.

Whether submitted on behalf of black women or black men, petitions for residency were all formulated in terms of what both free people of color and their white supporters expected white legislators would want to hear. This clever framing conveys a black awareness of legislative debates and legal changes and of considerable free black initiative in seeking to improve their lives for the better. From the perspective of free people of color, then, applications for residency related first to their desire to remain with beloved family members; these motivations contrast sharply with the more economically minded white views on free people of color's residency rights. The often poignant residency requests from free blacks, therefore, have much in common with the enslavement petitions described in chapters 4 and 5, where affective ties were of paramount significance.

For example, James Butler of Petersburg, Virginia, was involved in three petitions, in 1810, 1811, and 1813. Butler labored for a decade as a miller before buying his freedom for six hundred dollars from his master, John Osborne. It was only after Butler's manumission that he "learned he would have to leave the state." But as he was "advanced in years" and did not want to leave his enslaved wife and children, in 1810 he requested special permission to remain in Virginia. One year later Osborne submitted his own petition in support of Butler, asking that he be allowed to remain with his family. Perhaps Osborne had been unaware of the law when he freed Butler. In 1813 Butler petitioned again, describing how leaving his family within twelve months would be "infinitely more galling" than bondage, although he did not suggest his own reenslavement as a possible solution.[36] Neither did "Tobias," who similarly petitioned for residency in 1811. Tobias had been freed on the understanding that he could also purchase his wife, but the reality was rather more horrific: "Your petitioner is informed that by a late law of this state he is bound to leave it in one year after his emancipation, which would not only defeat his desirable object of gaining her freedom but must separate him from her, which would be worse to him than slavery itself."[37] Both men prioritized their immediate families above all, and neither could bear the thought of separation from their wives and families. Petitioning before the era of legislative debates about voluntary enslavement, though, they only implicitly suggest that they would prefer reenslavement to separation.

In 1815, a white slaveholder named Bolling Vaughan submitted a petition asking permission for "Ben" to be emancipated and to remain in Virginia, having "served the Vaughan family for more than fifty years." But Ben had an enslaved wife and seven slave children. At his advanced age, it can also be assumed he had some enslaved grandchildren. Vaughan wrote that leaving his wife and family would be "worse than slavery" for Ben, who wanted both his freedom and the right to live in Virginia.[38] James Butler, Tobias, and Ben all believed there was one thing in the world worse than bondage: separation from their beloved families. The various petitions submitted on behalf of these three men can thus be compared with the petitions of Burk and Lucinda, who also lived in Virginia and requested enslavement in the 1810s. The rather loose wording of the residency requests of James Butler, Tobias, and Ben (coupled with their references to enslavement) suggests these men might also have considered bondage an option if their requests were denied, because it was the only way they could remain with their wives and children. Thus the distinction between slavery and freedom was not as absolute for black people as white society preferred to believe.

RESIDENCY REQUESTS AND COLONIZATION

Julius Dabney hinted at his fear of colonization in his residency petition, and although there survives no date for his request, by the 1850s the colonization movement was well entrenched in Virginia.[39] Moreover, legislature debates about colonization display considerable parallels with those over the expulsion of free people of color, if only because removal to Africa was seen as a long-term solution to the "problem" posed by free people of color in the South. The Virginia legislature, for example, passed an act in 1850 granting an annual sum of thirty thousand dollars for the removal of free blacks over a five-year period "to the colony at Liberia, or other place on the Western coast of Africa."[40] Colonization had its origins in what are now regarded as racist concerns as well as humanitarian ones because it grew out of rising hostility toward the very existence of "racially inferior" free blacks. Historian William Link argues that by the 1850s, the Virginia branch of the American Colonization Society perceived expulsion to West Africa as a "political and social necessity" even though the numbers involved were small. He estimates that between 1820 and 1853 only twenty-eight hundred free people of color had left the state for Africa, and attempts to enforce removal through legislative act also failed. Some also expressed humanitarian concerns about civil liberties, while others, especially in urban areas, were worried about the economic consequences of removal.[41] Petitions presented by Virginian whites in favor of colonization certainly support the latter hypothesis, because most of the free blacks they wished to exempt from exclusionary measures were skilled or semiskilled workers.

A number of surviving petitions written by various white people consider in some detail the reasons for and implications of migration to Liberia by free blacks. In 1830, thirty-six Virginia signatories described in a fairly compassionate manner how the state's increasingly restrictive laws passed since 1806 had caused free people of color considerable problems. In addition, other states were imposing similar prohibitions on the immigration of free blacks. Excluded from Virginia yet forbidden from entering other states, the petitioners wondered where free people of color were expected to go; they also argued against enslavement as "inhumane" and recommended instead African colonization as an inexpensive and "humane" remedy.[42] Other petitions, however, were less charitable, especially following the Nat Turner insurrection of 1831, which did much to harden attitudes against free blacks. In 1832 there was a flurry of anxious petitions that convey white Virginians' rising concerns about the "problem" of free blacks within the state. For example, in Gloucester County, 184 residents requested money from the state to pay for free blacks' removal to Africa, which could then be reimbursed via taxation. The petitioners argued the very existence of free blacks made it difficult for owners to keep their slaves "in proper subjection," making explicit a link between slaves and free blacks' fraternization and insurrection.[43]

Likewise, residents of Fauquier County somewhat hysterically worried that the safety of white persons would be at risk should free people of color be allowed to remain in Virginia and suggested 1 January 1837 as a cut-off date, after which all free blacks should be sold into bondage.[44] Free blacks incited "discontent and insubordination" among slaves, according to thirty-two petitioners from Northumberland County. Colonization in Africa, however, would place free people of color "upon a footing of liberty and equality." The petitioners' language suggests enforced migration to Liberia would be mutually advantageous for all southerners—both black and white.[45] Indeed, such "humanitarian" concerns were intrinsically bound up within a broader racist framework of expulsion. Other Virginia petitioners were concerned more with the practical—urging the state to fund through taxation the removal of free blacks to Africa.[46] Isle of Wight County residents displayed some sophistication within the discourse of their petition, arguing that free people of color were neither freemen nor slaves. "The mark set on them by nature precludes their enjoyment, in this county, of the former; and the laws of the land do not allow them to be reduced to the condition of the latter." Free blacks were therefore "trapped" between freedom and bondage in an unhappy compromise whereby they "benefitted" from neither situation. Migration to Liberia was thus again cited as an "ideal" solution to the "problem" of this "ill-fated class."[47]

From a free black perspective, too, the idea of migration to Liberia was sometimes an attractive one. Africa had symbolic connotations of an ancestral home and a place of freedom from racial oppression. Yet, Africa was not home, and some free people of color bitterly regretted moving there. Such individuals begged to be allowed to return to the United States, even if that meant reentering as slaves. For them, "Back to America" was a more appropriate slogan. In a broader geographical context, other states followed Virginia's lead in debating colonization. For example, Mississippi considered the removal of some free people of color to Liberia at a more local level. In 1854 the Pike County Board of Police was authorized to hire out at public auction all free blacks in that county with the surname Lundy, with 8 percent interest charged on their labor costs. This policy was deliberately designed to create a fund of some six thousand dollars to ship the Lundys to Liberia and provide "for said negroes comfortable lodgings and provisions for one year."[48] A note of paternalism is clearly visible in this legislation, yet it remains unknown whether the Lundys themselves were instrumental in initiating the request. Census evidence from 1850 shows that many Lundy family members were already hired out before the 1854 legislation and provides fascinating insights into the Lundys and their household composition.

There were twenty-six black or mixed-race people with the surname Lundy in the 1850 census, fifteen of whom lived in a large, multigenerational family in Police District 2. Headed by Robin Lundy, a black farmer of twenty-eight, this household also contained three other black men in their twenties, described as laborers; a woman of fifty-seven (Dolly); and four women in their twenties and thirties. Four children ranging in age from eleven years to three months old also lived in this extended family; across time and space it has been fairly typical of families for whom poverty is an issue to reside together.[49] Extended families provide additional labor for financial support, and women can share childcare duties within a domestic environment. However, a trawl through the other Lundys in the Pike County census reveals something rather more unusual. Spread throughout eight additional white-headed households were a number of Lundy children—of whom the eldest, John, was fifteen, and the youngest, Celia and Bob, were both six.

These children all lived either alone or in pairs with these white families, of whom many had the surname "Quin." The Lundy children seem to have been sent to labor in white households either in return for money or to spare the adult Lundys the day-to-day costs of raising them. These children probably performed small domestic chores and helped with childcare, with the older children perhaps doing farm work. In short, their labor was practically the same as that of enslaved children, and the very notion that the Lundy children were "free" people of color is rendered rather meaningless by their day-to-day existence. The plight of these poor children shows how slavery and freedom were at opposite ends of a whole spectrum of exploitative unequal relationships that had many manifestations in between.

Family formations within free black households—such as those of the Lundys—were malleable, rendering the search for familial structures within census data often elusive. But it is clear that familial structures transcended the nuclear, that extended kin networks were highly significant for free blacks, and also that affective ties bound free people of color to the enslaved. Take fifteen-year-old John Lundy, for example. He lived with the Stallins, a farming family whose head of household, James, owned five slaves.[50] John Lundy would have lived within this small enslaved community as if he were part of it. Likewise, a lawyer named John T. Lamkin, in whose household eleven-year-old Sarah Lundy resided, owned forty-two slaves.[51] The Stallin and Lamkin families would have treated John and Sarah Lundy much the same as their chattel, meaning that the Lundy children were slaves in all but name. And the same can be said of the other Lundy children. William and Stephen, both just ten years old, lived with the McNabb family, farmers and owners of a family of six slaves.[52] The merchant George Nicholson owned one thirty-five-year-old enslaved woman yet also had living in his home Cindarilla and Jane Lundy, aged eleven and nine respectively.[53] Bob Lundy, just six years old, lived with rather elderly Daniel Quin, Quin's wife, and his eight enslaved people who no doubt cared for the young Bob.[54] In a similar situation was six-year-old Celia Lundy, residing in the household of a farmer named H. Murry Quin, who owned six slaves.[55]

Complex racial and class relationships were intertwined in the case of Goober Lundy, aged just seven. Lundy resided in the household of an overseer, Peter H. Quin, Quin's wife, and his infant daughter.[56] The plantation owner for whom Peter Quin worked is unknown, but certainly Peter Quin, his family, and Goober Lundy came into contact with the enslaved on a daily basis. That Quin was an overseer also suggests the family was not terribly wealthy. The Quins possibly hired free black children because they could not afford slaves of their own. The service of Lundy children within Peter Quin's household would, therefore, have increased the family's sense of their own status and prestige, as well as providing helpful additional household labor. Like the other unfortunate Lundy children, Goober was essentially enslaved. In the longer term, attempts to raise enough money to ship the Lundys to Liberia seem to have failed. Twenty members of the family appear on the 1860 census for Pike County, many of them still laboring within white households. Bob, now sixteen, resided in the home of Frank, not Daniel, Quin and his family, while Celia and Goober remained with the same white families. Sarah Lundy had left the Lamkin household and lived alone with her two infant children, Wallace and Charles.[57] The Lundys' experiences, accessible only through detailed investigations into census evidence, confirm the existence of de facto slavery for southern free people of color before the Civil War.

Like Mississippi, South Carolina encouraged migration to Liberia. In 1831 a group of educated free people of color formed an organization designed to promote emigration there, and they had some success in encouraging both the enslaved and free blacks to leave the United States.[58] Jehu Jones Jr. provides a famous example of such attempted emigration. A member of Charleston's free black elite, he left the state to work as an editor on a Liberian newspaper. But the job appears to have fallen through, and Jones never traveled farther than New York. To add insult to injury, he was also banned from reentering South Carolina as a free person of color, and he had to submit a residency petition asking to be allowed return to the state and his home. In his 1840 petition, Jones described how he was "induced to leave his happy home in South Carolina in 1832 by promises of great remuneration in money and valuable lands, made by the Friends of the American Colonization society to engage my services for Liberia." However, such promises were "merely a delusion," and the society cruelly "abandoned me to my fate, among strangers . . . without friends, without funds and without employment." Now living in Philadelphia, Jones wrote that he wished "to visit the grave of my father, the spot where I was born, grew up and lived respectfully for nearly half a century." Finally, he "begs the legislature of my Native state to permit my return to South Carolina."[59]

A second 1840 petition submitted on behalf of twenty-four Charleston residents also requested that Jones be permitted to return to his beloved home: "They are fully satisfied that his character is fair and his deportment such as to render him not merely harmless but exceedingly well calculated to diffuse useful knowledge and inculcate proper principles in our colored population."[60] The sad experience of Jehu Jones, stuck in northern geographical "limbo" between South Carolina and Africa, again illustrates how black motivations behind residency petitions were related to a love of "home" and "family," both necessarily flexible terms connected to one's sense of "belonging." That "northern" always equaled "better" can also be questioned by exploring the perspectives of free black southerners for whom being "at home" in the South assumed priority. Finally, Jehu Jones reveals something of the complex ironies for "free" black people in the antebellum south, where "freedom" sometimes meant banishment from one's home and family, from where one belonged, and from where one really wanted to be.

BETWEEN SLAVERY AND FREEDOM

A free black woman from Richmond, Virginia, named Judith Hope perceptively picked up on the irony of being a free person of color in the antebellum South, as well as the incredibly hazy line between slavery and freedom, in her two legislative petitions of 1820. In the first, Hope claimed her freedom because her father (a free black barber named Caesar Hope) had provided for the emancipation of his enslaved children in his will. Hope believed she was entitled to be free, but there was a caveat. She also wrote, quite understandably, that she was not prepared to leave her mother, presumably recently widowed, to whom she was dearly attached. Poignantly and eloquently, she described how leaving Virginia would be "severing every connection and every habit and partiality of her life." She also worried about an 1816 law that required "meritorious service" as a precondition for remaining in Virginia after manumission. Rather over-honestly, Hope stated that she could not make such a claim.

Records indicate Hope's petition was rejected, though it is unclear whether it was her request for freedom or her desire to remain in Virginia which was denied. The legislature may have forbidden both.[61] She wrote a second petition, couched in much stronger tones. Brimming with anguish and eloquence again, she described how freedom would be a "cruel mockery" if she could not live where "her every friend and natural connexion upon earth" resided, and "where her every habit and association which years had fostered and matured remained."[62] But the legislators remained unmoved and rejected this second petition as well. In desperation, in 1821 Judith Hope petitioned the Virginia legislature for a third time. Her anger clearly evident, she described how the efforts of her late father had been "totally frustrated" even though an injunction had been taken out against the executor of his estate (by whom is unclear). By 1821, Hope herself had been bought by her mother, Tenar, obviously anxious to protect her daughter from future sale or separation. Again "in line with her father's wishes," a clearly impassioned Judith Hope requested both her freedom and residency rights.[63]

Judith Hope's passionate petitions reveal how she clearly felt she had been immensely wronged by the legal process. She believed it was her fundamental right to be free *and* to continue to live in Virginia at home with her mother. Affective ties between the enslaved and the free took many different forms. Tenar Hope's purchase of her own daughter shows that strong men and women were prepared to seek legal recourse to keep their families around them, regardless of their legal status as enslaved or free. Judith Hope's insistence that her father's wishes be "respected" also conveys her absolute refusal to acknowledge that people of color were not able to (or worthy of) using the machinery of law. The experiences of the so-aptly-named Hope family that crossed the hazy line from slave to free sum up in a nutshell the complexities of race, class, and gender interactions in the early-nineteenth-century South. Caesar, Tenar, and Judith Hope exemplify the broader struggle of black people—enslaved and free—to fight for what they perceived to be their rights as people who lived in their homes, with their families, in beloved communities.

Other free people of color fell, like Judith Hope, somewhere between the statuses of slave and free in legal terms. Lucy Wright and Lucy Claibourne had been manumitted in 1813 but remained in Virginia, contrary to the law, as "they did not have the means to emigrate." By the time of their joint residency petition in 1821, each woman had two children, "ranging in age from seven years to ten months." Apparently "the overseers of the poor took them up as slaves," but now the two women were scared of being separated from their children, all of whom had legally been declared free. Both Wright and Claibourne had been told that they had "forfeited their right to freedom . . . and should be sold as slaves." They therefore requested that they be able to stay in the commonwealth as free women of color. The two women also used whatever bargaining power they had to frame their petition. Ingeniously, yet also honestly, they situated their petition in the context of their roles as loving and nurturing mothers. This was obviously at odds with most contemporary ideologies of black womanhood, yet it was one Lucy Wright and Lucy Claibourne hoped would have resonance with white legislators.

Wright and Claibourne were also aware of the economic dimension of their expulsion. They wondered who, exactly, would provide for their children should the two mothers be enslaved: "Your petitioners were to be converted into slaves and separated from their infant children yet two of whom are dependent upon them for their sustenance which nature has provided the mother should for a time afford her offspring."[64] Both women performed to racial and gendered expectations in the discourses of their petition. The quality of their impassioned prose (whether they received assistance in writing their appeal or not) is testament to the strength of their desire to remain in Virginia with their families as free people of color, as they believed they were entitled to do.

Lucy Wright and Lucy Claibourne existed somewhere between enslavement and freedom in part because they were taken up as slaves by the overseers of the poor. Elected officials, overseers of the poor, began in the late eighteenth century to "make policy, levy and distribute public money, and deal with paupers as they thought best."[65] Although they dealt with cases of poverty among both black and white people, in taking responsibility for needy free people of color, the overseers of the poor actually diluted the distinction between freedom and enslavement. This sometimes created complications for the legal system. For example, Wright and Claibourne could have ended up enslaved, while their offspring were technically free. The two women were therefore quite right to wonder about from whence their children would be provided. The overseers of the poor also caused complications for Jim Outten, a free black man forced into bondage by his refusal to leave Virginia. He had been sold at a public auction in Accomack County in 1826 alongside other free people of color. Overseers of the poor conducted these sales, and the money raised was paid to the public treasury.

Jim Outten was bought by a man named Littleton Henderson, and here the story might have ended. But crucially, Outten was not in Virginia at the time of his own sale but in Baltimore; thus, he was bought without having been seen. He was also capable of using the legal system and prepared to do so as a means to protest his involuntary move into bondage. Claiming it was against the law to sell a black man not in custody, Outten sued for his freedom. Henderson subsequently petitioned the legislature in December 1827 for financial reimbursement and was probably very concerned about the "troublesome" nature of his new property. Henderson's petition was unsuccessful, so in 1828 he again petitioned the legislature, claiming he had bought Outten in good faith "for fifty dollars." He wanted his money returned. Notably, too, Henderson described how he had been wrongly accused of "being a speculator in slaves."[66]

A third petition relating to Jim—now described as James—Outten, survives from 1834.[67] Littleton Henderson had sued a man named John G. Joynes for selling Outten when the latter was in Baltimore, and Joynes was now seeking compensation himself, having had to reimburse Henderson. Outten's actions, his initiative before the law had important financial ramifications for these two white men, both of whom were forced to use the law themselves in the face of financial losses. Jim Outten seems to have been released from bondage, and, by 1850, aged thirty-eight, he worked as a sailor and still lived at home in Accomack County, with a young black woman named Amris Purkins. If Outten's age on the census is correct (his birth year was only given as "about 1812"), he would have been but a teenager at the time of his sale.[68] This makes his efforts to use the law as a vehicle to shift himself away from slavery toward freedom all the more commendable.

Finally, some residency petitions simply offer a desperate reminder of the meaning of home as a place of belonging for free people of color. Howard Cash was born free and lived in Hinds County, Mississippi, with a wife who had purchased her own freedom. Both rather aged, in 1859 they requested a "special act" to allow them both to stay in the state. "If it may please the almighty to spare their lives, they will endeavour to demean themselves as good and loyal subjects to the state."[69] Howard Cash and his wife were perhaps both unskilled workers, with their ages also affecting their abilities to labor. Being "good and loyal" was, therefore, all they had left to offer. But offer it they did.

The residency requests cited within this chapter display striking parallels to the enslavement petitions of free people of color. Both show that people's interests, needs, and desires remained broadly the same over time. For free people of color, the desire to stay with beloved kin was paramount, whether that kin constituted immediate family members or more distant relatives from extended family networks. Ties of affection, especially spousal, crossed the blurry divide between slavery and freedom in the early antebellum era as much as the late. White people viewed the residency rights of free blacks in a much more pragmatic way that prioritized their own economic objectives. Free people of color who had an economic input were deemed "worthy" of residency, and racism was couched in terms of degrees. Some free blacks were "better" than others, but the march of the proslavery ideologues held no place for a relative conception of race because it upset visions of a biracial South of free whites and enslaved blacks. As sectional tensions rose through the 1830s, 1840s, and 1850s, then, a new and chilling alternative to the idea of "exceptional" residency requests moved to the forefront of legislative discussion, that of the expulsion or enslavement of all free people of color.

3

"Traditional" Motivations and White Perspectives on Voluntary Enslavement

The aptly named Daniel Freeman from Orangeburg, South Carolina, requested that the House of Representatives permit him to become enslaved to John B. Murrow. Freeman was apparently "assured that the condition of slavery would be preferable to his present condition as a free person of color. That he is anxious to relinquish his present dubious condition and grant to himself the benefits of protection and support which will arrive from the relation of master and servant." Freeman then marked his request, for which there survives no date, with an "X," so indicating that the "real" writer of his petition remains unknown.[1] But the choice of words is vitally significant. Freeman's petition defined bondage as "preferable" to freedom; the latter was but a "dubious condition" without the "benefits of protection and support" granted by masters. Like Daniel Freeman, many other enslavement petitioners couched their requests in terms of proslavery ideology, where bondage was suggested as a positive good. Such petitioners were typically seeking to appeal to white lawmakers by performing to expected racial roles.[2]

Daniel Freeman does not appear to have any familial ties to the Murrow family slaves, as John Murrow owned only four: a twenty-year-old woman, an eighteen-year-old man, and two young children, apparently a nuclear family grouping.[3] Neither did Freeman live within the Murrow family's household. In the 1860 census, he appears as a thirty-five-year-old "mulatto" who lived in the household of the non-slaveholding white Howel family.[4] So Freeman's motivations for enslavement remain elusive. Indeed, the impetus behind his petition could have come from John Murrow himself. Master of only four slaves, Murrow would significantly increase his chattel through his acquisition of Daniel Freeman. This particular petition, therefore, also hints strongly at the typical socioeconomic profiles of potential owners, who tended not to be wealthy men.

Surviving petitions such as this one have been interpreted too literally by contemporary proslavery ideologues and subsequent generations of historians. Typically, both the expulsion and enslavement of free people of color have been viewed through a prism of issues that include impoverishment, debt, and the notion of enslavement as a positive good. This chapter will show that all three areas constitute "traditional" explanations for the phenomena of expulsion and enslavement and that all dwell exclusively on white, rather than black perspectives. While poverty, financial debt, and proslavery ideology can all offer some partial explanations for free blacks' expulsion and enslavement, all three factors ignore the significant role free blacks' more intimate sentiments played, and they fail to address free black volition where people were fighting to remain where they belonged, with beloved kin.

This chapter takes as its starting point the use of enslavement requests as proslavery propaganda in southern newspapers. It also probes more deeply the framing of slavery petitions in terms of proslavery discourses, and it will also consider those petitions submitted by free blacks who had fallen foul of the law and those who were poor, impoverished, or sickly. The chapter also assesses the socioeconomic profiles of potential owners by tracking their slave ownership. What sorts of people cajoled or tricked or otherwise encouraged free people of color into requesting bondage? The broad conclusion is that most potential owners, like John Murrow, held only a few slaves (if any at all). They regarded voluntary enslavement initiatives as a way into the slaveholding class, with subsequent economic gain. White potential owners did not seek voluntary slaves for benevolent reasons, despite their public framing of petitions in such a way. Finally, the chapter will comment on the financial transactions involved in enslavement requests and the economic value of free people of color to their potential masters.

ENSLAVEMENT REQUESTS AS PROSLAVERY PROPAGANDA

Situated within the contexts of poverty, debts or ill health are the traditional historical explanations for enslavement. John Hope Franklin saw voluntary slavery as a means by which "free negroes" could avoid legal difficulties and cited the example of John Stewart, who moved to Cincinnati, Ohio, after having purchased his freedom in Raleigh, North Carolina. In 1854 he was sentenced to a chain gang after he entered a plea of guilty to stealing. He apparently expressed regret that he was now a free man and vowed to return to the South and slavery.[5] Stewart's story was picked up by southern newspapers, which took great pleasure in couching these enslavement requests within broader proslavery rhetoric. Slavery would be much "better" for free people of color than freedom would. Indeed, the experiences of men such as John Stewart confirmed white beliefs in free blacks' inability to cope without masters. Such propaganda explains why skeptical historians have regarded enslavement petitions as having little value. Historians have often believed these petitions to be mere rogue examples that convey nothing other than the development of proslavery thought.

For example, in 1852, the *New Orleans Daily Picayune* described two free people of color who "preferred slavery to freedom." The first story explained how a white man, Mr. J. Ridge, traveled to California from Arkansas with his "negro" man whom he subsequently freed. However, Mr. Ridge's "negro" did not wish to partake in the delights of the West Coast and apparently returned home. The newspaper argued he preferred "perpetual slavery in Arkansas to freedom in California." The second (suspiciously?) similar story appeared later that year. This time, another freed Arkansas slave, named Kent, who had once belonged to William Pennington, returned from California to the South. He was arrested in New Orleans for not having the "necessary papers," but the authorities then allowed him to return to Arkansas and reenslavement. The newspaper noted, rather pompously, that "the above facts are submitted for the reflection of the Abolitionists of the North."[6] Both stories focused on bondage as preferable to freedom per se. But from the perspective of the free black men involved, familial and community affective ties may have assumed priority over legal status.

Likewise, Hannah Dodds was emancipated by James Dodds in Shelby County, Tennessee. She later petitioned the Shelby County Court requesting that she be able to remain there through reenslavement, writing: "She was born and reared in a slave state—all of her relatives and associations are here." So while this request can be compared to many enslavement petitions, where the maintenance of familial relationships was placed above all other concerns for free blacks, Dodds also cleverly played on white sentiments in the hope that her request would be granted: "If she is driven from this state she will be compelled to settle in some of the free states . . . in no portion of our government is the condition of the free colored race more deplorable than in the free states."[7] The *New Orleans Daily Picayune* also picked up her request, describing her as: "sensibly saying that she preferred being a slave and [to] remain in Tennessee . . . that she wanted a kind master to take care of her and provide for her wants. The Court therefore ordered a decree, in accordance with the prayer of the petitioner and the law of Tennessee."[8] Dodds may, like Kent, have wanted to stay enmeshed within her broader familial and community networks. However, the depiction of her motivations, in both the petition itself and the newspaper, reveals more about "benevolent" proslavery ideology. In making claims about the superiority of southern bondage to northern freedom, Hannah Dodds conformed to white racial expectations where her own familial bonds mattered little. According to proslavery discourse, under bondage she would be "cared for" by a "kind master," a depiction notably at odds with the reality of life for enslaved women, with their constant fear of sale, separation, physical punishment, and sexual abuse.

Another New Orleans newspaper, the *Daily Delta*, also covered enslavement requests, including the local petition of John Clifton, who chose Green L. Bumpass as his master.[9] Historian Judith Kelleher Schafer claims Clifton first appeared in the *Daily Picayune* in 1853 for "stealing clothing" and was sentenced to a chain gang. But just two years later, he had committed another offense and appeared before the first district court for "contravention." He posted bond to leave Louisiana within sixty days but seems to have remained within the New Orleans area, from where he requested—and was granted—bondage in 1859. John Clifton's case was elaborated on at this time in the *Daily Delta*. Here, his attorney wrote: "John Clifton naturally seeks a protector and guardian, and the law furnishes him with one of his own choice, who by acceptance of this guardianship incurs the obligation to protect and support him." Schafer argues John Jefferson Earhart (Clifton's attorney) represented at least four other enslavement requests, including that of John Wells, who requested enslavement to Benjamin F. Litterall, as cited in the *New Orleans Daily Picayune* in 1859.[10] The paper wrote: "Slavery cannot be such a bad thing after all, when we see free men accepting it voluntarily. The negro sometimes understands his own interests better than his would-be white friends."[11]

Enslavement requests provided the proslavery ideologues with a powerful tool of support for their cause. That slavery was better than freedom was even recognized by some black people, they believed. "Incapable" of survival without masters, perceptive individuals such as John Clifton and Hannah Dodds soon understood where their "real" interests lay. But enslavement petitions are not cited in southern newspapers as extensively as might be expected, because of the ultimate irony at the heart of voluntary enslavement: while slavery petitions can be seen as testament to white slaveholder benevolence, they are also illustrative of free black initiative. The petitions were as controversial to white southern society as they have been to subsequent generations of historians attempting to assess the motivations behind them. Newspaper features about free people of color who asked for bondage are, therefore, difficult to evaluate, because enslavement petitions opened up the mechanisms of law to black people at a time when, ironically, southern states were attempting to restrict free blacks' involvement in civil society. A systematic investigation of all southern newspapers is beyond the scope of this study (and also, as explained, inherently problematic). However, the sentiments conveyed within these requests illustrate much about whites' attitudes toward voluntary enslavement. While enslavement was "best" for poor free people of color incapable of providing for themselves without sliding into poverty, debt, destitution, or crime, their slavery petitions also caused whites fundamental unease about the divide between freedom and bondage.

Free black initiative (considered more fully in the introduction) appears throughout the enslavement petitions of free people of color, who showed independence of thought through their choice of language. Performing to white ideas about race and the desirability of enslavement, the petitioners used every tool available to them in their attempts to get their requests passed; they framed their petitions to play upon white sentiments by couching their enslavement requests in proslavery rhetoric. An exploitative element is also apparent in slavery petitions. Sometimes potential owners wrote petitions on behalf of free people of color whom they wanted to possess, and they gave their own reasons about why slavery was preferable for the free blacks involved. Because the "real" writers of enslavement petitions are mostly unknown, in order to hypothesize and speculate about the motivations behind enslavement it is vital to build up profiles of both free blacks and their potential masters using supplementary evidence such as that in the census.

Voluntary enslavement requests that cited proslavery propaganda (where slavery was apparently "better" than freedom and potential owners were described in positive tones) equaled 11 percent of the total number of prime motivations given in the enslavement petitions, and examples other than those cited above include Abisha Locus, of Wayne County, North Carolina. Locus claimed he wanted "the protection and support of a master" and had identified D. H. Bridgers as his new owner.[12] Henry Reed of Jackson County professed to be "tired of liberty and its ills and inconveniences" (he specified no further as to what these might be) when he asked the Western Circuit Court of Florida to enslave him to Sidney S. Alderman.[13] Two free women of color named Rachel and Anarcha, of Fort Belknap, Texas, wrote in their 1858 petition that they "wished to be made slaves for life" of Major George H. Thomas, "a man of good character and a humane master." Thomas paid court expenses of thirty dollars before the request was granted.[14]

"TRADITIONAL" MOTIVATIONS FOR ENSLAVEMENT

Some free people of color facing economic concerns or legal difficulties petitioned for enslavement in the hope that it might provide an escape from their problems.[15] But, economic or legal challenges were not the only motivating factors when it came to seeking bondage, as subsequent chapters will show. Indeed, free people of color who asked for slavery because of legal or economic concerns were in a considerable minority. Impoverishment instead served as a backdrop—an undercurrent—in cases where poor petitioners strove to live with beloved kin, and there are parallels between the experiences of free blacks in the late antebellum South and other impoverished workers across time and space. All faced the same fundamental problem of how to secure subsistence.[16] Some free people of color decided that subsistence was only possible under enslavement.

More specifically, court costs, being aged or in ill health, and issues of poverty or debt contributed just 12 percent to the prime motivations cited in the petitions themselves, as shown in table 1 of the introduction. For example, in 1795 three free black men petitioned the Kent County Court of Delaware asking for slavery following their conviction for felony. These were the earliest enslavement petitions found, about which little information survives. Jesse Brooks was apparently "entirely destitute of property" and asked to "be sold into slavery in order to pay the costs incurred by his conviction."[17] Thomas Dennis, who was over seventy, similarly sought bondage in order to "satisfy court costs." At his age, Dennis probably thought he would not have much time left in the world and hoped his service would be brief.[18] Isaac Jessops, who had three felony indictments adjudged against him, also requested enslavement to meet court costs.[19] All three men appear to have viewed enslavement in relation to these specific costs rather than impoverishment in a more general sense, although for younger men the relative costs of a lifetime of bondage would be very high. Billard Filmore also requested enslavement because of specific legal difficulties. He petitioned the Mississippi State Legislature in 1859 after being charged with the attempted murder of a slave. Filmore wanted to belong to a lawyer named James J. Lindsey, of Fulton, writing that he was "desirous of procuring counsel in his defence."[20] It seems as though Filmore's petition was successful; James J. Lindsey of Itawamba County appears in the 1860 slave schedules owning one slave, a twenty-four-year-old mulatto man.[21] Billard Filmore could have been this man, although whether Lindsey defended his new slave in court is unknown.

Occasionally, enslavement requests were framed in terms of petitioners' ill health and the alleged belief that bondage would somehow be "better" for sickly free people of color incapable of looking after themselves. Such public sentiments would have gone down well with proslavery ideologues who stressed the benevolence of "caring" masters. For example, Henry Wilson of New Orleans requested enslavement to William Barrett in 1860. His petition described how he was "in infirm health and desirous of taking advantage of the act of the legislature . . . of March 1859 entitled an 'Act to permit free persons of African descent to select their masters and become slaves for life.'" William Barrett was a forty-year-old "shipping master" in the 1860 census, living with his family and two enslaved women of twenty-four and fifteen. Henry Wilson could not be traced.[22] So although Wilson's petition stressed declining health, he may well have been related to one of Barrett's enslaved women.

Henry Wilson (or the "real" writer of this petition) was also obviously familiar with recent enslavement legislation in Louisiana and thought reference to it would cast the petition in a good light with decision-makers. However, there was an unusual twist: "After hearing pleadings and evidence, on motion of C. M. Bradford, District Attorney, it is ordered and adjudged that the whole proceedings be dismissed at applicant costs."[23] Why this case was dismissed is unknown, although historian Judith Kelleher Schafer suggests a couple of possibilities, including Henry Wilson's death and fraud.[24] However, forcing a poor and sickly black man to pay the costs of these proceedings (rather than his potential owner, William Barrett) strikes at the very heart of antebellum racial injustice.

The New Orleans courts were unusually keen to both reject enslavement petitions and force the costs of proceedings onto free people of color. Twenty-one-year-old Julia Elliot asked for enslavement from the First District Court of New Orleans. Elliot was allegedly "desirous of having the benefit of the act of the legislature of said state to permit free persons of African descent to select their masters and become slaves for life," and she identified John D. Lackie as her prospective master (neither could be found in census records). But the district attorney denied her request: "The petitioner is not entitled to the relief asked for and the privilege of selecting a master for among other reasons she is not one who comes within the law, that she is not a good and moral subject, and that criminal proceedings are now finding against her . . . on a charge of living in contravention of the law, she having been long previous notified to leave the state and that her present action is only brought to evade said prosecution and the law applicable to her case." Elliot's application was therefore dismissed, and she was required to pay costs.[25]

This tragic story starkly reveals the multiplicity of contradictions at the heart of enslavement requests and their relationship to proslavery ideology. The district attorney's prose suggests Julia Elliot sought bondage as an "escape" from prosecution because she lived illegally in Louisiana. She must have lived elsewhere in the South and at some point arrived in the state contrary to law. Why she did so may never be known. Perhaps as a poor free woman of color she hoped the bustling port city would offer better opportunity to provide for herself (and her family, if she had one). She might also have had affective ties to the enslaved or other free people of color within New Orleans, and she might have been in love with someone from the city from whom she was reluctant to be parted. Elliot's motivations for enslavement would have differed sharply from those of the district attorney, and much can be gleaned from a consideration of his perspective. Undoubtedly, this man believed bondage was a "positive good," describing enslavement as a form of "relief" and a "privilege" for which Julia Elliot (an "immoral" woman) was not worthy. Rejecting Elliot's enslavement request, therefore, denied her any "initiative" and placed the court in a position of overall control. However, in rejecting such enslavement requests, the New Orleans courts unwittingly conveyed their fear of free black initiative in their voluntary enslavement.

The New Orleans courts also rejected the enslavement petition of George Stephens (or Stevens). Stephens had asked in 1862 to become the property of James P. Frank, who was "willing to become the master of said George Stevens, as prayed for in his said petition." Found by the district attorney to be "in violation of law, not being a native or resident of the state," Stephens had apparently been "under arrest before and at the time of his application." He was ordered to pay costs, and the case was dismissed, with Stephens "remanded in prison to await his trial for being in the state."[26] Julia Elliot and George Stephens were both caught residing illegally in Louisiana, and they both tried to enter bondage as a means of remaining in New Orleans. Their punishment was financial, but as it is likely both were unable to pay, they would have been imprisoned instead. This course of action adopted by the New Orleans legislators is in marked contrast to the treatment of free black people in Arkansas caught residing in the state illegally after the expulsion ruling of 1860. In Arkansas, some free people of color were subsequently forced into bondage against their will but according to state law. In New Orleans, the courts chose to deny bondage to free people of color living there illegally because it was the free blacks themselves who offered their enslavement as a viable option. The courts' actions in fining and imprisoning Julia Elliot and George Stephens are again testament to a fear of black initiative driving enslavement requests. However, viewed from a more economic perspective, an opportunity to acquire more slaves from among the ranks of free blacks was missed.

Seeking enslavement as a means of escaping legal difficulties therefore occurred across the southern states, and such petitions complicate the notion that moves into bondage were voluntary. For example, in 1860 in Copiah Country, Mississippi, the legislature permitted a free black man named Thomas Crenshaw to "go before the probate judge of said County and voluntarily to select a master, and go into slavery for life: Provided, that the master so selected by him shall also appear before said judge and accept said slave as his property. . . . And provided also, that the master selected as aforesaid shall pay said judge and clerk a reasonable compensation for making and recording said decree, and for any other costs and charges lately incurred in the apprehension and imprisonment of said free man of color, for the purpose of selling him into slavery."[27] One day later, Thomas Crenshaw appeared before Copiah County's judge of probate and allegedly "selected" D. W. McRae "of said County to be my master and consent that the relation of master and slave to henceforth subsist between me and the said D. W. McRae in accordance with the provisions of the said act referred to." Crenshaw marked the document with an "X." McRae then testified before the judge "that the relation of master and slave subsist between me and him." The judge, Jackson Millsaps, noted that McRae had "paid said Judge . . . all reasonable compensation for making and recording this decree and all other costs and charges lately incurred in the apprehension and imprisonment of the said Thomas Crenshaw for the purpose of selling him into slavery." Jackson Millsaps hence decreed that Thomas Crenshaw become the slave of McRae "for life."[28]

This sad story, like so many of the other enslavement requests, invites questions about its petitioner's "true" motivations, and the reference to Crenshaw's "apprehension and imprisonment" is particularly intriguing. Whether Crenshaw was in prison for residing illegally in Mississippi or for some other crime is unknown. McRae's willingness to pay the "costs and charges" associated with his imprisonment suggests that acquiring a slave from the ranks of imprisoned free blacks represented something of a bargain for potential owners. Perceived in this way, the notion that Thomas Crenshaw voluntarily chose slavery is rendered meaningless. And there was a sting in the tale for Crenshaw. In 1860 D. W. McRae was a thirty-year-year-old lawyer, living in a hotel run by Mary Morgan—probably a widow—and her seven children. Three other lawyers lived in the same hotel, as did the judge of probate—Jackson Millsaps.[29] McRae and Millsaps were thus acquaintances, if not friends. They could have hatched a mutually beneficial scheme to spare Copiah County the cost of Crenshaw's imprisonment while giving McRae an opportunity to buy a slave.

THE PROFILES OF POTENTIAL OWNERS

Some of the possible motivations behind enslavement requests can be deciphered through an analysis of the socioeconomic profiles of potential owners. Free people of color with affective ties to the enslaved were more likely to cite as potential masters planters with many slaves, as shown in chapter 4. In contrast, chapter 5 will show how single white men involved in intimate relationships with free black women would sometimes submit enslavement requests on the latter's behalf. Methodological concerns about census data notwithstanding, the number of slaves held by white people named as potential owners in enslavement petitions illustrates that, for the most part, less-wealthy whites used slavery requests as tools in achieving their socioeconomic aspirations. Most potential masters (they were usually men) were attempting to either buy their way into the slaveholding class or consolidate their positions as slaveholders. More broadly, then, the enslavement petitions lend support to the claim that antebellum southern society was bound through white planter hegemony. Less wealthy whites envisaged their progression in society in terms of acquiring slaves or becoming slaveholders, and they did not identify with poorer whites along the lines of social class. These less-wealthy whites increasingly perceived free people of color only in terms of their economic value as potential chattel.[30]

So the ultimate victims of enslavement requests designed by whites anxious to increase their chattel were free people of color. Often, too, these potential masters were white people with whom free blacks had previously been acquainted. This is vividly illustrated by two enslavement requests: the first submitted on behalf of Jane Miller, the second by the Short family. In the case of the former, the Georgia Assembly authorized Jane Miller of Clarke County "to sell herself into perpetual slavery" in 1862. Jane and her potential owner, E. S. Sims (who could not be traced as a slave owner), were to

> go before the Justices of the Inferior Court, or a majority of them, in said County, who shall faithfully and fully examine her as to her willingness to become the slave for life of the said E. S. Sims; and upon being satisfied of the same, they shall pass an order to the effect that the said Jane Miller be held, deemed and considered the slave of E. S. Sims for and during her natural life, subject to all incidents of slavery, except the liability of being sold during the lifetime of said Sims, by himself or his creditors for his debts; the sole consideration for which voluntary enslavement on her part, shall be obligation thereby incurred by her master of feeding, clothing and protecting her.[31]

Census evidence for 1850 shows twenty-year-old Jane Miller residing in the same household as "Edward S. Simms," a farmer, some twelve years before her enslavement petition. Sims was thirty-five years old, married, and with three young children. Other free people of color also lived in the Simses' household. Nathan Miller, aged three, and Ephraim, an "infant," were probably Jane Miller's children, while a twenty-year-old man named William Rutledge was most likely her husband.[32] Sims might have cajoled Miller into enslavement because of her desire to remain with her family. But Sims's perspective was different. Having Miller enslaved to him would have brought him considerable benefits. It would increase his material wealth and his labor force, especially significant if he previously held no slaves. Rather rare was the restrictive clause about her being exempt from sale for debt, although this occasionally crops up in slavery petitions, presumably to convey a sense of enslavement as "benevolent" instead of "exploitative," in the "best interests" of free blacks. But Edward Sims was only forbidden from selling her "for his debts." Presumably then, if he wanted to relinquish ownership for profit—to make a "quick buck"—he was apparently at liberty to do so.

The Short family's enslavement request can be read similarly to that of Jane Miller, although petitions for bondage submitted on behalf of family groups were much rarer than those written for individuals. The Shorts all requested to become enslaved to Young Edwards, of Russell County, Alabama, in February 1860. This free black family consisted of "Charles Short, Jim Short, Hezekiah Short, Sarah Short, Harriet Short and Adeline Short, with their children, to wit: Henry, John, Smith, Willson, Anderson and Frank." From this evidence, contained within their petition, the familial ties among the Short adults and children are not entirely clear, but all were permitted by legislative act to enter slavery, with the caveats that "said negroes . . . shall never be sold for the debts or liabilities of the said Edwards or his heirs or distributees: and, provided also, the court must be satisfied that the said Edwards is a man of good moral character."[33]

Young Edwards, like Edward Sims, could thus presumably sell any of his new chattel for profits, if not debts. This wording, carefully chosen by the Alabama legislature, is testament to the desire to present the enslavement cases as valid, legitimate, and legal processes given serious consideration by policymakers. The prose, while rather defensive proslavery rhetoric, suggests free blacks were treated fairly, being enslaved only to "caring" whites. Alabama, like Georgia, thus introduced clauses restricting the sale of newly enslaved people to maintain a public image of benevolence and not because either state acknowledged the devastating impact upon enslaved families of debt and the subsequent division of estates.

Prior to their bondage to him, the Short family lived within the household of Young Edwards. In 1850, Edwards lived in an extended household consisting of himself (a fifty-year-old farmer); his wife, Mary; and five other white people (probably his children and grandchildren) whose ages ranged from twenty-five to six. Several black people also lived in this household, including Charles Edwards, aged twenty-one, and a woman (perhaps his mother) named Betsy, aged forty. There were also five black children, ranging in age from eight to fourteen, named Sarah, Harriet, James, Heseliah, and Adeline. They were probably Charles's siblings. Although this family was transcribed by census enumerators with the same surname as the white head of household (Edwards), some of their names match the "Charles, Jim, Hezekiah, Sarah, Harriet and Adeline" in the Short family enslavement petition of 1860, and the two families are unquestionably one and the same. Notable for their absence in the 1860 petition, however, are Betsy and the children "Henry, John, Smith, Willson, Anderson and Frank." Betsy may have passed away, while the children, if very young, were unborn in 1850.

Evidence from the 1860 census illuminates further the plight of the Short family. Young Edwards, who appeared to own no slaves in 1850, had over the course of a decade acquired fifteen people. There were also fewer people living in his household. By 1860, he lived with only his wife and two children. Significantly, the 1860 census was enumerated on 19 July, the Short family having been permitted to enter slavery in February of that year. So the free black family residing within Young Edwards's household in 1850 was by 1860 reduced to chattel, appearing in the slave schedules only as a list of ages and genders.[34] This change in status rendered the family practically invisible as enslaved people, nor could any of the family be traced after emancipation.

Rooted to their homes, families, and communities, some free people of color were cajoled, tricked, or deceived into enslavement. Young Edwards's actions support the proposition that non-slaveholding whites were supportive of the slave regime and, moreover, wanted to buy into it for their own economic gain. Ambitious individuals like him could dramatically increase their supply of productive and valuable slaves through the opportunities that voluntary enslavement debate and legislation provided. Moreover, the absence of a solid delineation between bondage and freedom meant that some potential masters had a ready-made supply of potential chattel already living within their own households.

And these slaves seem to have been obtained at practically no financial cost. While, unfortunately, there survives only scant evidence about the financial arrangements involved in the purchase of free blacks, in the case of the Short family, it seems as though Young Edwards obtained all twelve family members for just twenty-five dollars (he appears to have bought the other three slaves through different means). Legislative records indicate he paid just five dollars for the services of the judge of probate and twenty dollars to a guardian appointed by the court to act in the interests of those enslaved under the age of eighteen.[35] Faced with the economic opportunities provided by voluntary bondage, less wealthy whites had every reason to regard free blacks as potential slaves. It is also easy to see how southern legislators could have perceived voluntary slavery as a tool with which to quell potential class conflict. Enslavement legislation offered a relatively easy—both financially and bureaucratically—route into mastery for men such as Young Edwards, who could cajole free people of color with whom they had prior relationships into bondage. In return, Edwards and other like-minded men gained both status and increased financial security through their mastery. Finally, the experiences of the poor Short family convey the extent to which notions of slavery and freedom represented a continuum rather than polar opposites. The everyday lives of the family members probably changed little when they began laboring as slaves rather than as free black people. With so much to be gained—from a white perspective—through the enslavement of free people of color, the timing of the Civil War provides a welcome explanation for the relative scarcity of voluntary enslavement petitions.

Other evidence contained within census materials about slave ownership among the potential owners of free people of color also offers insights into the economic and social status of potential masters and the relationships of their new slaves. Florida Bright, of Escambia County, Florida, was apparently "desirous of going into a state of slavery" and in 1861 requested that Captain Walter L. Cozzens become her owner.[36] A free black man named George Gowan also apparently petitioned for Cozzens to become his master; Bright and Gowan may have been a couple. In the 1870 census, there was a thirty-three-year-old "mulatto" woman in Escambia County with the name "Florida Gowan."[37] It was unusual for families or couples to request enslavement; perhaps they were in financial difficulties. Switching perspective, since Cozzens owned only six slaves in 1860, he had every reason to want to bring two additional people into his possession. Moreover, a married couple was also likely to bear valuable children. Similarly, but rather more tentatively, the Mississippi legislature permitted Jim Wall, of Wilkinson County, to become enslaved to Daniel Williams in 1860. Wall was a laborer, married to Susannah with four young children under the age of nine. He became "the slave for life of the said Daniel Williams . . . as if he the said Jim Wall had been born the slave of the said Daniel Williams." But Daniel Williams does not appear to have owned slaves, and Jim Wall was married to a free black woman. Wall did not then, have spousal ties of affection to someone enslaved. Williams probably cajoled Wall into his enslavement petition for Williams's own financial gain because Wall was struggling to provide a subsistence level of support to his wife and children.[38]

Surviving enslavement petitions from New Orleans are somewhat skewed in their profiles of potential masters because most slaveholders in urban areas held fewer slaves than those who resided on plantations. But, like their more rural counterparts, free blacks in New Orleans were also victims of attempts to cajole them into bondage through the legislative provisions for voluntary enslavement. For example, in October 1859 the Fourth District Court received a petition from twenty-seven-year-old Joseph Thomas who "desires to avail himself of the benefits of an act of the legislature of this state entitled an act 'to permit free persons of African descent to select their own masters and become slaves for life.'" Joseph Thomas had, apparently, "taken pains to inform himself and has full knowledge of all the consequences of his actions . . . and it his determination, without fraud or collusion, to become a slave for life, and to that end he has selected and chosen Mr. John E. Florence with whom he has been acquainted for many years, who is a man of good character and who resides in this city and parish to become [the] petitioner's master."[39]

It initially seems as though Thomas had signed the document himself (rather than marking it with an "X"), and this is not the only unusual difference between this enslavement petitions and others. Census evidence from 1860 suggests rather exceptional economic profiles for both Joseph Thomas and John Florence. The latter appears as "Joh Florence," a fifty-two-year-old laborer who lived with his family and apparently owned no slaves. The only non-white Joseph Thomas was a twenty-nine-year-old black man and a dairy owner.[40] If these two men are indeed the individuals concerned in the enslavement petition, it is very strange that a property-owning free man of color would seek bondage to a white laborer; some sort of collusion may have taken place. There was a further unusual twist when Florence was cited as a potential owner in a different enslavement petition. This second request was submitted on behalf of a twenty-five-year-old free black man named William Gray. And although

Gray, like Thomas, allegedly signed the petition himself, Gray's petition is written in exactly the same hand, and phrased in exactly the same way as Thomas's request. Both petitions were also submitted to Fourth District Court in 1859 by free black men in their twenties. While William Gray could not be found in census records, the overall number of similarities between these two petitions renders them highly suspicious. As a relatively poor white laborer anxious to improve his wealth and status and jealous of free black men with a degree of economic success, in his attempts to trick both men into bondage, Florence may well have forged the signatures of Thomas and Gray.[41]

Using the 1860 census, it was possible to calculate the number of slaves belonging to sixty-seven of the potential owners cited in enslavement requests, representing just under half the total number of petitions. Of these, twenty held fewer than five slaves (29.9 percent), and thirty-seven (55.2 percent) held fewer than ten. Fifty-four (80.6 percent) held fewer than twenty slaves, the great majority, with the reminder (thirteen, or 19.4 percent) possessing over twenty.[42] Historian Peter Kolchin places the median holdings of slaves for the total South at twenty-three in 1860.[43] So, over three-quarters of the potential owners of free blacks possessed fewer than twenty enslaved people, and these white people who sought to bring free people of color into the system of bondage did not come from the ranks of the super-wealthy. Instead, they were attempting either to consolidate their positions as slave masters or to buy into the slaveholding class.

Financial Transactions and Enslavement Requests

Surviving evidence about the monetary exchanges involved in the movement of free people of color into bondage is frustratingly scant. Nevertheless, such testimony indicates that it was relatively easy for less wealthy white men to buy their way into slave-owning via legislation on voluntary slavery. Some examples of the prices paid for free blacks are included in chapter 4, but here the value of new voluntary slaves is explored in relation to surviving evidence for some Virginia counties. For example, the circuit court of Amelia passed a request from Lewis Wilkinson to become enslaved to James W. Ellis: "The court having proceeded to examine the said Lewis Wilkinson and James W. Ellis, . . . it appearing to the Court that the said Lewis Wilkinson is more than seventy years of age, that there is no fraud nor collusion between the parties, and that there is no good cause to the contrary, doth grant the prayer of the said petitioner." Wilkinson had probably been forced into a life of impoverishment or even destitution because his advanced age made it difficult to achieve a subsistence standard of living. He may well have thought enslavement preferable to freedom. But there are other considerations here. As he was over the age of seventy, Lewis Wilkinson was extremely cheap. The Amelia court ascertained he was worth just ten dollars, of which James Ellis paid only five. He was obliged to pay the remaining amount (plus an additional fifty dollars for court costs) by entering into a bond, "as decreed by Virginia law." The acquisition of new slaves was, thus, actively enabled through legislative provisions for voluntary enslavement that permitted the purchase of chattel through a system of credit. James Ellis was not a wealthy man. A farmer in 1860, he owned only one slave, an eighty-year-old man who was probably Lewis Wilkinson.[44] Ellis must have been very grateful to the State for its system of bonds, which facilitated his purchase of Lewis, who would otherwise have remained too expensive.

Other free black people involved in enslavement petitions in Virginia were notably more expensive than Lewis Wilkinson. Circuit court records include reference to a man named Caesar, valued at 375 dollars, who was permitted to enter bondage as the slave of Robert Smith. But Caesar was not the only slave Robert Smith obtained; he also bought the rather expensive "William," valued at 950 dollars.[45] James Smith of Gloucester County was valued at 300 dollars in his enslavement petition, while James, or Jim, Booker was apparently worth 850 dollars and "Absalom" was worth 1,200 dollars.[46] Another enslavement petition from Madison County shows that Nathaniel S. Wayland acquired two enslaved people (Jeptha and Thadeus Chapman). Each valued at 550 dollars, Jeptha and Thadeus tripled Wayland's chattel, because he owned only one slave prior to acquiring them.[47]

Women could also command high prices. Martha Brown of Giles County requested enslavement to William McComas and was valued at 500 dollars, of which McComas paid 250 dollars in cash. It can be assumed McComas entered into bond for the remainder. Somewhat differently, Margaret Price, who petitioned for enslavement in Richmond, was valued at only 150 dollars and may well have been rather elderly. She was permitted to become the slave of John H. Tyler in November 1859.[48] This very rare evidence about the financial value of free people of color allows for only impressionistic assertions. However, a common pattern seems to have been that following the "pricing" of free blacks, their new owners would pay just half their values (or even less) to the court before entering into bond for the rest, plus any additional court costs. The potential owners of these free blacks were not poor: they were mostly able to pay up to half of the value of their new chattel and obtain bond for any subsequent amount. But the important point is that their slaveholding was facilitated financially by southern states keen to promote the ownership of people for all.[49] Increasing their supply of chattel during the uncertain decade of the 1850s and even thereafter is also testament to slaveholders' confidence about the future of their beloved regime, because such men and women continued to perceive slaves as a worthwhile investment.

The evidence presented in this chapter illustrates that while ideas about voluntary enslavement fitted neatly into the rhetoric of proslavery ideology, white southerners were somewhat wary of the phenomena and voluntary slavery did not receive as extensive press attention as one might expect. This chapter has also shown how explanations of the primary motivations for enslavement—related to impoverishment, legal difficulties, or ill health—provided the basis for the initial historiographical understanding of enslavement requests, an understanding that for too long has remained unquestioned. Finally, a combination of census evidence and surviving documentation about the financial transactions involved in enslavement petitions illustrates the extent to which southern lawmakers intended their legislation to be used for *extending* slaveholding to a broader cohort of the white population. Taken as a whole, the findings presented here point to the significance of interpretation: free people of color in the antebellum South perceived the entering of bondage very differently than their white contemporaries did. The next two chapters argue that enslavement petitions represent more than mere white "ventriloquism" through passive black bodies.[50] Moreover, the first generation of historians to consider this controversial concept picked up on only one strand of enslavement motivations and failed to address those that came from a more private and personal space.

4

FREE PEOPLE OF COLOR
AND THE ENSLAVED

Born free, because although her father was enslaved, her mother was white, Lucy Andrews from Lancaster District, South Carolina, petitioned the South Carolina State Assembly for enslavement in the late 1850s. She described how, as a sixteen-year-old mother: "she is dissatisfied with her present condition, being compelled to go about from place to place to seek employment for her support, and not permitted to stay at any place more than a week or two at a time, no one caring about employing her." Andrews wanted to raise a family, yet said she was unable to provide a subsistence standard of living for them. She also emphasized slaveholder benevolence by professing to believe that "slaves are far more happy, and enjoy themselves far better than she does in her present, isolated condition of freedom, and are well-treated and cared for by their masters, while she is going about from place to place hunting employment for her support. She therefore prays that your honorable body would enact a law authorizing and permitting her, to go voluntarily into slavery, and select her own master." Fifty signatures appeared on the petition in support of her request, but Andrews herself could only provide a cross.[1]

Andrews's request appears not to have been granted, as she again requested enslavement in 1860. This petition described how she was "isolated from both the free whites and the slaves, that she has no one to protect, provide for or take care of her, in her ignorant, destitute and helpless state, and she is convinced it would be far better for her to relinquish and give up her freedom to become the slave of a kind master and thus secure to herself the benefits of the relation of master and slave." Three witnesses had apparently examined Lucy Andrews, and they vouched she was "fully informed of the purpose, nature and effect of said petition and that she expressed herself willing and desirous to go into slavery . . . that she has been induced to take this step of her own free will, without any compulsion." The witnesses were also well acquainted with Mr. Henry Duncan "and recommend him as a worthy clever man and state that we know of no undue influence nor have we heard of any having been exercised to unduly influence the within named Lucy Andrews."[2]

This petition also seems to have failed, because more than three years later, during the wartime upheaval of 1863, Lucy Andrews was still legally requesting enslavement. The rhetoric employed in this request focused much more explicitly on her need for subsistence as she had no family to support her in a challenging economic climate. Aged "about twenty one" with a daughter of three years old, and a fourteen-month-old boy, Andrews described how "for the last six years she has made her home at Mr. Henry H. Duncan's . . . and has had a comfortable living at his house, much more so, indeed than she had previously; for having no relations of her color in the state and District she found it extremely difficult to procure sustenance." She also wrote how she wished to belong to Henry Duncan, who "owns her husband Robbin, with whom she, together with her above mentioned children, [are] comfortably fixed and situated." Moreover, "in these times of scarcity of provisions and clothing and the consequent high prices of the same," she requested that she and her children—Emily and Robbin Jr.—be enslaved to Duncan.

In the same handwriting (so revealing himself the writer of her petition), Henry Duncan provided his written consent to take Andrews as his slave and, before signing his name underneath, further stated he had "no objection to the prayer of Lucy Andrews being granted." Duncan's prose is eloquent throughout all of the legislative requests, and his reference to economic difficulties during wartime conveys how he had put real thought into the framing of these petitions. Lucy Andrews lacked a wider familial support network, and her enslaved husband was unable economically to provide for his wife or children. If he took the responsibility for Andrews, her enslavement would have facilitated Duncan's sense of his own benevolence as well as been justified on economic grounds. He would relieve society of the "burden" imposed by Lucy Andrews.[3]

Andrews appears in the 1860 census as a sixteen-year-old "mulatto" (no occupation is listed) living in the household of Henry Duncan, a farmer, along with his wife, Susan, and daughter, Matilda.[4] Duncan owned five slaves in 1850 but cannot be traced as a slaveholder in the 1860 schedules.[5] Thus, he fits the pattern of typically small-scale slaveholders attempting to increase their supply of property through voluntary enslavement, as has been shown. Lucy Andrews's petitions are also fairly typical in that the legislature appears not to have adjudicated in her case, despite her repeated requests for slavery. No doubt in 1863 the men of South Carolina's government had more pressing concerns.[6] However, what is striking about these petitions is the sheer love Lucy had for her enslaved husband, Robbin, and her paramount desire to remain with him at all costs in the face of the limited choices available. She was prepared to subject herself and her children to bondage so her immediate family could remain together, and her ties of affection superseded her status before the law in her consideration of how she wished to live. Because Andrews lived in the same household as her potential owner, Henry Duncan, she probably labored for him and anticipated that her day-to-day life would change little if she became enslaved. For Lucy Andrews, as well as many other free people of color, there was no sharp delineation between freedom and bondage but a continuum of racial oppression.

This chapter focuses on emotional ties across the slave-free divide, the love and affection that bound free people of color and the enslaved within the context of their attachment to their families, homes, and communities in the antebellum South.[7] Such terms convey the meanings and significance attached to the everyday lives of free people of color and the enslaved, what historian Ben Schiller has referred to as the "experiential, processual versions of identity and belonging."[8] Put more simply, a sense of place in which one belonged underscored the petitioners' alleged desire for enslavement, and while their rhetoric often focused on economic benefits of slavery to whites, free people of color were prioritizing their own personal relationships. Love and affection for family members with whom the petitioners wished to live was cited as the primary motivational factor in many enslavement cases, and the petitioners' often poignant testimony reveals the extent of romantic attachment to spouses as well as love for wider kin networks within affective communities. Testimony from the petitions supports the specific assertion that families who crossed the line from slavery to freedom prioritized nuclear kinship ties, yet it also suggests that broader kin networks were significant. While the specific details of family structures within such networks remain elusive, enslavement petitioners were searching for a sense of belonging within wide kin networks in the place they knew as home, regardless of their status as slave or free.[9]

It is often assumed that in the prewar nineteenth century people married for reasons of property and pragmatism, but this is a white paradigm. The enslaved were early pioneers in setting up life partnerships for romantic reasons, and the enslavement petitions also illustrate the importance of romantic love across the divide between those enslaved and free people of color, albeit through sometimes impressionistic evidence.[10] Some considered the immense love felt for an enslaved spouse—and for children such as Emily and Robbin Jr. too—more important than the benefits of liberty. Enslavement petitioners therefore made pragmatic decisions about their legal status that facilitated their affective ties. While it was not uncommon for free people of color to buy, or to attempt to buy, their enslaved loved ones—what historian Larry Koger refers to as "nominal slavery"—to submit oneself to bondage for the love of another was surely the ultimate sacrifice.[11] Of secondary concern for the petitioners was the urge to maintain broader familial or community relationships. Malleable and flexible notions of "home," "family," and "community" all fell under the broad remit of "belonging," and all were prioritized by people of color who believed these sacred institutions might be under threat. Petitioners wanted to keep beloved family and kin together in the face of outside hostility.

Enslavement requests were complicated, and they reveal similar complexities about late antebellum society. Considered here, for example, are various petitions from individuals wanting to remain with spouses, children, and wider kin networks. Also explored are petitions submitted on behalf of family groups anxious about possible future separation. Finally, there were a number of petitions submitted from free people of color who had experienced life in Liberia and were anxious to return to the United States—even if that meant entering slavery. As shown in table I.5 of the introduction, "love of family" constituted a majority of enslavement (and residency) requests where motivations could be established, and these petitions convey the extent to which family was prioritized above all else. For example, 39 percent of all enslavement request petitions and 65 percent of those for residency were framed in terms of kin ties.

But further quantification about the specific detail of kin networks is difficult, especially when the numbers involved are so small. Sometimes petitioners did not offer clear rationales for their bondage requests; in such cases, supplementary evidence, such as that obtained from census materials, is used to decipher information about potential owners' slaveholding. For example, where a prospective master of an adult man owned one single adult female and her offspring, it can be hypothesized that spousal relationships were at play. More firmly, twelve of the thirty-eight petitioners included in the love-of-family category stated explicitly that they wanted to enter bondage to remain with spouses, and some of these also made reference to enslaved children. All others commented on their family ties in a more general sense, although one petitioner, William Bass, described how his prospective master also owned his stepfather. This chapter also includes evidence from enslavement petitions in which the nature of familial ties has been necessarily speculated based on available testimony. But, on balance, the importance of spousal relationships within nuclear households for free people of color and the enslaved is clear, with broader familial relationships being of secondary concern. The enslavement requests are considered on a state-by-state basis, as the wording therein facilitates understanding of how individual southern states framed enslavement and expulsion issues. Petitions from Virginia, many of which were very early, are considered first. Sometimes written prior to legislative action on enslavement, such requests are testament indeed to love against all odds, where people put their families first.

From the 1810s onward, free people of color in Virginia submitted enslavement petitions because they were unwilling to leave family members. These requests, whether for enslavement or residency, can be grounded in a context of fear. In 1806, the state decreed all manumitted people of color had to leave Virginia within one year or relinquish their freedom, unless county officials gave them special permission to remain.[12] Undoubtedly, the prospect of forcibly being parted from kin led some free people of color to question their priorities, and their legal status was not always deemed of paramount importance. For example, in an 1812 petition to the Washington County Court, a free black man known only as "Burk" reluctantly acknowledged the undesirable choice he faced. Having been emancipated by his late master's family, Burk wrote that he would rather be "reduced" to slavery than leave his enslaved wife and children. "Sooner than relinquish the first [his family] he will submit to the latter [slavery,] heavy as the sentence is." He therefore "prayed" that he might be allowed to remain. The framing of Burk's petition is interesting; he did not explicitly ask for enslavement but raised it as a possible outcome if he were forced to choose between his family and his freedom. The former took priority over the latter, but, poignantly, all he could offer was "a prayer" that the county legislators might allow him to remain on compassionate grounds.[13]

Lucinda, from King George County, petitioned the Virginia legislature for similar reasons in 1813. She had recently been emancipated with some other slaves by the will of Mary Matthews, on condition that they were all relocated to Tennessee. But Lucinda stubbornly refused to leave: "All the slaves so emancipated (except your petitioner) were removed this year to the state of Tennessee, but your petitioner declined going with them." Lucinda's petition also explained at length how her husband was enslaved to Captain William H. Hoe in the same county and that

> the benefits and privileges to be derived from freedom, dear and flattering as they are, could not induce her to be separated, that in consequence of this determination on her part, a year had elapsed since the death of her late mistress, and your petitioner, informed that the forfeiture of her freedom has taken place under the law prohibiting emancipated slaves from remaining in this state, and that the overseers of the poor might now proceed to sell her. . . . [Y]our petitioner, still anxious to remain with her husband, for whom she has relinquished all the advantages of freedom, is apprehensive that in case of a sale of her by the overseers of the poor, she may be purchased by some person who will remove her to a place remote from the residence of her husband. To guard against such a heart-rending circumstance, she would prefer, and hereby delivers her consent, to become a slave of the owner of her husband.[14]

The wording of this petition, unlikely to have been written by Lucinda but reflecting her emotional sentiments, is incredibly poignant, romantic, and eloquent. Lucinda's love for her husband radiates through the prose, and Lucinda herself seems passionately in love, if not even infatuated. She was an emotional woman who simply could not imagine being without her spouse. This is important; whoever wrote the petition acknowledged strongly and freely the existence of romantic love among people of color, whether enslaved or free. Yet such marriages were not recognized by law, and the cruelty of slaveholders in separating spouses has been well documented. That white people might also exploit black romantic love in their desire to acquire slaves is, therefore, ironic to say the least, and it reveals much about the callousness of slaveholders in their bids to acquire chattel by any means. But, importantly, Lucinda also requested enslavement to her husband's owner, not the family of her previous mistress, Mary Matthews. Whom Lucy belonged to was less important to her than whom she remained with. Like Lucy Andrews, Lucinda made a pragmatic decision to enter slavery so her spousal relationship could continue. She lived in a cross-plantation marriage with her husband prior to her emancipation, so she viewed enslavement as an opportunity for the two of them to live under the same roof. In contrast, the other men and women Mary Matthews freed could have been married to each other, so the consequences of removal to Tennessee would have been less stressful for them.[15]

Eliza (or Lizzie) Purdie of Isle of Wight County petitioned the Virginia legislature for enslavement in the late 1830s. She had been freed by her late master, Thomas Purdie, and given "a small property." She was, therefore, reluctant to leave, and she described how, at the advanced age of fifty-eight, she had ties in the state, "with friends and relatives nearby . . . going to a foreign land at her advanced age would be an evil to her much worse than slavery, and she would take upon her now a state of bondage with a good master of her choice rather than go away." It is unclear what exactly Purdie meant by "a foreign land." She might have been referring to American soil outside Virginia, or she could have had Liberia in mind. Neither is it known what would have happened to her property if she was enslaved: presumably she would have to relinquish it to her new owner. The text of this petition is also framed rather cleverly. Purdie stressed the perceived benevolence of the slaveholding class by referring to "good masters," but she also sought to retain a degree of control by requesting that her new owner be a man of her own choosing. This balance between accommodation and individual initiative was common throughout the petitions. Like others, she marked her petition with a cross and provided a long list of supporters.[16] Moreover, although she did not refer specifically to any spousal ties, she expected her general sense of kinship and community—her desire to remain with "friends and relatives"—to be worthy of serious consideration. From the perspective of white lawmakers, though, such concerns were of little significance; more important was Purdie's economic value as a slave.

An 1837 petition from Amherst County is also testament to the strength of familial ties among white and black families and the option of enslavement as a last, pragmatic resort. Here, Leanty, aged forty-six, and her two children, Mary and Henry, requested of the Virginia legislature that they be able to remain in the county as slaves following their emancipation by their late owner, Richard Smith. Smith requested that his executors petition the legislature for this family's residency and that, should this request fail, Leanty and her children should be "at liberty to choose new masters among Smith's blood relatives."[17] So this petition is rather different. Assuming that a prior residency request had indeed failed in the legislature, Richard Smith's relatives would have had a real economic incentive to push through the enslavements of Leanty and her family, especially as Smith had outlined this course of action in his will. He could have acted out of "benevolence," perhaps knowing that Leanty and her children were attached to his other slaves. He might also have thought his own family would treat them better than others would have. Finally, the idea that Leanty was "at liberty" to "choose" a master illustrates the inherent ironies of voluntary enslavement. More broadly, then, although Leanty's petition was motivated by white economic concerns as well as "benevolent" ones, it also hints at white slaveholders' considerable awareness of the ties that bound black families together.

The southern press, which tended to describe enslavement requests in rather gleeful tones, often picked up the notion of white slaveholder "benevolence." The *New Orleans Daily Picayune* noted in 1850 how Peter Beason, emancipated by his mistress (Mrs. Farrow) in Fauquier County, petitioned the county court to be "at his own insistence, sold into perpetual servitude." The paper went on to explain: "The laws of the state forbade his remaining within its limits more than twelve months from the date of his manumission, but all the ties which rendered existence desirable were intimately connected with the place of his birth; so after making a fair experiment of all the blessings attendant upon freedom, he finally determined upon the course he would pursue. He entreated that he should be publicly sold to the highest bidder, and Peter secured a good home for life."[18] Whether Beason entered slavery and went to a "good home" is unknown. He might have fallen into the hands of a ruthless master or slave trader who condemned him to a life of misery and brutality. However, the vague reference to "all the ties which rendered existence desirable" was essentially a comment on Beason's own sense of belonging to a family and a place. Thus, the ultimate irony is that the newspaper was happy to humanize Beason as a person with emotional attachments to home and kin at a time when most black people in America were regarded as "subhumans" suitable only for enslavement. Moreover, slavery would rob him of his freedom and render him more at risk of familial disruption than he was in his free status. Such contradictions expose fundamental flaws in a system of oppression based on perceived racial difference where not all black people were enslaved.

Various requests for enslavement also exist from those who had experienced life in Liberia and apparently found the prospect of bondage in the United States preferable to freedom in Africa. Homesickness and the desire to be reunited with kin were the primary motivations here, because it was hard to adjust to Liberian life. Twenty-six residents of Sussex County, Virginia, appealed to the County Court in 1850 requesting that Mark, Claiborne, and Eppes Collier be returned to slavery. The three men had departed for Liberia in 1848 along with sixty others by the will of their mistress, Nancy Cain, but professed to prefer "American slavery to Liberian freedom."[19] "Claiborn" was twenty-eight years old, "Epps" thirty-five, and Mark twenty-five.[20] Because the Colliers were colonized alongside Cain's other slaves, the men must have been separated from their immediate nuclear families rather than from their broader community networks. Most probably, they were parted from wives and children with whom they lived in cross-plantation unions. Being forced to live in a foreign environment, perhaps against their will, it is not surprising they expressed a desire to return to their previous lives, although surviving records offer only a snapshot of these.

Others, like Lizzie Purdie in 1839, requested enslavement before they were sent to Liberia. In 1854, two years before the Virginia legislation enabled voluntary enslavement, the state considered an enslavement petition submitted by Willis and Andrew Doswell, two "free persons of color in the County of Lunenberg" who had been emancipated through the will of David Doswell. Their petition, signed by at least forty-five supporters (the document is a little damaged, and it is hard to gauge an exact number), noted how, since their freedom, the two men had conducted themselves "honestly and industriously" and stated that they wished to remain in the Commonwealth of Virginia, "rather than go to the northern or northwestern free states, believing from what they can learn, their condition would be worse than in this state, and fearing that their situation in Liberia would be still worse, fearing the consequences of ill-health or loss of life in going."[21] The Doswells, like other petitioners, performed a racial role that played on white sentiments and proslavery ideology as a tactic to preserve affective ties and remain within homes and communities where they belonged. Like other petitioners, they fought for a degree of control over their destiny, notwithstanding their fear of expulsion, because they suggested choosing new masters from among the next of kin of David Doswell, their deceased owner.[22]

So their petition, like that submitted in 1837 on behalf of Leanty and her children, is testament to the ties that bound black and white families as well as black communities that crossed the line from slavery to freedom. No doubt the Doswell family would have been very grateful for the return of Willis and Andrew to bondage, and this was not just because of the economic benefit the two men would bring. The white Doswells also would have congratulated themselves on their own "benevolence" because Willis and Andrew "wanted" (in the face of limited choices) to become their property again. The men were freed prior to 1850, and in the census of that year they are listed as carpenters, aged thirty-two and thirty-four. Both lived in an all-black household alongside forty-year-old Milley Ragsdale and her two young children (Ragsdale's relationship to the Doswells is unclear). But Willis and Andrew Doswell disappear from the census in 1860, suggesting their petition was successful and they had rejoined the ranks of the Doswell slaves. Freedom was a temporary aberration.[23]

Virginia law formalized voluntary enslavement in 1856, after which there was a small flurry of enslavement requests from individuals who apparently placed their familial ties of affection above their status before the law. So the act became public knowledge, at least in the minds of some potential owners. In 1856, petitions included that of Thomas Grayson, a thirty-year-old black laborer living with a white family, named Settle, in Culpeper County. John J. Settle owned twelve slaves in 1850, so Grayson most likely would have had familial affective relationships across the slave-free divide.[24] This request was referred to several times in legislative records, and eventually the legislature passed an act allowing Grayson to "choose a master" (no name was given). Like Willis and Andrew Doswell most likely, Thomas Grayson vanished from the 1860 census as he joined the ranks of the enslaved.[25]

Other petitioners of this year included "Simon" of Southampton County, who asked for reenslavement on behalf of himself, his wife, Martha, and their two daughters, Judy and Margaret, all of whom were previously freed by John Williamson. In 1856, the legislature passed an act permitting all four to become the slaves of Willis Bradshaw, providing they "followed the procedures" identified by the assembly in its "act permitting voluntary enslavement."[26] Willis Bradshaw, of Nottoway River, owned ten slaves in 1850 and nine in 1860. Whether his chattel in 1860 included Simon and his family is unknown, because the slave schedules give no names. The motivations behind these requests for enslavement submitted on behalf of families (which are rare, with only eleven petitions for enslavement and eight for residency found for this study as a whole) were often more complex than those submitted by individuals. Simon and his family did not want to belong to their previous master or any member of the Williamson family. Why they became enslaved to Willis Bradshaw is unknown, but a likely explanation is that the family had broader kin ties to the Bradshaw slaves. Economic factors might also have played a role in familial enslavement petitions, where adult free blacks were unable to provide a subsistence standard of living for their nuclear families and made pragmatic choices about how best their families might be provided for.[27]

Also from Southampton County was the enslavement petitioner Lewis Williamson. In 1856 the general assembly permitted him to become the slave of A. B. Urquhart.[28] Urquhart lived in the East Side of Nottoway River, in the same locale as Willis Bradshaw (who acquired Simon and his family as slaves). The two men may have been acquaintances who discussed free people of color's enslavement and then "encouraged" both Thomas Grayson and Simon to submit petitions. Unlike most of the slave owners discussed here, Urquhart was a major planter, who owned 112 people in 1860.[29] That he possessed so many slaves increases the probability of Lewis Williamson being bound to Urquhart's broader enslaved community through familial ties. Similarly, in 1857 Armistead Currie requested bondage to Addison Hall, of Lancaster County. Although Hall owned only seventeen slaves in 1860, Currie may well have had affective kin ties to these slaves.[30]

Joseph Lee had been manumitted through the will of William Miller. He later petitioned the Circuit Court of Rockbridge County, asking to belong to David Kyger. The latter appeared in the 1860 census as David "Kiger," the owner of eleven slaves; it is again probable that Joseph Lee was attached to Kyger's enslaved people. In the documentation relating to this petition, the proceedings of the court state that "the rights and liabilities of said David Kyger, and the condition of the said Joseph Lee, shall in all respects be the same as though the said Joseph Lee had been born a slave."[31] But Joseph Lee *was* born a slave. The careless generic wording of the Court fails to acknowledge that freedom, for Joseph Lee and others who reentered slavery, was a temporary aberration. There was more fluidity between slavery and freedom (and vice versa) than has hitherto been recognized.

In 1860 Frank Harman requested enslavement to Anthony Owens of Pulaski County, the owner of four slaves. Harman had been indicted for remaining in Virginia after his emancipation because he failed to leave the state within a year, as decreed by law: "He is advised that he will either be compelled to leave the commonwealth or be again sold into slavery, that if he can have the selection of a master he prefers to return to a state of slavery rather than leave the state and that with this view he has selected Anthony Owens of said county as his master." His choices were limited. Faced with the prospect of either leaving his family or becoming enslaved, he decided on the former. Like other petitioners, he acted pragmatically in prioritizing kin networks and glimpsed freedom as only a fleeting phenomenon. Of Owens's four slaves, one was a thirty-three-year-old enslaved man. This might well have been Harman, having returned to slavery to live with his family.[32]

The last Virginia petition concerned with familial ties of affection was in 1861. In this year, Walker Fitch of Staunton, Augusta County, petitioned the legislature, claiming to be "weary of freedom" and requesting enslavement to Michael G. Harman, the owner of his wife and children. In 1860 Fitch was twenty-one years old and lived with his mother, Margaret, and sister, Elvira, both of whom were washerwomen. Harman owned twenty-four slaves. Impoverishment was significant here; Fitch was a laborer, and washerwomen were unlikely to be wealthy. Thinking pragmatically, Fitch probably considered he had little to lose by entering slavery, and he would also gain the ability to live within his own nuclear family. Moreover, Fitch's working life would have changed little, because he was already bound to the Harman family in an economic sense. Michael Harman confirmed in Fitch's petition that he owned Fitch's wife and children and "has had him in his employment for several years, and is willing to accept said Walker as his slave upon equitable terms."[33] Harman believed his possession of Fitch's family was worthy of mention and might make it more likely the request would be granted because familial references gave the petitioners and their potential owners a sense of "respectability" they hoped would work in their favor. Also notable is Harman's indication that he would be "willing to accept" Fitch as a slave. The wording selected is typical of slaveholder "benevolence," as though the responsibility of owning Fitch would outweigh the benefits of having him as an enslaved worker. Finally, while nothing survives of the "equitable terms" on which Walker Fitch entered bondage, his everyday life would have been broadly similar. Fitch labored for Haman both before and after slavery, and there was no sharp delineation between his life as a free man and that of a slave. Yet as a slave he was able to reside with his family.

A pattern by which free people of color petitioned for enslavement after the passing of laws facilitating voluntary slavery was repeated across the South, and while some of these requests do not explicitly state that the individuals (or families) involved wished to live with kin, potential masters' slave-owning suggests this was the case. For example, following the 1860 voluntary enslavement ruling in Alabama, the legislature "received and permitted into slavery" Ned Adkins, "a free man of color about sixty years old, now living with Thomas Williams, of Coosa County." He asked to become "a slave for life to Mistress Inda Ware, of the city of Selma, in the county of Dallas, to her sole and separate use."[34] Whether Adkins was attached to any of the fifty-one enslaved people belonging to Thomas Williams (or to any slaves belonging to Inda Ware or her husband) is unknown, but most likely he labored for Williams under a kind of "informal" slavery, in the same way as Walker Fitch worked for Michael Harman.

Adkins may have had familial ties to slaves belonging to the Ware family, though he is unusual in requesting enslavement to a woman. (The number of free people of color requesting such enslavement within this study was only ten, and eight of those were women themselves.) In 1860, Inda was twenty-eight years old and married with three young daughters. Her husband, H. H. Ware, owned six slaves, one of whom was a forty-five-year-old woman. It can be speculated that this woman might have been "Cealy Adkins," Adkins's fifty-six-year-old wife, according to the 1870 census. Certainly her age profile matches that in the 1860 slave schedule.[35] That Adkins might have been tricked or cajoled into petitioning for enslavement is also unlikely. Elderly men were not valuable, and members of the Ware family no doubt congratulated themselves on their benevolence in taking on Ned, who gained the opportunity to live with his wife. Evidence such as this thus allows for some speculation about affective familial ties and facilitates greater understanding of the complex and intertwined relationships among slaves, free people of color, and white families in the antebellum South.

The only other enslavement request where a man requested enslavement to a woman also came from Alabama. In 1860, James Fagin, a "free
mulatto," petitioned the County Court of Lowndes seeking bondage to
Ann Reese, "a white person of high moral character and good standing."
Under Alabama law, potential owners had to be both "respectable" and
"permanent residents" of the state. Two weeks after his initial petition,
James Fagin "appeared in open court," where he was examined, and he
then confirmed he wished to "surrender freedom . . . voluntarily and free
from any undue influence." The court then decreed he could become enslaved to Anne Reese.[36] In 1850, Anne was thirty-five, the mother of eight
young children, with a rather elderly husband, George, aged sixty-four.
By 1860, she appears to have been widowed and left to run an extensive
plantation with more than two hundred slaves. George Reese's estate,
therefore, seems to have remained intact, although his eldest son, Perry,
who was also a legal witness to James Fagin's petition, owned twenty-five
slaves in 1860. With such a high number of enslaved people on her plantation, it seems extremely likely that James Fagin was attached to one of
Anne Reese's slaves, with whom he wanted to remain.[37] Fagin's age and
occupation is unknown. By 1870 James worked as a carpenter and lived
with his wife and five children in Montgomery.[38] Caroline, his wife, was
perhaps a former Reese slave, and it is touching to see this family survive
the upheavals of enslavement and war.

Other Alabama enslavement requests were also clustered around the
time of the state's voluntary enslavement ruling. In this year, John Williams petitioned the Probate Court of Madison County asking to belong
to Thomas Douglass. The latter is described in the census as a farmer with
five slaves, three of whom were women over eighteen. John Williams
was probably attached to one of them, with their marriage bridging the
hazy line between freedom and bondage.[39] Likewise, the legislature also
permitted Pike County resident Lewis Wetherspoon, aged forty, to "select
and choose William Croswell [Crosswell], of said County, for his owner
and master." William Crosswell appears in the census as "William Craus-
well," a farmer with only three slaves. One was a forty-year-old woman,
perhaps Lewis Wetherspoon's wife. The other slaves were twenty-five-
year-old men, and it is not unreasonable to speculate they were the sons
of Lewis and his wife, had she borne them when she was fifteen.[40]

One year later, the same county received two enslavement petitions
from Nat Gunter. The first was "filed in writing by his friend Jonathan
Jones," the second allegedly written by another "friend," named Billy

Jones. In both petitions, Nat Gunter requested enslavement to Presley Davis, a married farmer with seventeen slaves. Testimony of "supporting witnesses" A. J. Lockard and Samuel Davis showed that "the facts set forth in the said petition are substantially true," and the court approved Gunter's request.[41] However, the witnesses were not entirely independent. Samuel Davis was an overseer for Presley Davis and maybe a relation; he was therefore unlikely to speak against Gunter's enslavement request.[42] White families sometimes asked their friends and relatives for help in enslavement petitions. For example, Anne Reese's son, Perry, served as a witness in James Fagin's enslavement petition. Such involvement reveals how the economic incentive to whites of voluntary bondage lay behind many enslavement petitions.

Another 1861 slavery petition, from Pike County resident Samuel Cobler, had an unusual outcome. A "free person of color over the age of twenty-one years," in May he asked probate court to enslave him to Wyatt Hogan. The hearing was scheduled for 1 June but was delayed twice— first because the judge of probate was absent and second because the witnesses were. Cobler thus petitioned again in August, "praying that he may become and be made a slave under acts of the legislature of 1859 and 1860 passed by deed of this Court choose James K. Murphree as a suitable person to become his master and prays that the same be granted." Another hearing was set for "the second Monday in September," but "Paper B" of surviving records claims the court dismissed the request prior to this date. Sam Cobler seems to have refused

> to become a slave, in accordance with the petition filed, therefore James K. Murphree consents to the withdrawal of the said petition. . . . It is further ordered by the court that said Sam Cobler, petitioner as aforesaid, pay all the costs of the proceedings and for which expenditure may issue in accordance with the acts in such cases made and provided. It is further ordered that the said Sam Cobler . . . is hereby this day noticed and required to leave this state within thirty days or he will be dealt with as the law requires; all of which is done in open court this day.[43]

Poor Sam Cobler faced either enslavement to Murphree or expulsion from Alabama in addition to paying for the costs of wasted court proceedings. Why he "refused" enslavement is unknown, but there are various possibilities. He might have been tricked into either or both enslavement petitions. Alternatively, his relationship with Murphree might have broken down, with the former preferring to belong to Wyatt Hogan. And why was Hogan cited as Cobler's potential owner in the first petition but not the second? Some of these answers remain elusive, although census records offer useful contextual evidence. James K. Murphree was described in 1860 as a "livery stable helper." Married with three children, he also owned three slaves, one of whom was an adult woman of twenty-eight, who might have been intimately attached to Cobler. This woman would provide an explanation for Cobler's second enslavement request, if not the first.[44] However, if Cobler was indeed tricked or cajoled into his petition, then his refusal to submit to bondage is commendable, even if the eventual outcome was not. Sam Cobler, a poor man of color, would not have the financial reserves necessary to pay court costs; therefore, he faced financial ruin, imprisonment, and forcible separation from his family.

One of the latest surviving enslavement requests was from Alabama in 1863.[45] In Chambers County, a free woman of color named Susan requested enslavement in June: "The said Susan desires voluntarily to surrender her freedom to the said Elizabeth Davis."[46] Elizabeth Davis was married to W. F. Davis, a farmer. They lived in a large, multigenerational household that included two free blacks—Susan Davis, aged sixteen, and George Davis, aged twenty-four. No occupation is listed for either, and their relationship is unclear. They might have been unrelated; however, they might have been a couple, or they could have been siblings. Also unknown is why Susan requested enslavement in the first place and why she sought bondage to a woman. But Susan's petition is still highly revealing. Like many other free people of color, Susan and George lived under a kind of quasi-slavery, where the distinction between bondage and freedom was hazy. They even shared the surname of their "master," W. F. Davis. Davis owned six slaves, so there were probably familial or other emotional ties of attachment among George, Susan, and Davis's slaves.[47] Extensive paperwork survives with this petition, including a note that Susan's request was approved in June 1863, she having waited for the "requisite ten days," solicited testimony from two witnesses, and obtained written consent from Elizabeth Davis.[48]

The relationships among Elizabeth and W. F. Davis and the two witnesses could not be deciphered, but the testimony of both men—Elliott H. Meese, the clerk of the county court, and William H. Vance—is significant. Neither could be traced as slave owners, but Meese was guardian to Robert Marter, a free man of color who lived within his household and worked as a blacksmith.[49] Meese and Vance had to answer the following questions:

> Are you acquainted with Susan the petitioner, a free person of colour? Where does she reside? What is her age? Do you know whether said Susan desires to surrender her freedom and become the slave of Elizabeth Davis? Do you know whether the said Susan filed the petition in this case voluntarily and free from undue influence? State how and why you know the facts above inquired about.
>
> Are you acquainted with the general character and standing of Elizabeth Davis? If yes, state whether the moral character and standing of the said Elizabeth Davis are good or bad, and where she permanently resides. Have you any interest in the result of this case?

Meese and Vance confirmed they learned Susan wished to enter slavery from a "conversation" they had with her. Vance declared he knew nothing of Elizabeth Davis, nor did he have a vested interest in the case. Meese declared that Elizabeth's "moral character and standing, so far as he knows and believes, is good." He also declared no vested interest in the case.[50] That both these white men supported the enslavement request is unsurprising, because most white people were conditioned to believe that the enslavement of free people of color was a good thing. There was, then, only a scant chance that Susan's petition would be rejected, although the relative wealth of evidence surviving from these Alabama requests reveals the time and attention devoted to enslavement petitions by Alabama lawmakers, who wanted to convey how such requests were taken seriously.

Arkansas was the only state to pass an expulsion law prior to the Civil War, so surviving enslavement petitions from this state can be read rather differently from those from elsewhere. Minutes of county circuit courts suggest, chillingly, that at least a handful of free people of color were forced into bondage because they refused to leave the state after their compulsory exclusion. For example, Robert, "of dark complexion," was arrested by the sheriff of Pulaski County "as a free negro residing in the State of Arkansas contrary to law." Robert appeared in open court, where he chose Thomas F. Yell as his owner, a "prayer" that was unsurprisingly granted. Yell filed his written consent, and three "responsible citizens of the County" were appointed to appraise Robert's value after having "viewed and examined" him. In a stark reminder of the sheer brutality of bondage, they declared he was worth only 250 dollars. But Thomas Yell had to pay just half Robert's value (125 dollars) to the Pulaski treasury, plus court costs. In return, "Robert shall be the property and slave for life of the said Thomas F. Yell."[51]

Faced with the stark reality of either expulsion or enslavement, both undesirable options, Robert chose to belong to the man who owned his family. The 1850 census shows that Robert Deam was a black laborer of "about" forty-five. He lived in Jefferson County with the Yell family—Thomas, a farmer of twenty-five; his twenty-four-year-old wife, Phliciann; and their infant daughter, Pricia. So, by 1860 Robert was fifty-five years old, which explains his rather low price. Robert also disappears from the 1860 census, which was taken after his enslavement, and becomes traceable only on the slave schedules. In the same year, Thomas F. Yell (now living in Pulaski) owned eleven slaves, one of whom was a fifty-five-year-old man, who probably was Robert. Also in Yell's possession was a sixty-year-old woman. She could have been Robert's wife, from whom he did not wish to be separated.[52] That Robert lived with the Yells both before and after his move from freedom to slavery again shows that the day-to-day lives of many free blacks who entered bondage changed little. Indeed, the ties that existed among whites of all social classes, free people of color, and the enslaved throw up interesting household formations that historians have not sufficiently analyzed.[53] Robert Deam (or Dean, as he appears in the 1870 census) was widowed. He worked as a laborer even in his mid-sixties and lived with his three children (Missouri, Jack, and Rachel Dean). Robert's children had probably all been slaves of the Yell family, but emancipation did not bring them true "freedom" from white society. Also living in the Dean household was a fifty-eight-year-old white woman named Lucy Yell.[54]

Two further enslavement cases survive within the minute books for the Circuit Court of Pulaski County. Mary Brock, a free "mulatto" woman, appeared before the court in May 1861. Like Robert Deam, she did not want to leave Arkansas and so was forced into bondage for living in the state illegally. William W. Adams filed his written consent to become Brock's master and gave "his bond for the sum of one thousand dollars." The court decreed Brock Adams's slave "for life" and demanded that he pay all costs accrued.[55] William Adams, of Little Rock, possessed five slaves in 1860 (one year before he acquired Brock), of whom three were adult men aged forty-three, thirty-seven, and twenty-seven. He also owned an adult woman of thirty-five and a male child of sixteen. Brock probably bore attachment to one of Adams's enslaved men.[56]

Another free "mulatto" woman who desired to stay in Arkansas was Elizabeth Keatts. Like Mary Brock, she appeared in open court in 1861 to "select" James B. Keatts as her master. He filed his written consent to both own Elizabeth and "take charge of her two infant children according to law." Elizabeth and her offspring cost one thousand dollars (the same price as Mary Brock), for which James Keatts filed bond.[57] A planter from Big Rock, James Keatts owned sixty-seven slaves, making it highly probably that Elizabeth Keatts was intimately attached to one of his enslaved men. Moreover, she shared his surname. She may well have lived on James Keatts's plantation with her husband and children in quasi-slavery prior to the Arkansas expulsion ruling and her subsequent slavery petition.[58] The enslavement petitions of Mary Brock and Elizabeth Keatts were linked: not only were the acts enabling bondage passed at the same time, but James B. Keatts confirmed the securities of William W. Adams and vice versa. The two men were probably friends or acquaintances. They also, of course, paid more money for their new slave women than Thomas Yell did for the rather elderly Robert Deam, because the women were younger and considered more valuable. But James Keatts did not pay any extra money for taking Elizabeth's children into his possession. Typically, slaveholders perceived their ownership of children "benevolently," and Keatts would have taken great pride in his "kindness" in taking them on. Robert Deam, Mary Brock, and Elizabeth Keatts all lived on the edges of slavery, and all chose not to leave the places where they belonged following the 1860 expulsion law. Their stark choice was either slavery or separation from their families. Faced with such an undesirable situation, all acted pragmatically in "selecting" bondage to exploitative and cajoling white men, and all three no doubt anticipated that their everyday lives would change little.

Other Arkansas cases also suggest something of the dilemmas facing free people of color forced to choose between expulsion and enslavement. Lewis Green petitioned the Phillips County Circuit Court in 1860 asking for bondage to Samuel Weatherley. Weatherley had four slaves, including one adult woman who may have been Green's wife. Weatherley paid a bond for twelve hundred dollars for Lewis Green.[59] Mark Dodd became the slave of General Gideon J. Pillow in 1860. Pillow was a wealthy man with fifty slaves, and he paid the not insignificant amount of fifteen

hundred dollars to the State of Arkansas for Mark Dodd. It can be speculated that Dodd was attached to one of Pillow's enslaved women.[60] James
Truman of La Grange, Lafayette County, and "over the age of twenty-one
years," requested slavery in 1862. He was "praying to reside in the State
of Arkansas, and that he be made a slave for life and the property of Lewis
B. Fort." The Lafayette court also spelled out that James Truman had "been
instructed by the Court as to what his legal rights are, he therefore chose
to reside in the State of Arkansas and fully voluntarily, and of his own
accord chose Lewis B. Fort as his master." Lewis Fort filed bond for two
thousand dollars "with two good securities," showing that he was a man
of some wealth highly anxious to obtain James Truman as his chattel. The
court decreed that Truman should "not be permitted to act for himself
or as a free person . . . [and shall be] subject to all laws that now govern
slaves in the state of Arkansas."[61]

For James Truman, as well as others, family came before legal status,
and this was especially apparent for free blacks who became enslaved to
wealthy planters on whose property they had previously resided. There
was also was a higher probability of spousal or other intimate relationships across the divide between slavery and freedom where new masters possessed many slaves. For example, Lewis Fort was described in the
1860 census as a "farmer," but owning fifty slaves actually made him a
prosperous planter. Also living on Fort's "farm" were seven free people
of color, all "laborers." One of these, nineteen-year-old Jim (the eldest)
could be the "James Truman" who entered bondage in 1862.[62] Regardless of restrictive legislation designed to keep them separated, slaves and
free people of color formed families, homes, and communities across
this often arbitrary divide, which they fought to preserve in pragmatic
ways. Many free people of color were de facto slaves in the households
of white families, families to whom some later sought enslavement. Ira
Berlin famously described free blacks as "slaves without masters," but in
reality, some antebellum free people of color were already subject to a
kind of quasi-slavery with masters.[63]

Similar patterns of voluntary enslavement in the late 1850s and early
1860s existed across the South. In Florida, a free woman of color named
Jane petitioned the Suwannee County court in 1860 requesting that she
and her son, Charles, "under fourteen years of age" become enslaved to
Mary Rowland. Unusually, Rowland had no husband. Described in the
1860 census as a forty-two-year-old farmer, she resided with her four
children and ten enslaved people, of whom one was a twenty-three-year-

old man who could have been Jane's husband and Charles's father.[64] If this is the case, Jane wanted to live with her husband against all odds. Jacksonville free black Cato Smith had a similar desire to be with his family. Although not enslaved, Smith entered a period of indentured servitude for his love of a woman, according to his son, Samuel Smalls. Smalls informed his Works Progress Administration interviewer in the 1930s that in his work as an overseer his father traveled all the way to Suwannee County from Connecticut, where he fell in love with an enslaved woman. Her owner told him, though, that to live with her as his wife he would have to labor unpaid on the plantation for seven years. He obliged.[65]

The latest enslavement petition found for this study was submitted to the interior court of Habersham County, Georgia, in 1864. This might be because Georgia itself did not legislate on voluntary enslavement until 1863. Here, John Sexton asked to belong to William H. Fuller. Like many other petitioners, he played on perceived benevolence of the slaveholding class in conforming to expected racial conventions. He professed to believe "that people of his color are more happy, more secure of support and more especially believing that he can better secure his wife and children a competent maintenance in a state of slavery, he is willing and hereby petitions said court to be allowed to sell himself into slavery." Sexton also marked the document with an "X," which was fairly common. More unusual, however, is the surviving level of detail about the financial arrangements of his petition. Court minutes show that

> the said John Sexton being present and having been examined by the undersigned privately, and having expressed to us his free and full consent to become the slave of the said William H. Fuller upon the payment of the sum of five hundred dollars to the wife and children of the said John Sexton, and the said William H. Fuller being present and expressing his willingness to accept said slave and to pay the sum of five hundred dollars to the wife and children of the said John. It is therefore ordered that the said John Sexton be and he is hereby declared to be the slave of the said William H. Fuller.[66]

Five hundred dollars seems a rather low sum to pay for John Sexton, a thirty-four-year-old skilled blacksmith, and this outcome is also unusual in other respects.[67] William Fuller cannot be found as a slaveholder, and if he indeed owned no chattel, then John Sexton would have had no familial incentive to belong to him. But, in selling himself for five hundred dollars, with the money going to his free wife and children, John Sexton was placing the economic well-being of his family before his legal status. In the 1860 census, John was married to Margaret, a housekeeper, and they also had eight children, ranging in age from fourteen to two. The family must have been impoverished, with John and Margaret unable to provide a subsistence standard of living, and it is desperately poignant that John Sexton made the sacrifice of selling himself into bondage to provide for them. And there is a final curious twist: all members of the Sexton family were described with the letter "M?" for "mulatto" except Margaret, who was not assigned the letter "B" for "black," either. Might Margaret Sexton have been John's *white* wife?[68] The case also raises further apparently unanswerable questions: Was Sexton not afraid of later being forcibly separated from his family? Why would William Fuller (who cannot be traced on the census) want to buy a slave in 1864, during the death throes of the regime? Why did he not simply employ Sexton so the latter could provide his family with a regular income? Why might Sexton have needed a lump-sum payment?

Unlike Florida and Georgia, Mississippi framed its legislative debates in terms of expulsion (though such a law was never passed), and the state did not legislate on voluntary slavery. However, within the state a number of enslavement petitions tended to be clustered around the years of legislative debate over expulsion. These petitions are further testament to familial ties between the enslaved and free people of color. For example, Johan Perrot, the twenty-three-year-old son of a white woman, requested of the legislature in 1859 that he become the slave of Charles Hailey, a man he regarded as a "kind master and friend," to whom he was formerly apprenticed. The petition is couched in the popular rhetoric of benevolence, but there may be another reason for Perrot's request.[69] Hailey (appearing as "Hale" in the 1860 census) owned nine slaves, of whom four were adult women and five were children under sixteen. Perrot was probably in an intimate relationship with one of these women, and some of the children could have been his own. That "John Perrit" appears as a single man on the 1860 census (enslaved spouses were not recognized by law or census enumerators) lends credence to this claim, while illustrating that Perrot's petition was rejected.[70]

Other petitioners were explicit about their spousal relationships with the enslaved. Wilson Melton (a farmer) and John W. Sproles (a merchant) petitioned the Mississippi legislature in 1859 on behalf of Wesley Moore, a "free man of yellow complexion." They wanted Moore to be exempted from a bill designed to expel free blacks from the state because he was married to a slave of "one of the petitioners," with whom he had several children, also enslaved. Melton and Sproles claimed Moore would prefer enslavement to expulsion, and their request was referred to a committee but seems to have never been decided upon. Melton owned three adult women and six enslaved children under the age of ten.[71] Melton and Sproles wrote their petition with public benevolence in mind. Moore preferred enslavement to enforced expulsion away from his home and family, and these sympathetic white men were helping him achieve personal happiness. But privately, white motivations could be very different from those expressed publicly, and Wilson Melton would have had real economic incentive to gain for himself an adult slave man.

Free black man Joe Bird requested slavery of the Mississippi legislature in 1859. Using typical proslavery rhetoric, he explained how he desired to "elevate himself from his present condition into slavery," a conception which would probably have been very popular with white legislators. Having lived in the state for more than twenty years, Bird described how he wanted to remain with his slave wife and children and belong to Robert Graham, presumably his wife's master. Bird considered any "elevation" to be in terms of his forthcoming day-to-day residence with his nuclear family. However, Graham, along with the white men of state government, would have regarded enslavement per se as an "improved" status for Joe Bird.[72] In Hinds County, also in 1859, Jesse Russell likewise requested enslavement, to James Tapley. In 1860, Tapley held only three female slaves, aged twenty-eight, sixteen, and nine, and it is highly probable that Russell had an intimate relationship with one of the older two. Although Russell seems never to have become enslaved to Tapley, the acquisition of an enslaved man would have significantly added to Tapley's property.[73]

From Tippah County, William Jackson also petitioned the Mississippi legislature for enslavement "on condition he may elect his owner." Citing James T. Craig as his proposed master, Jackson appeared well aware of his legal rights and seems to have regarded the process of enslavement as a site of negotiation within which he held a degree of bargaining power. Craig owned thirteen slaves. Perhaps Jackson's wife was the only adult owned by Craig, a woman of thirty-two. His other twelve slaves, some of whom may have been Jackson's children, were all aged sixteen or under.[74]

Emmarilla Jeffries's 1860 petition explicitly referred to the expulsion law "about to be passed" by Mississippi, although it never was actually put into law. Jeffries described how her potential owner, E. W. Ward, had "kindly provided for her wants" and explained her husband and sister were enslaved to him. She also asked for Ward to own her children, Ida, Thomas, Ann, and Curtis. Ida, the eldest, was but six years old and "very much disabled from an injury."[75] This desperate-sounding petition conveys how familial ties extended beyond the spousal and also shows that free black women had to make heartbreaking decisions about their children's futures as well as their own. Mississippi did not legislate on the enslavement of children, so requests here were dependent on individual initiative. Jeffries found it difficult to provide for her four young children and was scared about having to leave the state. She therefore put her family first so she could remain in the place she belonged regardless of her legal status.

A more ambiguous Mississippi enslavement petition, in which motivations are hard to evaluate, was submitted to the legislature in 1860 by William Webster of Charleston, Tallahatchie. There are several possible explanations for Webster's request, in which he explained how he was "indebted" to a white physician named Dr. Atheral Ball. "Indebted" can be read in either a personal sense or a financial one; Webster might have been bound to Ball through affective ties, as he wrote that he was "attached" to him and "does not wish to be removed from his possession."[76] So Webster was apparently living within Ball's household prior to his enslavement request, although he does not appear on the census as a household member for either 1850 or 1860. Ball was married with children, and he owned nine slaves, including two adult women. The most likely explanation, then, is that Webster was intimately involved with one of Ball's slaves, although it is strange that he chose not to refer to his spouse—which would have given him an aura of "respectability" with which to impress legislators—and instead described only his "affection" for Atheral Ball. The majority of enslavement requests engaged with proslavery ideology, but most tended to be couched in terms of the "care and provisions" of white slave owners rather than affective ties between potential slaves and owners of the same gender. Webster's petition was accepted, and Ball was given "full, complete and absolute ownership of the said William Webster, as if he the said William Webster had been born the slave of said Ball."[77]

Like Mississippi, North Carolina did not pass laws enabling voluntary enslavement or exclusion. But enslavement petitions survive from this state, also, in which free blacks prioritized their familial relationships above all else. Submitted to the legislature in 1862 was a petition from a white man, C. A. Featherston of Gaston County, who wished to enslave a thirty-five-year-old black man named Wyat, who had had lived with the family for "several years" (though in the 1860 census he does not appear in Featherston's household), and Featherston claimed "the said boy preferring a life of slavery with the master of his choice and with the woman he had taken up with and his children to the life of a free negro." Wyat's wife was also one of Featherston's seven slaves. Featherston referred to Wyat as a "boy" to typically diminish his status as an adult man. Featherston also belittled the familial relationships of black people when he wrote that Wyat had "taken up" with (rather than married) one of his slave women, who had then borne Wyat's enslaved children. Wyat could have been tricked or cajoled into this petition, which does not even bear his "X," and no outcome was ever decided upon.[78] Featherston displays some of the inherent contradictions of slaveholding: he framed the petition in terms of Wyat's personal ties of affection while at the same time giving scant regard to their significance.

In a similar vein, Nelson Patterson requested enslavement to Davie County slave owner William Marsh in 1861, who already owned his wife.[79] Likewise, Percy Ann Martin of Davidson County allegedly wanted to become enslaved to her husband's owner, Henderson Adams, in 1860. She described how she had been married for five years and explained that "she is attached to her husband and does not wish to be separated from him."[80] Unlike C. A. Featherston, who submitted his petition "on behalf" of Wyat, Patterson and Martin did not shy away from reference to the marriages of black people, even if they did not write the petitions themselves, which suggests they had at least some involvement in deciding how their enslavement requests should be framed. Other North Carolina petitioners included Julia Dickinson and Susan Lewis (their relationship unknown), who became enslaved to J. G. Holiday of Northampton County in 1860. Holiday owned eleven people, all of whom were over the age of twenty. Dickinson and Lewis might have been married to two of Holiday's seven adult men.[81]

Finally, the North Carolina legislature received an enslavement petition on behalf of a free black family from Jones County named Garnes. Consisting of a husband, a wife, and six children, this family apparently wished to belong to Joseph A. Hartley, who was already in possession of fourteen people. The Garnes family was probably enmeshed within a broad enslaved and free black community within which Hartley's slaves also lived. But this familial request failed in the North Carolina senate in 1861. No doubt local government efforts were diverted toward rising sectional tensions, although the enslavement of children remained a contentious issue in this state as it did elsewhere.[82] More broadly, the petitions submitted in states where no legislation providing for enslavement was passed are revealing. They convey how expulsion and enslavement were being debated throughout the South and show that free people of color were fearful about the future, providing for their families, and being separated from kin. Some free blacks, therefore, took the desperate preemptive measure of seeking enslavement.

South Carolina permitted voluntary enslavement through special legislative acts in individual cases, and within the Palmetto State some petitions survive that, like that of Lucy Andrews, convey the importance of affective ties between free people of color and the enslaved. This is true regardless of who (explicitly or implicitly) wrote the petitions, be it prospective owners or others. For example, the Reverend William P. Hill, a Baptist clergyman of Greenwood, curtly and confidently wrote, "you can consider this as a petition" in his 1859 request for ownership of Elizabeth Jane Bug. Bug was mother to an eleven-month-old child, whom Hill thought should also be enslaved "in connection" with its mother. Elizabeth herself had apparently "been anxious to become his [Hill's] slave for about a year" and had "been persuading Mrs. Hill and myself [to enslave her]." Referred to a committee, no outcome was ever recorded for this petition.[83] Hill, who lived with his extended family at the time of the 1860 census, owned four slaves, including a thirty-eight-year-old woman; a twenty-five-year-old man; and two boys, aged sixteen and nine.[84] Although Bug's motives are elusive, it is perfectly plausible to speculate that she was married to the twenty-five-year-old slave man. Significant, too, is that William P. Hill simply assumed her infant child should be brought into bondage with her, even though South Carolina did not legislate on children's enslavement. Hill presented a public discourse of benevolence in "taking on" Elizabeth's child, but he also had a more private incentive of future economic gain.

Rather curiously, there survives another enslavement petition from an Elizabeth Bug in Edgefield District, and this second request also sheds light on white attitudes toward the enslavement of children.[85] This second Elizabeth Bug (if, indeed, they *were* different women) was aged forty-one and "the wife of a negro man named Nat, the property of A. B.

Dean." Elizabeth and Nat had three children, "Pickens, about eleven . . . Harriet a little girl about eight . . . and Sally about two." Bug described in her enslavement request, marked with an "X," how "it is inconvenient, if not impossible for your petitioner to provide suitable and sufficient food and [illegible word] for her and her children under these circumstances. Freedom is a burden to her." She therefore asked for herself and her three children to belong to A. B. Dean, her husband's master.[86] Her petition was framed similarly to Lucy Andrews's. Both were concerned about providing their children with subsistence standards of living, and "freedom" was unquestionably difficult for free black women in the antebellum South. But both also had enslaved spouses with whom they wanted to live, so they also had emotional rationales for entering bondage, prioritizing their spousal relationships above their legal status. The second Elizabeth Bug's request was rejected in 1859. The report of the committee on the judiciary stated "that they . . . are of the opinion that no enactment can be made whereby upon the petition of another, infant free persons of color can be reduced to the condition of slavery. The committee recommends that the passage of the petition not be granted."[87] The South Carolina legislature, like that of North Carolina, therefore accepted that the enslavement of free children of color was controversial; there are parallels here with the Virginia and Tennessee legislatures, which also forbade free black children from entering bondage.

Like William P. Will, slaveholder W. G. Gore was transparent about writing an enslavement petition on behalf of a potential chattel: "The petition of the subscriber, citizen of Laurens District, and the state aforesaid, respectfully showeth that the within named William Jackson, free man of color, wishes to go into slavery, and voluntarily offers himself to your petitioner, W. G. Gore. Your petitioner therefore prays that he may be made the lawful owner of said William Jackson." Attached to the petition was a statement, in a different hand, allegedly written by William Jackson (although he had marked the document with a cross). The statement read: "That I, William Jackson, a free boy, am tired of freedom and wish to become a slave. I do, therefore, voluntarily give myself to W. G. Gore and his heirs during my life, to be treated as any other of his slaves." Here again, "boy" was a typically derogatory term used to infantilize black men and probably not a reflection of Jackson's youth. And there are other common examples of proslavery rhetoric in this petition, including the notion that freedom was "tiring" for free people of color, for whom an enslaved life would be "preferable." However, since Gore owned eleven slaves, including seven children aged sixteen or under, three adult women, and one adult man, it is likely that William Jackson was tied to one of the enslaved women through marriage.[88]

The wording of the 1859 petition of William Bass of Marlborough District also contains typical proslavery discourse about the hardships of freedom and benefits of bondage. Bass's petition to the general assembly read:

> His position as a free person of color, a negro, is more degrad-
> ing, and involves more suffering in this State, than that of a slave,
> who is under the care, protection and ownership of a kind and
> good master. That as a free negro, he is preyed upon by every
> sharper [con man] with whom he comes in contact, and that he
> is very poor, though as an able bodied man, and is charged with
> and punished for, every offence, guilty or not, committed in his
> neighborhood; that he is without house or home, and lives a
> thousand times harder, and in more destitution, than the slaves
> of many of the planters in this district.

William Bass asked for enslavement to Philip W. Pledger "who has consented to receive him if he can do so lawfully . . . and who owns his
stepfather and some other relations." He also marked the document with
an "X."[89] Historian David Dangerfield notes that Bass's petition was published in a newspaper prior to its legislative debate, with the publicity generated being used to support the notion of slavery as a positive
good.[90] Like those of other petitioners, William Bass's request was framed
in terms of both economic hardship and familial ties of affection between free blacks and the enslaved, specifically that Pledger possessed
Bass's "stepfather and other relations." A prominent planter, Philip Pledger owned forty-two enslaved people in 1860. Bass was enmeshed within
this broader enslaved community while straddling the divide between
freedom and bondage.[91]

Two surviving enslavement requests from Tennessee are also testament to the strength of affective familial ties between slaves and free
blacks. In 1861, James Johnson asked to belong to Edward West, of Washington County. Johnson was probably bound up within West's small enslaved community; West owned five adults and one infant. Relationships
between the Johnson and West families also stretched back over time.
James Johnson described how Edward West had manumitted his mother,

Cynthia.[92] This makes Johnson's enslavement request all the more ironic, but it also suggests that any distinction between slavery and freedom for Johnson and his mother was rather arbitrary. Similarly, in 1858, a free man of color named Benjamin requested enslavement to William Miller of Hawkins County. While Miller cannot be traced as a slave owner, Benjamin was (or had been) married to a slave. He wrote in his petition that he had "several children who are slaves residing here." Presumably "here" meant the household of William Miller, where Benjamin believed he belonged and where he had paternal responsibilities. Benjamin, who marked his petition with an "X," had a value stated at eight hundred dollars. Following the approval of the circuit court, James Miller paid just one-tenth of his value (eighty dollars) at the outset.[93] Arrangements such as these, where prospective owners paid only fractions of their new slaves' values, were obviously designed to facilitate slave ownership among less wealthy people.

Finally, in Texas, in 1858 a free man of color known as Daniel petitioned the County Court of San Augustine requesting bondage to B. Milam Watson. Frightened of expulsion from the state, Daniel had as his priority to remain in the place he called home, with his family around him. His petition was worded in a rather fulsome, if eloquent, fashion and was obviously designed to appeal to the white slaveholding men of local government. He poignantly yet glowingly described how Watson was: "in every day fit to receive this gift of my freedom. . . . The object of life is happiness—freedom is only useful when it tends to secure it. For my part I can only say that it has great terror for me as it robs me of my family and forces me from the spot to which I am so much attached. If I only share the lot of other slaves around me I feel that I not only have not relinquished, but have gained an advantage by changing my condition." Desperately reaching out to slaveholder "benevolence," Daniel also described in disparaging tones how life in the North would "bring ruin and misery to myself. . . . [T]he laboring classes are equally indigent and infinitely more selfish and exclusive than the slaves here—I should be starved out or driven off to the Canadas." Such lamentations must surely have curried favor with the white lawmakers, although no outcome survives for Daniel's petition.[94] Daniel's choice of owner is also interesting. Watson was a twenty-two-year-old man (no occupation is listed) living in the household of the "merchant and planter" Richard Waterhouse. Watson could have been an overseer wanting a share of slaveholding for himself. Although the number of people belonging to Waterhouse cannot be traced, his being described in the census as a planter suggests he owned more than twenty slaves, increasing the likelihood Daniel bore ties of affection to one of them.[95]

Finally, in another enslavement request that conveys both the strength of familial ties between the enslaved and free blacks and the desire of white men to increase their chattel, Gabriel Todd of Polk County asked in 1860 to belong to Edward D. Martin. Todd wished "to avail himself of the law permitting him to select a master and become a slave," indicating his awareness of recent legislation on voluntary bondage. Although any outcome is unknown, Todd may well have been successful in his request for enslavement. He submitted his petition in March 1860, and by that August, when slave schedules were enumerated for the census, Edward D. Martin appears as the master of ten slaves, four of whom were over eighteen, including one forty-year-old man. This age profile matches that of the fifty-one-year-old Gabriel Todd, who in 1870 lived in Harris County with his family.[96]

Southern states can be characterized in terms of their similarities in their treatment of free people of color rather than their differences. Whether or not states passed legislation on expulsion and enslavement, the clustering of petitions around the late 1850s and early 1860s is testament to free people of color's rising sense of fear that they would be forcibly separated from enslaved family members. Discourses within the petitions themselves also reveal performances that matched racialized expectations through repeated emphasis on the "benevolence" of slaveholding. They also starkly display the extent to which poverty characterized free blacks' lives. In particular, free women worried about their ability to provide for their children. Finally, the petitions show in a very tender and touching manner the strength of marital, familial, and community affective ties that cross the slave-free divide for the antebellum South's black population. To live in a place that was home with people one loved was the ultimate priority for enslavement petitioners, many of whom already lived along an arbitrary line dividing freedom from bondage that rendered their legal status rather meaningless in their everyday lives.

5

Expulsion, Enslavement, and Ties across the Color Line

A rather complicated case, which encapsulated many of the racial concerns of the day, went before the general assembly of Virginia in the early 1830s. Lucy Boomer was a free woman of color emancipated through the will of the late John Winn, to whom she had been enslaved. Lucy's 1833 petition to the legislature asked not for slavery but for "permission" to remain in Virginia, framing her request in terms of her relatively advanced age and her "faithfulness," as defined by whites. She claimed to have always worked hard for the Winn family before her "reward" of freedom. Her petition reads: "[She] has always borne an excellent character, she has spent her life in the faithful discharge of all duties incumbent upon her, and for which . . . her master, by his last will and testament, gave to her freedom, making also a provision for her support during her life." Sensibly, Lucy included with her petition a copy of John's Winn's will, confirming his desire to free her and then to provide for her thereafter. Her request then described how "the said Lucy is now so advanced in life, that a removal from this Commonwealth in pursuance of an Act passed March 2nd 1819—concerning slaves, free negroes and mulattoes, is totally impracticable." She therefore "prayed" the legislature would pass an act permitting her to remain in Virginia and provided twenty-three signatures in support of her request.[1]

Two copies of John Winn's will survive, although these are written in a different hand. The will explained how Lucy should not be freed immediately after his death but should instead be bequeathed to Winn's wife, Susanna. Upon Susanna's death, Lucy was to be liberated "and not to be subject to the control of any person whatsoever. I also give her a bed and a sufficiency for her support during her life to be provided by my representatives hereafter named." In contrast, Winn's other slaves, plus his land and property, were distributed among Susanna, her children, and her grandchildren. So Winn singled out Lucy for liberation; she was most likely a favored slave.[2] Such requests were not unusual. However, this case took a complicated and unusual turn when Winn's family submitted a counterpetition, opposing Lucy's request to stay in Virginia. They described how it would be an "injustice" and a "great impropriety" if Lucy's request for residency was granted because of her "moral character." The family argued Lucy should be compelled to leave the state because she caused "wounds" within the family, and "violated their faith." They described how "the heart of a helpless female [has] been made to bleed at every hour under such circumstances. We can't believe for a moment that your honorable body will doubt upon the subject but will spurn her petition with the contempt that it deserves from every lover of virtue."[3]

Various members of the Winn family also included their own personal affidavits with their rationales for opposing Lucy's request for residency. For example, John and Susanna's daughter-in-law, Charlotte Winn, submitted a lengthy document explaining why Lucy should be expelled from Virginia. Lucy had apparently "demanded" her freedom upon Susanna's death, claiming "she would not serve them any longer." Lucy had apparently insisted that a man named Colonel Bacon had told her about her freedom, although Charlotte wrote that Bacon had denied having "told Lucy any such thing—that he was sorry he did not have her whipped for saying it." Lucy had also again "demanded" of the second John Winn (Charlotte's late husband) "his protection as he was left an executor of his father's will." Charlotte recalled how her husband told Lucy "if she behaved herself he would treat her well . . . , if she did not behave herself he would make her remember what she had made his mother [Susanna] suffer."

After this unpleasant encounter, Charlotte wrote, her husband was taken sick and died, and, curiously, at the same time another family member, Priscilla Winn, had also passed away. Lucy had apparently confided in Charlotte that Chaney, the plantation cook—along with her enslaved husband—had poisoned Priscilla. But Charlotte believed Lucy was somehow responsible for both deaths and possibly others. Charlotte described how some years previously a white man named James Brown "had made Lucy mad and afterwards said Brown and two of his negroes were taken sick and attended to by Dr Richard May." Brown and one of the slaves subsequently died, but the other slave, a woman, was sent to Susanna Winn's "for Lucy to nurse." She regained her health and was then sent home. However, Charlotte wrote, "Lucy went to see her the next Sunday and . . . gave her a biscuit which she ate and within half an hour she was taken sick and died within ten days." Charlotte also claimed that Lucy had confessed to poisoning John Winn: he "died within half an hour after she had given him biscuit to eat."[4] Charlotte's sometimes convoluted testimony therefore combines a consideration of Lucy's "impudence" and her "demanding" nature with more widespread contemporary fears about poisoning.[5] In total, she suggested Lucy may have poisoned six people, namely her husband John Winn, Pricilla Winn, James Brown and two of his slaves, plus John Winn her father-in-law. Lucy may also have tried to pass the blame for two of these deaths onto Chaney, the plantation cook. The tone adopted within Charlotte's affidavit suggests she was rather fearful of Lucy but believed she had firm grounds upon which to question Lucy's petition. Obviously bitter about the manumission of a "troublesome" slave, Charlotte seemed to want to "punish" Lucy by expelling her from Virginia.

That Lucy had strength of character and an awareness of her "rights" as outlined in John Winn's will is clear, and the view of her as "demanding" crops up in other Winn family affidavits. Charleen, a grandchild of John and Susanna Winn, described how Lucy had "demanded support" and said her "Aunt Pricilla Winn had to whip her and whip her before she would submit."[6] Whether Lucy did indeed poison Pricilla after this bout of physical punishment may never be known, but further affidavits explain why the family did not take the poisoning claims into a more public realm: Lucy was having a sexual relationship with John Winn the elder. Sophia A. Winn (the elder John Winn's daughter), for example, recalled a conversation she had once had with Lucy, who lamented her "mistreatment" and vowed never to allow it to happen again: "She 'would not take such treatment from no man living.'" Lucy asserted how she had "never had taken it but from one, and she would not take it from no other." Although Lucy denied that Sophia's father, John, had "abused her," she refused to divulge a name. Sophia's description of her conversation with Lucy is testament to the close relationships that sometimes formed among southern women, with the enslaved Lucy feeling comfortable enough to confide in Sophia, at least to an extent, as another woman.[7]

More explicit in his own affidavit was James Winn, another son of the elder John. His own mother, he wrote in disgust, had to "give up her bed to Lucy, the negro woman set free by my father, John Winn, deceased, in [the] lifetime of my father for twelve of fifteen years."[8] The bitterness among Winn's children about his relationship with Lucy is understandable, especially as the elder Winn had granted Lucy her freedom and provided financially for her support. Winn's singling out of Lucy in this way was undoubtedly hurtful to his wife. Moreover, Lucy's recourse to the law in an attempt to gain residency rights aggrieved John and Susanna's children, especially because she adopted a "demanding" tone, couched firmly in terms of "rights" within her petitions. Lucy wanted both her freedom and the promised financial support, and the right to remain in Virginia, her top priority. But this was a step too far for the Winn family, which responded to Lucy's seemingly excessive claims by putting into a more public domain difficult and private issues. Her behavior was deemed inappropriate and "uppity," and the Winn family thus sought to punish Lucy for her demands.

Other surviving documents suggest something of Lucy's status in her local community as a trusted house servant with a long history of working for the Winn family. Other members of the family, as well as other whites to whom the family had ties, saw fit to come forward in support of Lucy and her claim for residency and probably caused a profound family rift. Edward Winn, for example, described how he had been acquainted with Lucy for "upwards of fifty years" and wrote that John Winn and his family spoke very highly of her. Edward claimed never to have heard of the poisoning accusations prior to the submission of the counterpetition. He also claimed James Winn had confided in him "that he never did believe the said Lucy was a poisoner and did not give his affidavit to that effect."[9]

Dr. Richard May, who tended to James Brown and his two slaves after Lucy's alleged poisoning, felt compelled to write a letter in support of Lucy, claiming: "She is a woman of uncommon character for a negro. The counter petition is signed by interested legatees [sic] exclusively. I am the Richard May alluded to in it [the affidavit of Charlotte]. I have known that family well, 18 years. This is the first I have heard of these charges. She acted as housekeeper before the death of John Winn, was on the best terms . . . with her mistress and the family. She continued in that capacity until the death of Mr. Winn."[10] May might have thought Charlotte's petition challenged his ability as a doctor, because she implicitly suggested he was unable to save Brown and his slaves from Lucy's poisoning. However, other individuals suggested an alternative explanation for the Winn family's counterpetition: they were hoping to keep Lucy for themselves. A man named David Tirrell (his relationship to the Winn family is unknown) wrote an affidavit in support of Lucy. Clarifying that John Winn had been dead for "about seventeen years," Tirrell described how, from his perspective, Lucy had "always appeared to be a very trusty servant" and John Winn always spoke "very highly" of her. Tirrell claimed never to have heard "of the said Lucy being accused of [or] been guilty of poisoning any person his life" and wrote that John P. Winn, a grandson of the deceased John Winn, once declared that should he not be able to "keep" Lucy for himself, "he would not approve her petition before the legislature" to remain in the state.[11]

This document provides a crucial time frame for the previous events. Susanna died in 1833, the same year Lucy petitioned the legislature. Lucy therefore framed her requests for freedom and residency within the same document and, significantly, to "prove" her freedom, she offered a copy of John Winn's will. However, to some of the Winn family members, the notion that a black woman might sleep with their father, use this intimate relationship as a tool to gain freedom, and then also seek special permission to stay in Virginia was simply unacceptable. John P. Winn spelled things out succinctly—if Lucy could not be "kept" as a slave, then she could not stay. The Winn family's motivations might have been economic: because John Winn's will stipulated that Lucy should be supported financially, this burden would have fallen on the surviving Winns if Lucy was allowed to remain in Virginia. Lucy was also of advanced age and perhaps unable to work as adeptly as in the past. Yet the passion and depth of feeling conveyed in the family's many affidavits also suggest exile should be enforced in a punitive sense. Lucy Boomer was a black woman who had forgotten her place.

Despite losing her residency request, Lucy Boomer remained in Virginia in 1835, and she continued to fight for the right to remain in her home. Perhaps acknowledging the futility of her previous efforts, she also changed her approach, and her petition of this year is rather different from her previous ones. Her petition of December read:

[Now] . . . about sixty years of age, in delicate health and wishing to remain here [in Lunenburg County] the remainder of her

life, she petitioned the general assembly at its last session for
leave to do so. But that body in its wisdom refused to grant it,
and she is now here at the mercy of the laws and without the
interference of some special act of your honorable body calcu-
lates ere long, to be sold. The relief your petitioner now asks and
prays for is that if she is compelled to be sold, that an act may be
passed authorizing her to make choice of a master.

An attached document provided the signatures of twelve individuals who
"for some time [have] been acquainted with the person and character of
Lucy Boomer . . . and believe to the best of our knowledge that the facts
therein stated are true—that as far as we know or believe she is a person
of good character, that the provision made in the will of John Winn,
deceased, is completely sufficient for her maintenance during her life."
Imagining Lucy's thoughts and "reading the traces of performance" in
her acting out of racial and gender identities is revealing here. Despite
her considerable initiative in reframing her petition to better fit with
contemporary racial ideologies (she undoubtedly hoped the idea of enslavement would have been more "appealing" to the white men of the
legislature), the case was referred to a committee on 23 December and
rejected on 15 January 1836.[12]

Lucy was likely expelled from her home against her will, and,
crucially, it was this desire to remain home—the place where she belonged—that assumed priority for her. She placed her home above her
legal status, regardless of all she had suffered there. The detailed testi-
monies of Lucy, the Winn family, and others involved in this case display
the lengths to which Lucy was prepared to go to "demand" her freedom
and support from the Winns and the measures they were prepared to
take to prevent both. Yet, losing her fight for residency forced Lucy into
using the only bargaining tool she had—the value of her freedom. That
she was prepared to relinquish this freedom is illustrative of the extraordinary lengths to which some free people of color were prepared to go
in their fight to remain within their families, homes, and communities,
even when surviving evidence reveals nothing about the scope and nature of these institutions themselves. That Lucy wrote her own petitions is
also unlikely, and there are more words about her from others than from
herself. Historians have to piece together her perspective from these few
fragile surviving documents. Lucy was a strong woman, not prepared to
go away quietly. As mentioned, she had a sexual relationship with John

Winn, consensual or otherwise. She perhaps partook in an extreme form of day-to-day resistance by attempting to poison the white family who held her in enslavement. Despite her advanced age, she grasped an opportunity for freedom with both hands, but in her opinion "freedom" was not worth more than the right to remain in the place she called home. Faced with the stark and limited choice of expulsion or enslavement, both undesirable options, she asked for a new master.

Lucy's applications to the Virginia legislature convey how the line between enslavement and residency requests could sometimes be blurred. Of course Lucy did not "want" slavery, but when she was forced into a harsh choice between selecting bondage or expulsion, she went for the former. Also blurry—both in the surviving testimony and more broadly—was the line between rape and consent. Without her words, one cannot know whether she shared John Winn's bed voluntarily or whether she believed that "tolerating" such a relationship might bring long-term material benefit. Black women such as Lucy Boomer, who demanded their legal rights in a public way, were not typical, but their behavior at the edges of the slave regime illustrate enterprise, initiative, and a great deal of courage. Lucy's petitions forced members of the Winn family to put their personal secrets into a very public realm, to admit their late father chose Lucy, rather than their own mother, to share his marital bed. For members of the slaveholding class seeking reassurance in their own benevolence and comfortable extended familial networks, Lucy Boomer served as a stark reminder of the dark underside of the regime so often ignored in contemporary accounts: the constant presence of interracial sexual liaisons.

This chapter explores cases like that of Lucy Boomer, where enslavement petitions submitted on behalf of black women were (or may have been) related to issues of interracial intimate relationships.[13] It also considers more broadly the extent to which issues of expulsion and enslavement highlight ties along the line of gender across black and white lives. Lucy Boomer confided in John Winn's daughter, Sophia, about her own sexual relationships, which suggests there was some friendship between the two women. Speculating about why free women of color sought enslavement to white men is inevitably contentious. Causal factors relating to free people of color's poverty, economic hardship, and familial ties within black affective communities across the slave-free divide have been dealt with previously, but there is still a space for exploring, albeit tentatively and speculatively, the notion that sexual relationships underpinned some enslavement requests. Moreover, notions about expected racial and gendered behavior exemplified in the language employed by the petitioners reveals something of the contours and complexities of slavery and freedom in the antebellum South.

These women's enslavement requests can be read in a variety of ways. A first hypothesis revolves around the assumption of interracial romantic love: free women of color were attempting to maintain or strengthen their intimate ties of affection with white lovers. Viewed through this prism, enslavement petitions brought women and men together under the law, across the divisions created by color, where interracial marriage was banned. A second interpretation relates to the theme of exploitation. Exploitative white men pressured into bondage poor free women of color, some of whom had children to raise. Third, enslavement could have played a distinctive role in the political strategies of free women of color who embraced legal action when seeking to improve their quality of life. Individual initiative and action are therefore paramount in this last interpretation. It took many years of sharing a bed with John Winn for Lucy Boomer to gain her freedom, and other free black women could have used their relationships with white men in a similar way. The threat of expulsion or economic hardship may have encouraged women to use their sexuality as a tool to improve their lives for the better. Believing their best hope in life was to remain where they were as slaves, some free women of color were, perhaps, prepared to sacrifice their own free status and that of their children.

A total of 28 percent of the enslavement requests for which motivations could be assessed (there were ninety-eight in total) came from apparently single free black women who may have been involved in intimate relationships (twenty-seven women in total). Indeed only "love of family" constituted a higher percentage figure in the ranking of possible enslavement motivations, as shown in table I.5 of the introduction. For all of these women, alternative reasons for enslavement—such as love of a spouse or family, poverty, or debt—could not be traced, and in the absence of alternative evidence, it can be speculated that intimate sexual relationships were at play here. This figure also constitutes, significantly, nearly half of all the enslavement requests made by women (there were fifty-six in total), and of the total petitions, all but one were allegedly made by the women themselves. In the case of the latter, Charles O. Lamotte of Laurens County, South Carolina, wrote that Lizzie Jones apparently wanted to become his slave. The petitioner "believes that such a course would have a salutary effect upon that class of the population, as well as the slave population in whom we are more particularly interested." Lamotte framed his petition in terms of the broader "public benefits" of enslaving free people of color, but the nature of his "private" relationship with Jones is unknown.[14]

Moreover, free black women and men who were married tended to mention their spouses in their enslavement requests, rendering it more plausible the women included here were single. The historian Suzanne Lebsock has argued that in Petersburg, Virginia, women headed more than half of the households in which free people of color resided, admittedly an urban setting, in which there was a relative shortage of free black men. Single free black women avoided "oppressive" marriage and protected their legal rights. Their single status was therefore borne largely out of choice.[15] But enslaved and free black women may have had husbands about whom no documentary evidence survives. Another study claimed that "single" free black women most likely did have men in their lives, but since most were enslaved, women were unable to marry them or to afford to buy them.[16] But black female petitioners did mention their husbands. Because they placed primary importance on their affective relationships and love for their family members, enslavement petitioners tended to mention their spouses—whether enslaved or free—where present. A textual reading of the petitions as performance also suggests the petitioners hoped their references to spouses and family would grant a sense of respectability. The petitioners hoped conforming to broader expected societal norms would help them curry favor in their attempts to appeal to the white men of state legislatures. Lawmakers themselves, however, were more concerned with free people of color's economic worth, as evidenced in their handling of residency petitions. Thus they did not respond very enthusiastically to humanitarian requests about their maintenance of familial relationships.

Seeking enslavement for themselves and their children were six of the twenty-seven women.[17] These women's offspring may have been the children of white men, perhaps even the potential owners cited in their enslavement requests. In the absence of firm evidence to the contrary, this was a distinct possibility. Additionally, one woman, named Kissiah Trueblood, desperately offered Henry Ritter her future children as slaves, "should she have any"—this was perhaps enticing, as the doctor owned no slaves at the time.[18] White men sexually exploited enslaved women horrifically and saw no shame in watching their own children be raised as chattel. That some free women of color might have been pressured into requesting enslavement by white men seeking to increase their property is not, therefore, surprising.

Poor and impoverished free women of color might also have perceived enslavement as a means of improving their (and their children's) material quality of life and economic security. It could also give their children a chance to forge ties with their fathers. The legalistic wording of the requests sometimes offers no suggestions about the motivations for enslavement. But in the absence of such written testimony, historians have to present their own tentative speculations and hypotheses as a way of understanding previously overlooked lives. As they were often impoverished workers seeking only to survive, it seems likely that free black women made decisions that prioritized their economic well-being and that such decisions were often dependent on white men. Amrita Chakrabati Myers has described how the liberty of Margaret Bettingall (a free black woman from Charleston) was "like that of other antebellum black women . . . both contingent and insecure. To live according to her vision of freedom and secure the manumission of her children, Margaret had to maintain a position of goodwill with a wealthy, connected man." For some forty years, she had a relationship that "looked like a marriage" with Adam Tunno, a wealthy Scottish merchant. Tunno's wealth facilitated her quality of life and enabled her to move away from the economic insecurity that characterized the lives of so many other free black women. She also prioritized the well-being of her children, hoping her long-term relationship would enable their long-term prosperity.[19]

Motherhood is also crucial in explaining the potential motivations of free black women who sought enslavement. Historians have stressed the significance of "economic" motherhood for black women, where providing for offspring in a practical sense was as important as more domestic ideals relating to care and nurture. Only privileged white women devoted attention to the latter, because they did not assume responsibility for their children's economic welfare.[20] It has also been persuasively argued that enslaved women who were subsequently freed "took up the instrumentalization of maternity . . . to reconstruct the meaning of motherhood and individual self-proprietorship through litigation aimed at securing their children." These women thus exploited their maternal roles in seeking their children's freedom.[21] And the mentioning of maternal roles within the different context of enslavement petitions—especially where a broader, more "economic" type of motherhood encompassing the ability to provide was paramount—is significant. Motherhood itself had connotations of respectability that the petitioners hoped would work in their favor when appealing to lawmakers was their primary aim; and finally, the petitioners' children also had an economic worth as potential slaves. Kissiah Trueblood was certainly aware of this when she offered her "future children" for enslavement.

SINGLE WOMEN WITH CHILDREN SEEKING ENSLAVEMENT BY WHITE MEN

Testimony about intimate interracial relationships is lacking in women's enslavement petitions because of the "culture of dissemblance" among black women. Census evidence can therefore be used to offer suggestions, if not firm evidence, about the possibility of intimate relationships between free women of color and white men, although it remains true that neither age nor marital status served as a barrier to white men seeking sexual satisfaction from black women.[22] For example, Elizabeth Chavers, a twenty-six-year-old from Wake County, North Carolina, requested bondage to thirty-four-year-old Benjamin Graham, along with her infant child, about whom she gave no more information. Census schedules suggest Graham was unmarried with no slaves. He lodged with another family, and his occupation cannot be deciphered.[23] Chavers's familial relationships are also rather difficult to analyze. She lived in a multigenerational "mulatto" household consisting of various people with different surnames and ages. Her request was put before a committee that ruled in her favor, although it did not permit her child to be enslaved beyond the age of twenty-one.[24] Graham and Chavers could have been a couple, and the infant child Graham's own offspring. That he lodged with another family suggests Graham had little wealth, and he may have frequented a world in which he came into regular contact with free people of color, such as Elizabeth Chavers.

In 1861, in the same North Carolina county, Sally Scott requested enslavement for herself and her infant son to Sidney A. Hinton. Hinton does not appear in the census as a slave owner, but was a twenty-six-year-old married farmer with two small children.[25] Ann Archie, of Marshall County, Mississippi, wanted enslavement for herself, aged twenty-two, and her daughter, Julia, to Andrew H. Caldwell, "with whom your petitioner has long been acquainted and whom she would prefer to live together with her offspring as slaves."[26] The nature of the "acquaintance" between this woman and man is unknown, although the fact Caldwell owned thirty-two slaves means Ann could have been attached to one of his enslaved people. More unusually, in 1861 Leah White gained the permission of the North Carolina Assembly for herself and her children to become the slaves of Morris McDaniel, in Jones County. Morris was only ten years old, so Leah and her children seem to have been acquired for Morris by his father, Elvin, a farmer. No one in this family appears to have owned any slaves.[27] Also in 1861, Rachel Hamilton petitioned the Court of Travis County, Texas, requesting that she and her two-year-old son, Jim, be enslaved to John D. Bowen. Her request also made reference to an 1858 law enabling enslavement, which suggests that knowledge of legislation did pass into the wider communities.[28] That some of these men were married does not negate the possibility that they were also engaged in relationships with the free black women petitioners. These men's status as slave owners or non-slaveholders is also significant. Someone without enslaved people would have had a real economic incentive to acquire adult females and their offspring as chattel.

Finally, Mary Walker, a "free person of African descent" aged "about twenty-nine," requested of the Louisiana legislature that she, and her daughter, Jane, "now about nine years of age," become enslaved to George W. Whitaker, "a man of good standing and character, with whom she has been acquainted for many years, and who resides in this city [New Orleans] and parish."[29] While no one involved could be traced using census evidence, the term "acquainted" has complex connotations, and Mary may have been involved in an intimate relationship with Whitaker. It is also of significance that all of these female petitioners with children requested enslavement in states where the entering of bondage for children was permitted under law, and not one came from Virginia or Tennessee, both of which forbade such bondage. Knowledge of state legislation, thus, made its way into free black households of various forms as well as into the homes of white potential slave owners, and both black women and white men used complex negotiations under new laws in an effort to achieve their economic and emotional aims.

SINGLE WOMEN SEEKING ENSLAVEMENT TO WHITE MEN

Other free black women requested enslavement to white men without mentioning any children or black spouses. Because petitioners tended to mention both their offspring and their marital partners, these were probably single women who had not borne any children. The cases are considered on a state-by-state basis, with those with the highest number of petitions being analyzed first, in conjunction with supplementary census evidence in order to cast light on the possible motivations behind enslavement. In North Carolina, Celia Lynch requested enslavement to Dr. J. T. Watson of Martin County in 1861. She described how she desired a "legal protector in health, in sickness, and old age," and it is rather ironic that her wording is similar to that of many wedding vows. Yet, in reproducing the discourse of marriage and in her desire to appear "respectable," notions of liberty and obligation are explained in a language that straddles both issues.[30] Lynch's performance of gendered and racial behavior would have obvious resonance for legislators: she sought to appeal both as an inferior "dependent" woman and as an ardent supporter of the material benefits of slavery. Watson was a married physician who in 1860 had five young children and a twenty-three-year-old "mulatto" woman named "Celie Watson" living within his home, though no occupation is given for Celie. Watson also owned sixteen slaves, so Celie/Celia may have been attached to one of his enslaved men.[31]

However, the ultimate point is that Celia's life would have changed little after her enslavement request was granted. Before this year and thereafter she was a black woman who lived and worked within a white couple's house. She even had the name "Watson" imposed on her before her enslaved status was legally granted. For women such as Celia, as was the case with many of the other petitioners, any distinction between slavery and freedom was rather arbitrary, and while Watson may have cajoled her into believing an enslaved status was preferable, because of the alleged "protection" it granted, Celia's life at this time can be best characterized by its continuities rather than its changes.

Twenty-eight-year-old Jenetta Wright of Guilford County requested from her county court that she belong to John Clark. Perhaps out of concern about how the legislature would interpret it, her petition was carefully worded to explain: "This request is made by her own free will and accord without force or compulsion from anyone."[32] There were four adult men named John Clark in the county in 1860, so he could not clearly be traced, though only two "John Clark"s appear as slave owners, with two and three slaves respectively.[33] Ellen Ransom, aged twenty-six, petitioned for enslavement to Leonidas Perry of Franklin County in 1861. Census records suggest she lived with her mother (they both worked as washerwomen) and her three children, and all had the surname "Ranson." Interestingly, Ellen did not ask for her children's enslavement, only her own. She probably was prioritizing economic factors. If Perry would provide for her material needs, then her children could be cared for by her mother and so spared slavery.[34] Other North Carolina women seeking enslavement included Eliza Hassel, aged twenty-five, who cited farmer and slaveholder Shepard R. Spruill of Martin County as her potential owner, although her petition was rejected.[35] Nineteen-year-old Cynthia Chavis of Warren County similarly sought enslavement to Alexander Jones in 1861.[36]

Four apparently single women from Virginia requested enslavement to white men. Judy Cullins had been manumitted through the will of John Cullins, but in 1858 she requested enslavement to a different man—William C. Scott, of Powhatan County, the owner of six slaves, two of whom were children.[37] It is particularly poignant that having experienced life as free persons, former slaves moved back into a system of bondage and vanished from the census. For example, Lavinia Napper's 1859 request of the circuit court of Fauquier County was to be owned by a merchant named Edwin Smith. The legislature permitted her request; Smith is listed on the slave schedules of 1860 as owning only one slave, a nineteen-year-old black female, who was most probably Lavinia Napper.[38]

Likewise, a twenty-two-year-old free woman of color named Mary Elizabeth reenslaved herself after having been emancipated through the will of William Miller, who had previously owned seven slaves in Rockbridge.[39] Minutes of the Rockbridge County Circuit Court show that Mary was granted enslavement in 1860 to Joseph Saville. Saville was a farmer who appears not to have owned any slaves.[40] But he was able to pay half of Mary Elizabeth's value of eight hundred dollars (it is very rare for an indication of the financial value of these people to have survived) and give bond for the rest, as allowed by Virginia law. The circuit court also decreed that "the condition of the said Mary Elizabeth shall in all respects be the same as though the said Mary Elizabeth had been born a slave."[41] Notably, though, as emancipated slaves, both Mary Elizabeth and Lavinia Napper were born in bondage, and their free status was sadly only a temporary aberration.

Like Lavinia Napper, Fanny Gillison requested—and was granted—enslavement through the Circuit Court of Fauquier County. In September 1860 she became the slave of William A. Bowen, following an "examination" of both by the court, although there survive no details about what this actually constituted. Gillison was described in the "Register of free negroes" as being thirty-five years old, with various scars, one "near the corner of her left eye," several "on the back of her right hand near the wrist, the little finger of same hand bent and shortened . . . several scars on the back of the left hand and wrist."[42] Bowen owned twenty-three slaves in 1860, and by the date of the census one of the adult women listed was Fanny, one hopes ensconced within a broader enslaved community.[43] A free woman of color with scarring more usually associated with enslavement again underscores the notion that there existed between bondage and freedom a very porous boundary.

Three surviving petitions from Louisiana offer a perspective on enslavement requests that were more urban; all come from New Orleans. The opening vignette of the introduction to this book cites the 1859 petition of Jane Moore, and a similar case went before the Third District Court of New Orleans later in the same year, when Elizabeth Jones petitioned for enslavement to John W. Musselman. Like Moore, Jones had been emancipated, in this case through the will of her previous mistress, in Hamilton County, Ohio. Jones had then traveled to New Orleans, having decided to live in Louisiana, but she found she was forbidden to do so under existing laws. However, slavery presented a way for her legally to remain in the city, and she described how John Musselman had apparently "consented to become her owner and to exercise the full and legitimate control of her" and to meet the "costs of the above suit," although no figures were given. Unfortunately, Jones gives no reason why, like Jane Moore, she migrated to New Orleans, and also hidden in history is the nature of her relationship with the white man desirous of her ownership.[44]

Finally, Emilia Stone petitioned the Fifth District Court of New Orleans in 1859, claiming she desired to be "the slave for life" of John H. Pope "who is willing to become her owner" and had agreed to pay all costs. Aged twenty-five and married with no children, Pope was described in the 1860 census as an apothecary.[45] Interestingly, this request and an 1861 petition by an "Amelia Stone" are both cited in Judith Kelleher Schafer's *Becoming Free, Remaining Free*. Schafer claims these were two different women, although they may actually have been the same person, with Stone requesting enslavement to a different man following the failure of her first request. Amelia asked to become the slave of Lucien Adams, impressively described in the petition as "the gallant recorder of the Garden District." He also appears in the 1860 census as the "recorder of the fourth district" and was married with several children. He also owned fifteen slaves in 1860, ranging in ages from fifty-four to six. She

might have been bound to this group of enslaved people through affective ties.[46] Her case also appeared in the *New Orleans Daily Picayune*. Proudly
headlined "A Note for Ward Beecher & Co.," the feature described how
Amelia Stone, aged twenty-four, was seeking to change her status from
free to slave: "The reason assigned by her for this step, which many other
free negroes have taken, is that she prefers the liberty, security and protection of slavery here, to the degradation of free-niggerdom among the
Abolitionists at the North, with whom she would be obliged to dwell,
and in preference to which, she has sought the 'chains' of slavery. Amelia
has selected Recorder Adams, of the Fourth District, as her master."[47] The
paper presented slavery as a kind of consumer choice, in which poor free
blacks could "select" masters who provided the "security and protection"
they were unable to provide for themselves. (The broader structural implications of racism and its associated limited choices were conveniently
forgotten here.) Furthermore, the ironic placing of the word "chains" in
quotation marks also conveys the newspaper's ardent proslavery message
as well as some of the inherent contradictions of voluntary bondage. Individuals could only request enslavement when they had the "liberty" to
do so. The idea that women such as Amelia Stone might seek out "chains"
seems to have been popularized deliberately to antagonize abolitionists.

In 1860, Alabama passed a law permitting "free negroes to select
masters and become slaves," and subsequent petitions tended to follow
its exact wording. For example, Mary Ann Randolph apparently wished to
become enslaved to James D. Randolph "under the provisions of the act
of the legislature of the said state," and her petition carefully explained
that both she and Randolph resided permanently in Alabama, that she
was over twenty-one years of age, and that James Randolph was "of good
moral character and standing." Potential owners, if not free people of col-
or themselves, were thus aware of local legislation and were prepared to
respond quickly to these new legislative provisions. Mary Ann appeared
before the Montgomery County Court to confirm her petition was made
"voluntarily and free from all undue influence" (another requirement
set out in the legislation) and was then allowed to enter slavery.[48] She
shared her potential owner's surname (indeed, she was the only petitioner for slavery who did so), as did many enslaved people. She may have
been living with the Randolphs as a slave "in all but name," supporting
the idea of there being a whole spectrum of oppression between slavery
and freedom. Although neither James nor Mary Anne Randolph could be
traced in the 1850 or 1860 census, a man named J. D. Randolph appears

in the 1860 slave schedules as owning five people.[49] James Randolph may have perceived the acquisition of Mary Anne as a means of boosting his property, consolidating their intimate relationship, or achieving both these aims at the same time. In the same year (1860), Lucy Green was permitted to become enslaved to Daniel Crawford, of Coosa County. This appears to be "Daniel Croford" in the 1860 slave schedules, owner of forty-eight slaves. Lucy may have been intimately involved with one of Crawford's enslaved men, if not Crawford himself.[50]

Across the South there were five other cases of women seeking enslavement to white men without offering clear explanations of their rationales for doing so. In December 1861, Elmira Matthews, of Greene County, Georgia, was permitted by legislative act to become enslaved to John J. Doherty "for life," and the wording in this case is significant and worth quoting from at length. The authorization reads: "[That] . . . Elmira Matthews be held, deemed and considered the slave of said John J. Doherty, for and during her natural life, subject to all the incidents of slavery, except the liability of being sold during the lifetime of said Doherty, by himself or his creditors for his debts: The sole consideration for which voluntary enslavement on her part, shall be the obligation thereby incurred by her master of feeding, clothing and protecting her." Doherty's obligations to feed, clothe, and protect Matthews is reminiscent of those in the petition of Celia Lynch from North Carolina, detailed previously. Both requests use gendered language that evokes notions of marriage vows and mutual obligation.[51] But Elmira Matthews's petition is unique, as it is the only surviving example found where an exemption from sale accompanied the admission into bondage. Such a restriction would undoubtedly have had financial repercussions for John Doherty, who owned Matthews in terms of her economic labor but not the value of her saleable person as chattel. Moreover, Doherty was prevented from selling her for any reason at all, including his own financial debt. This was highly unusual. Georgia, like South Carolina, permitted voluntary enslavement by special act of the legislature, and local lawmakers were undoubtedly keen to illustrate their own "benevolence" in attempting to prevent the subsequent exploitation of free people of color who entered slavery.

But it is highly questionable whether Matthews would have been able to impose the restrictive conditions of the Georgia legislature. Who would regulate her subsequent movements? Would she, as an enslaved black woman, have had the power to prevent her own sale if Doherty was inclined to get rid of her? Did she have access to documents outlining her more "privileged" enslaved status? Elmira Matthews's uncertain future raises many hypothetical questions, but unfortunately relevant census evidence confuses more than it clarifies. Living within Greene County was a twenty-two-year old "mulatto" woman named "Elmira Pierce" who lived with a white family named "Doherty," where she worked as their house servant. Like many other free women of color, then, Elmira Matthews probably lived somewhere on the porous boundary between enslaved and free. The Doherty family consisted of forty-three-year-old Charlotte Doherty and a man of twenty-two (her son?), named Charles. Neither had any occupation listed. Also included in this household was five-year-old John J. Doherty. Charlotte and Charles may have wanted to push Elmira into slavery by requesting she be given to a child.[52] However, there was also another "J. J. Doherty" appearing in the 1860 slave schedules for Greene County (his relationship to the first Doherty family is unknown). J. J. Doherty owned just two slaves, a fifty-year-old woman and forty-year-old man, and he may have been the John Doherty involved in Elmira's enslavement petition.[53] Yet whoever ended up in possession of Elmira Matthews would have had in their charge a unique slave, unable to be sold.

Other cases of black women requesting enslavement to white men include a woman known only as "Roseanna," from Hinds County, Mississippi. She petitioned for bondage to Calvin Bolls.[54] Another request came from Elizabeth Bickley, a free "girl" of color, aged twenty-two years. The *Abingdon Democrat* enthusiastically reported how she "voluntarily went into slavery at the present term of the Abingdon Circuit Court [South Carolina]. She was bought by Captain Samuel Skinner, Sheriff of that County." Rather proudly, the paper also noted, "The woman is very intelligent, and was fully aware that a kind master was better able to provide and care for her than she was herself. This is a nut for Yankee philosophers to crack."[55] For such enslavement requests to be couched in proslavery rhetoric in the southern press was common, but a sense that voluntary bondage was a kind of philosophical problem remained. Here the paper simply avoided the issue all together, instead handing it over to the "Yankees" to solve.

In a failed 1858 petition to the county court of Williamson, Tennessee, Sarah Cheatham, aged just eighteen, claimed to desire enslavement, although the testimony shows only that she had "chosen a resident of Williamson County" as her new owner. Cheatham appears in the 1860 census as a "mulatto," "about twenty-two," living with her parents and three younger brothers (no occupation is listed for any family member). In the absence of her words, why she chose to petition for bondage must be questioned. A bill proposing enslavement or expulsion for all free people of color in Tennessee did not go before the legislature until 1859, after Cheatham's enslavement request. She might have known the bill was under discussion. Alternatively, she and her family might have been in financial difficulty, struggling to survive. Cheatham could have taken brave and desperate action to try to help her parents by sparing them the burden of providing for her. Her attempted move into slavery might also have involved some sort of intimate relationship with her potential master or one of his slaves.[56] Finally, in Gillespie County, Texas, Ann Jackson petitioned her county court, asking for W. C. Lewis of Mason County to be her "lawful master." Married, with a wife and young child, Lewis appears not to have owned any slaves. He might have been more generally attempting to buy his way into the slaveholding class, or he might have particularly wanted ownership of Ann Jackson.[57]

Surviving testimony about all these women—whether petitioning for their own enslavement or for that of themselves and their children— offers only clues about the possible motivations behind their requests, and as such, this chapter is necessarily speculative. However, one striking conclusion adds further credence to the notion that these women were involved in intimate liaisons with white men. All the women shared similar age profiles, and of the sixteen whose age is known, twelve were in their twenties, three in their teens (aged eighteen or nineteen), and one in her mid-thirties. These were sexually mature females of childbearing age. They were also vulnerable, both in an individual sense, from sexual assault by white men, and at a societal level, from the wider movement to enslave all free black people in the 1850s. That some of these women either reentered slavery or had lived prior to enslavement in the households of their prospective masters is also significant. These women were slaves in all but name who lived on the fringes of the institution, somewhere between bondage and freedom.

ENSLAVEMENT REQUESTS INVOLVING WHITE WOMEN

In contrast, only ten enslavement requests survive from black people seeking enslavement to a white woman. This is not surprising, considering the nature of southern society at this time, where few white women were both single and financially independent. However, that men made two of these ten requests supports the notion that intimate relationships were at play in petitions involving single black women.[58] The eight enslavement requests by women who asked to be bound to other females also shed light on the idea that women were bound together by their gender across the racial divisions.[59] As Lucy Boomer confided in Sophia Winn about her own interracial sexual liaisons, so other black women were similarly close to white females.

For example, a curious petition went before the Alabama legislature when a group of white people from Coffee County sought residency (and perhaps enslavement) for Narcissa Daniel in 1857. Narcissa had entered the state from Georgia with a man named Alen Daniel, described in the request as a "highly respectable citizen," and his wife. Unusually, the petitioners claimed Narcissa to be "the offspring of a white woman of high family," though they gave no clues about this family's name. Alen's wife was apparently Narcissa's "best friend," to whom Narcissa "would prefer a state of bondage to that of separation" although the request was denied.[60] This residency request, like that of Lucy Boomer, illustrates the permeability of the divide between "enslavement" and "residency" petitions.[61] Narcissa Daniel's petition was also the only example found of a residency petition that placed primary significance on interracial intimate affairs, and it offers a tantalizing glimpse into the world of free people of color borne to white women.[62] What this case does not reveal is as fascinating as what it does. Without her words, one can only assume that Narcissa agreed with the sentiments of Mrs. Daniel, who may, in fact, have been attempting, for her family's personal and economic gain, to trick the legislature into believing Narcissa wanted either enslavement or residency. The nature of the relationships among Narcissa, Mrs. Daniel, and Alen Daniel is unknown, as is Narcissa's parentage. Who was her white mother? Narcissa might have been the sibling of Alen—they have the same surname—and raised as part of the white family despite being unable to pass as white. The wording of the request, in its claims about Narcissa's status, also conveys how issues of respectability were intrinsically bound with notions of race and class. Frustratingly, none of the individuals involved could be traced using census evidence, but Narcissa's experience suggests that white women could be just as exploitative as men when it came to enslaving free black people.

Other enslavement requests similarly show how white family ties sometimes affected the framing of petitions. In 1852 the Virginia legislature received a petition from Flora Jones, emancipated by the will of John

James Henry Gunnell, a planter with twenty slaves. Her request read: "Your petitioner is tired of the conditions of a freed woman and prefers to be again a slave." She asked that she and her child become the property of Annie E. Wagner, described as a physician's wife and the niece of her former owner, John Gunnell. Also written on the petition was that "the above was signed by the said Flora Jones and she adheres to all its declarations in our presence after being cautioned of its effects." Being unable to see exactly what "effects" Flora was cautioned about is frustrating.[63] Flora most likely had maintained contact with the extended Gunnell family after her manumission and possibly with John Gunnell's enslaved people as well. Whether Flora had a genuinely close relationship with Annie Wagner (described, as is typical, in terms of her marital status) or was cajoled into an enslavement petition by her is also unknown. The Gunnell family might have believed that framing Flora's petition this way would present a more "benevolent" view of bondage, characterized by "friendly" ties of affection between black and white women.

Emily Hooper was another free black woman allegedly "disappointed" by freedom. In 1858, the North Carolina legislature passed a bill permitting her, as "a citizen of Liberia," to "return into a state of slavery as the slave of her former owner, Miss Sally Mallett of Chapel Hill."[64] Hooper was not alone in finding it difficult to cope with life in Liberia. She was highly unusual, however, in seeking reenslavement to her former owner; this was the only such case found for this entire study. Moreover, Flora Jones was the only petitioner who asked to be reenslaved to a relation of her former owner. Former slaves did not want to belong to their "old" masters or mistresses. Instead, they strove to use their own initiative in shaping their new lives as slaves by attempting to use their limited amount of choice to select their own masters or mistresses. These owners, as has been shown, often possessed free blacks' beloved spouses or other family members. Emily Hooper's new mistress, Sally Mallett, is also unusual because she was single in the 1850s. Sally appears to have been single in the 1850s, and, according to the census, she ran a boarding house for students. In 1850 she owned one twelve-year-old female slave, and in 1860 she possessed three enslaved people, a fifty-five-year-old couple and a ten-year-old girl.[65] Unfortunately, because of the impersonal nature of the slave schedules, without knowing Emily Hooper's age it is impossible to decipher whether the twelve-year-old girl listed in 1850 was she. Neither is it known whether Emily Hooper requested reenslavement to Sally Mallett because she regarded her favorably or simply because she saw enslavement to her as the only available option.

Two women from New Orleans asked permission for enslavement to white women. Ann Barney requested of the Fourth District Court that she be enslaved to Ann Johnson Dickens, the wife of Samuel B. Dickens, and marked her petition with an "X." As with many of the other New Orleans enslavement cases, a lot of paperwork survives, including the notice to be pinned to the courthouse door. This stated: "Now therefore notice is hereby given to all whom it may concern to show cause within 30 days from the first publication hereof why the prayer of the petitioner be not granted." It appears that no one did object, and Ann Barney's petition was approved by the district attorney in 1860. His report read:

> It appearing from the evidence that the petitioner Ann Barney is a free person of African descent, and over the age of twenty-one years and now residing in this state, and that all the formalities described in the act approved March 17th 1859, entitled "An act to permit free persons of African descent to select their masters and become slaves for life" have been complied with, and it further appearing after a careful examination of each party separately, as well as the subscribing witnesses in open court and in the presence of the District Attorney . . . [illegible word] . . . the allegations and prayer of said petitioner, and the court being satisfied that there is no fraud or collusion between the parties, and that the proposed mistress is of good repute and of a kind and humane disposition, and that it is the real and voluntary intent and purpose of the said Ann Barney, a free person to enslave herself for life to the said Mrs. Ann Johnson Dickens, wife of Samuel B. Dickens. It is therefore ordered adjudged and decreed that the said Ann Barney be and is hereby adjudged and decreed to be a slave for life, and the legal and lawful property of Mrs. Ann Johnson Dickens, subject to the laws of this state regulating slaves.[66]

The wording of this report is worthy of some consideration. Taken collectively, the New Orleans enslavement requests suggest that cases were explored in depth over time and scrutinized at various levels. There seems to have been genuine concern that free people of color were not "tricked" into enslavement by exploitative and cajoling whites. Each person involved in each request was examined separately, and a period of time prior to acceptance was set aside in case objections were raised. Since petitions needed to follow the legal processes outlined in the Louisiana act that permitted enslavement, some knowledge of the law, or the taking of legal advice about enslavement would also have been necessary for all interested parties. Finally, Ann Barney's request, like that submitted on behalf of Narcissa Daniel, reveals something about contemporary notions of gender and the "performance" of female gender and "respectability" as manifested in the text itself. Ann Johnson Dickens is, like most other women, referred to only in relation to her husband, Samuel, and she is also described as being "of good repute" and having a "kind and humane disposition." Both were highly desirable attributes for "benevolent" slaveholders. However, it is not known whether Ann Barney chose Anne Dickens because of her "kindness" or whether she perceived that enslavement to another woman was preferable to belonging to a man. Certainly, it was more common for enslavement petitioners to request male owners.

Records of the Fourth District Court of New Orleans also show one other similar surviving enslavement request: when Mary W. Green sought bondage to Eliza Ann Haslip, described as the "wife of Jacob Haslip." Notably, too, Jacob Haslip apparently "authorized" his wife to appear in court and become the owner of Mary Green.[67] Despite that white women could and did become independent slave owners, most of those involved in enslavement requests were defined in terms of their relationships to men, and most seem only to have become involved with the permission of their husbands. For example, in Hinds County, Mississippi, Elizabeth G. Purdom became the owner of Ann Mataw following a legislative act on 11 February 1860.[68] Elizabeth was described as the "wife of a lawyer," so, as was the case for other women in similar situations, her credibility as a slaveholder was granted through notions of respectability awarded through her husband's status. Elizabeth's husband also played a more practical role in acquiring Ann Mataw. He was a clerk in the county circuit court and so would have been more knowledgeable than others about enslavement laws. Also noteworthy is that Elizabeth owned three slaves in 1860 (the census data was collated on 15 June, after Ann's request), so one of the two women listed—aged either thirty or seventeen—would have been Ann Mataw.[69] Ann probably had familial ties to these enslaved people, with whom she wished to reside above all else.

A complicated enslavement case survives from Chambers County, Alabama, from where, in 1860 "Cora" asked of her county court that she be enslaved to Elizabeth Witter "because of the attachment and affection she has and bears to [her]."[70] The two women could have been of similar age; Elizabeth Witter appears on the 1860 census as a twenty-five-year-old living in the household of her in-laws, James and Mary, plus her own twenty-seven-year-old husband, Henry. Father and son were cabinetmakers. Elizabeth was, rather unusually, described as a "teacher of painting." No one in this rather artistic household appears to have held any slaves in 1860.[71] Court minutes show Cora petitioned for enslavement to Elizabeth, "Henry's wife," in February 1860 and that Elizabeth also filed her written consent "to become the owner and mistress of the said Cora." A man named A. G. Lemar also appeared before the court as "the next friend of, and on behalf of said Cora" who, somewhat bizarrely, asked that the case be delayed until 25 February; this was granted despite both Cora and Elizabeth having objected to the delay.[72]

Ties that bound black and white households can be deciphered through census materials relevant to this case. Alfred G. Lemar was a blacksmith, born in England, and living in the household of a white farmer named Charles Easley, alongside Charles's wife, Mary, and also a twenty-year-old black woman—Cora Bellenger—and Cora's two "mulatto" children, one-year-old Samuel R. and two-year-old George. Lemar might have fathered Cora's children, although there is no surviving evidence to corroborate this.[73] At the meeting of 25 February 1860, Elizabeth and Henry Witter were instructed to pay the costs of the proceedings, and Cora was permitted formally to apply for enslavement to Elizabeth Witter because Alabama passed a law enabling voluntary enslavement on that same day. Cora, the Witter family, and Alfred Lemar must therefore have been aware of the changes being discussed within state legislatures, which explains why Lemar wanted the hearing delayed (though it fails to explain why he might have wanted his own children enslaved. Did he genuinely believe they might have had a better quality of life? Might the Witters have offered him financial reward for supporting the petition?). The Probate Court of Chambers County also seems to have been awaiting permission from the State before it allowed the case to proceed: Cora's request is referred to in preceding legislative records for the county. These all indicate she had been given permission to apply for enslavement to Elizabeth Witter by "making application to the judge of Probate of Chambers County."[74]

That the Chambers County Probate Court was reluctant to proceed reflects its uncertainty over the issue of voluntary enslavement without guidance from the State. As was the case elsewhere (most notably in North Carolina), no systematic procedure for enslavement was in place, and hesitance on the part of lawmakers reflects the controversial nature of the phenomenon. Moreover, within Alabama guardians had to be appointed for enslavement petitioners under the age of eighteen—presumably to protect them from further exploitation. Henry Witter applied, and was then permitted, to become the guardian of a free person of color described only as "George," "under fourteen years of age" in February 1860.[75] This was almost certainly Cora's son, George, aged only two. So, presumably both of Cora's boys were included in her enslavement request, although no documentation survives for Samuel R. It is also likely that because the "guardian" of the two boys was the husband of their potential owner, he would have favorably considered their future enslavement. Such nepotism made a mockery of the idea of independent guardians who would represent free black children's interests.

In the longer term, despite the time and attention devoted to their potential enslavement, Cora and her family seem never to have belonged to Elizabeth Witter. So the "attachment and affection" between the two women may not have been so strong after all, especially as the case took an unusual twist in 1861. The Probate Court of Russell County, neighboring Chambers, received an enslavement request from "Cora Bellema" on behalf of herself and her two children, "George Bellema, about three years of age and Rice Bellema . . . about seven months old." Ownership was asked of a Mr. J. M. Kennedy. Without any reference to her previous application—and apparently convinced "that this application is the free and voluntary act of the said Cora Bellema for herself and on behalf of her two minor children"—the Russell court decreed "that the prayer of said petitioner be granted," and Cora and her boys were thus enslaved.[76] Whether the Russell County Court even knew of Cora's previous application for enslavement is unknown, but the important point here is that Cora's request to be a slave took priority over the inclinations of her potential owners. It is also significant that her second petition went before the Russell County Court, when Cora lived in Chambers County. Kennedy's line of work could not be deciphered, but he also lived with his wife and children in Chambers, not Russell, County.[77] Perhaps Kennedy and Cora thought the new petition would have a greater chance of being passed in a new county, particularly if they lived somewhere along the border between the two.

Probing more deeply into available census evidence enables the reconstruction of a broader picture of the lives of free people of color on the porous boundary between slave and free, as well as some of the ties that existed between black and white households. In the 1850 Alabama census was a young black girl named "Cora Belanny." Eleven years old, she lived in a household with her mother, Lavinia, and her siblings, Henry, Prince, Zarah, William, and Joseph.[78] Evidence suggests this girl was the Cora Bellenger requesting enslavement to the Witters in 1860, because the families were connected. For example, "Prince Belanny," thirteen in 1850, had been under the guardianship of a man named George A. Witter (another cabinetmaker). Court minutes for Chambers County describe how George Witter offered his "resignation as guardian of Prince, a free person of color over the age of twenty-one" in early 1860.[79] The Witter, Lemar, and Belanny/Bellenger extended families were thus bound across racial divides by their attempts at formal enslavement and through the guardianship of free people of color. It is unsurprising that after the Alabama government passed legislation on voluntary enslavement, white families already involved in the "supervision" of free blacks should utilize the law in this way.

Cora was not the only member of her family to ask for enslavement. In February 1861, Prince, released from guardianship for just one year, petitioned the Probate Court of Chambers County for enslavement to John B. Barrett. Apparently "he desire[d] voluntarily to surrender his freedom, and . . . the said John B. Barrett . . . [was] of good moral character and standing."[80] Henry, another one of Cora's brothers, submitted a similar petition to belong to the same man. There was also a third petition asking for enslavement to John Barrett from Lavinia, Cora's mother, and her son, "Alick," who was "under eighteen years of age." Alick does not appear on the 1850 census with the "Belannys," but he does appear in an 1860 "mulatto" household, misspelled as "Alexandra," aged eleven, alongside a "Savina" (which can be read as "Lavinia"), Henry, and Prince Bellenger.[81]

The five witnesses called in relation to these enslavement requests are also significant. The first was named Henry Wilkinson. The second was Henry Witter, the husband of Elizabeth Witter, cited as the potential owner of Cora in her first enslavement petition. William C. Allen was the third witness, and, importantly, he was also appointed as "guardian" to Lavinia's son Alick, to represent his interests in the enslavement request of his mother. Oliver S. Barrett (presumably a relative of John B. Barrett, the potential owner of Prince and Henry) was the fourth. The fifth was named David Rosenberg.[82] It seems unlikely that any of these men, some of whom had ties to the Witter and Barrett families, would raise objections to the enslavement requests, even that of the young Alick, but no doubt their appearance as witnesses lent a sense of "professionalism" to the application process. The Chambers court would also have wanted to convey the impression it took its enslavement requests seriously and gave them due consideration. This is evidenced by the list of questions posed to witnesses. For example, in relation to Henry's petition, all witnesses were asked the following:

> Do you know a free person of color named Henry Billinger [Bellenger]? Do you know John B. Barrett? Where does he reside? Is said John B. Barrett of good moral character and standing?
>
> Do you know whether the said free person of color really desires to surrender his freedom and to become the slave of the said John B. Barrett? If so, state your means of knowing these facts. Do you know whether the petition filed in this case by said Henry Billinger was filed by him voluntarily and free from undue influence?

All the men confirmed they knew both parties and that both resided in Chambers County. Henry Wilkinson, Henry Witter, and Oliver Barrett also confirmed John Barrett was of "good moral character and standing," although William C. Allen, perhaps a little "off-script," explained he "knows nothing of the moral character and standing of said John B. Barrett of his own knowledge, but is informed that it is good." All four men also professed to know that Henry Bellenger personally wanted enslavement, "derived from a conversation had with said free person of color privately." John Barrett also gave his consent in writing "to become the master of said Henry."[83] Although the outcome of Henry's request is unknown, ten days after Prince's application, the probate court decreed his application should be accepted, and Prince became the slave of John Barrett. Lavinia and Alick's petition also seems to have been passed. They entered slavery on 20 February 1861.[84]

What initially appears as a relatively simple enslavement request by Cora to belong to Elizabeth Witter opens out into a whole world of complex familial and household ties and interactions among white and black communities on the edges of slavery. And the status of the white people involved is highly relevant. John Barrett was a physician who appears on slave schedules as only an "employer" of slaves, while a man named George Brockman was cited as a slave "proprietor."[85] Furthermore, the Witters do not appear to have held slaves. Like some of the potential owners detailed earlier, these white families may have used voluntary enslavement laws to try to consolidate their status through the owner-ship of black people. Moreover, the sense of fluidity between enslavement and freedom for some free people of color facilitated their movement in the direction of bondage when the opportunity arose, and formal and informal systems of guardianship also enabled such movement. This ra-cially based oppression notwithstanding, though, some free people of color used enslavement petitions as strategies of survival in their efforts to maintain family and kin networks, and subsistence standards of living.

A system of guardianship (rather than one in which white men were appointed to represent black children in enslavement cases) was more common in the upper South. A few surviving petitions in Maryland are from free people of color requesting either to be "bound out" or made apprentices of whites.[86] While this is not the same as enslavement, much of the motivational rationale was similar. Both examples involve young black women seeking association with white women, again perhaps be-cause of familiarity between the two. Mary Brown, "a free colored wom-an about sixteen" years old, explained to the "honorable judges" of the Orphans Court of Baltimore County how she had once been a slave of "the late Mr. Spence" but had subsequently lived with a Mrs. Mary Ann Pfeltz, though she gave no more information about her manumission. Brown asked formally to be bound to Pfeltz before law: "She is now anx-ious, with the consent of the said Mrs. Pfeltz, to be bound to her to do housework and to make herself generally useful, until she shall arrive at the age of twenty-one." In return, Pfeltz agreed to provide "suitable food and clothing." Both marked the petition with an "X," suggesting Pfeltz was not particularly wealthy or well educated, either. The two women might have been friends or had more of a mother-daughter-type rela-tionship.[87] Why either of them wanted the move into a more formal sys-tem of guardianship is unknown, but the fact that Brown had been living in Pfeltz's household as a free girl of color conveys the extent to which, yet again, there were various permutations of slavery and freedom for free blacks, and a whole spectrum of unequal relationships in between.

Another poignant petition was submitted by a free black woman named Eliza Cullison, in which she sought to bind out her six-year-old daughter, Frances, whose father was, apparently, dead. Cullison described:

"That your petitioner is poor, and unable to maintain said Frances, and is desirous that said Frances should be bound out by your honors [of the Orphans Court] . . . to some responsible person, and your petitioner further prays that your honors will bind out said Frances to Mrs. Maria Sanders of the city of Baltimore." She marked the petition with an "X," but a man named Charles Marshall also signed it on her behalf. The request was dismissed with costs, although no explanation is given, nor could any of the individuals involved be found on census rolls. However, Eliza Cullison's sheer desperation is striking. This impoverished mother would do anything at all to help improve her daughter's prospects and enable a subsistence living. Cullison might have been close to Sanders and have genuinely believed that Frances would be well cared for. However, the plan appears to have backfired. The Maryland legislature may have felt uneasy about free people of color choosing which white people they wanted to provide for them. Cullison was ultimately liable for the costs of her case, which she was certainly unable to pay.[88]

This chapter has explored complex and often hidden motivations behind the enslavement petitions submitted by and on behalf of single black women both with and without children. It has considered petitions requesting enslavement to white men and white women and suggested that there could be very different rationales for explaining the potential enslavement of black men and women to men and to women. Prioritizing gender as a tool of analysis in the consideration of legal documents offers an often surprising avenue into areas of life where documentary evidence is lacking. These include more private and intimate spaces, such as sexual relationships between free black women and white men, as well as broader explorations into the ties between black and white families and households on the edges of slavery in the late antebellum era. While some questions are still unanswered and some of the hypotheses suggested here are inevitably speculative, it does seem likely that free black women could be exploited into enslavement by men with whom they were intimately involved and that there is still a lot to explore in terms of interactions among free people of color, the enslaved, and white families who themselves were on the fringes of the slaveholding class at best.

A total of 133 enslavement petitions cited men as potential owners, and only 10 cited women. White men were thus very much at the forefront of enslavement campaigns, and when white women got involved in voluntary slavery cases they tended to do so only in terms of their status as wives. However, the petitions also reveal a lot about the perspectives of free people of color. Only 10 requests for bondage were clearly identifiable as people seeking reenslavement, and of these, only Emily Hooper asked for enslavement to her former owner. Free blacks who sought slavery did indeed want the freedom to choose white owners who would either represent their material interests or to whom their beloved family members (mostly spouses) belonged. While the line between bondage and freedom was blurred, free blacks made calculated, pragmatic decisions about their futures. Using whatever degree of initiative they had in the face of undesirable choices, free blacks looked for practical solutions to poverty and threatened familial separations in which they prioritized relationships within their affective communities. Whether they were requesting residency or enslavement, the significance of this motivation for free people of color is clear.

CONCLUSION

An 1854 novel, *The Planter's Northern Bride*, contains an oblique but starkly revealing reference to an enslaved woman, Judy. Although living as free in Kentucky, having escaped from her master, Judy was far from content. In a plaintive request to Crissy, an enslaved woman, Judy laid bare her determination to return to bondage:

> "You jist sit down, one minnit, Crissy, and let me say someting ben on my mind dis long time. Spose you ask your massa to buy me?" She uttered this in a low voice in Crissy's ear, who had seated herself at her request, pressing her clothes close to herself, to avoid the contact of Judy's soiled garments.
>
> "You!" cried Crissy in astonishment; "I thought you free!"
>
> "So I be—dat is, dey call me so; but dat don't make me so. I run way from old massa, 'cause he treat me bad. He live way over de river, in old Kentuck. I thought if I got among free folks I'd be de fine lady, equal to de white folks; but I'm noting but a nigger arter all—noting but poor Judy. . . . What o' dat?—no matter. You got good massa and missus—wish I had—den I'd have somebody to take care of me. Don't know how to take care of myself—folks 'pose on me. White folks call us niggers brudders and sisters way off; but when dey close to us I find out we noting but niggers. Please ask your massa to buy me, and say noting 'bout it."
>
> "He's no use for you; he's got plenty now," said Crissy; "and Mars. Russell don't approve of buying or selling. He jist keeps what he's born to, and won't have nothing to do with speculators."[1]

Judy's plea for enslavement betrays much about the familiar discourse of proslavery rhetoric. In keeping with the ideology of slavery as a benevolent, paternalistic institution, Judy finds herself in a "worse" position as a free black woman than one who is enslaved. She cannot even keep her clothes clean. "Mars. Russell" is also cast in a positive light as a "typical" kindly master who disapproved of the domestic slave trade.[2] The similarly striking air of benevolence found in the enslavement petitions of the late antebellum era provided the proslavery cause with valuable ammunition. It is therefore surprising that neither proslavery advocates nor proponents of the later Lost Cause drew greater attention to free blacks' enslavement requests as a propaganda tool. But the explanation relates to contemporary discourses about slavery and freedom; unhindered by bondage, free people of color were at "liberty" to attempt legally to change their status, but this choice provoked among slaveholders feelings of unease about black initiative, even when the requests were for slavery itself.[3]

Conceptualizing enslavement petitioners as workers attempting to secure subsistence who were engaged in a process of individual bargaining, which was itself limited by coercion and discrimination, therefore facilitates the rejection of what O. Nigel Bolland has described as the "simplistic antinomy of 'slavery' and 'freedom.'" The actions of the petitioners for enslavement display some real parallels with the enslaved's limited ability to bargain, for example, in negotiating their free time, geographic mobility, and hiring out.[4] Moreover, through their attempts to secure enslavement, free people of color can be brought into a more complex picture of evolving systems of racial oppression, where the division between "slave" and "free" was more than the mere distinction between "black" and "white." Viewing enslavement petitions from the perspectives of free people of color thus explains their relative absence from discussions among proslavery ideologues, the tactics of the defenders of the Lost Cause, and subsequent southern historiography.

Historians have felt uncomfortable about using enslavement petitions for three main reasons. First, the very notion that individuals might want slavery causes unease, because it suggests bondage could be "better" than freedom—an interpretation with stark connotations of the widely held proslavery defense, because for people of color that bondage trumped freedom. Second, the difficulty of establishing the identities of the real writers of enslavement petitions and their true intentions points to the methodological dangers inherent in such evidence. Finally, the relative scarcity of enslavement requests renders them atypical. These points notwithstanding, however, slavery petitions offer true insight when situated within the broader context of antebellum movements toward the expulsion and elimination of free people of color. They should not be neglected or dismissed as mere rogue examples, because atypical historical phenomenon is not necessarily synonymous with insignificance. Indeed, the historian Peter Parish some time ago advocated further research into the so-called edges of the slave regime. Such endeavors, he believed, "illuminate many features of slavery and of southern society generally—its racial attitudes and compromises, its internal pressures, its readiness sometimes to subordinate economic to racial and social priorities, its combination of inflexible rules with flexible application."[5] Historians can also overcome problems of evidential reliability by offering multiple hypotheses, consulting and comparing various sources, by raising questions as well as answering them. Imagination and speculation are also particularly helpful for historians concerned with the personal—with feelings and emotions across time and space.[6]

The sheer desperation shown by the petitioners should also quell any unease historians might have about exploring enslavement requests. The free black petitioners "wanted" slavery only because their circumstances left them feeling like they had no alternative to bondage. Accordingly, rationales for enslavement lie within free blacks' personal, familial, community, and economic circumstances. Impoverished free people of color developed individual strategies for survival in which families came first. Their affective communities assumed primacy within a climate of ever more hostile racial oppression. The motivations of the enslavement petitioners were multifaceted, but beyond the performance of perceived white benevolence expressed in the immediate language of petitions, they also expose the complex ties that existed among free people of color, the enslaved, and white society. For free black petitioners, family dynamics assumed priority over legal status.

This research into the expulsion and enslavement of free people of color invites the conclusion that the severity with which free blacks were treated in the years preceding the Civil War has been overlooked. During this anxious time, there was a flurry of debate and legislation over excluding or enslaving free people of color, and callous slaveholders—anxious about their futures—cajoled, tricked, or otherwise persuaded desperate and impoverished free blacks into petitioning for enslavement. In particular, in a bid to increase their chattel, they exploited free people of color's emotional ties within a changing legal climate. Some white men also pressured free black women with whom they were having intimate relationships—consensual or otherwise—into petitioning for their own enslavement and sometimes for the bondage of potential owners' own mixed-race children. These examples serve as stark reminders of the harsh market at the heart of American slavery, despite a public language of benevolence.

The act of requesting enslavement under American law (regardless of the desperation of those involved) meant being prepared to relinquish the freedom fought for and desired by many others. This willingness to cast aside freedom exemplifies a degree of initiative that white slaveholding society was ever-more anxious to suppress. Although methodologically problematic, enslavement and residency petitions offer myriad fascinating insights into marital and other familial ties across the slave-free divide; relationships across the color line; economic conditions and the impact of legislation upon free people of color; the relationships among gender, race, and the law; attitudes toward and notions of legal citizenship; and the broader proslavery defense in the Old South. Requests for enslavement, although highly unusual, testify to the desperation of some free people of color to improve their quality of life by whatever means necessary and against all the odds.

Free people of color possessed an ability to request the removal of their wider liberties and move yet further away from idealized notions of "freedom" and citizenship. And this movement has its own broader significance. A restriction of enslaved movement was at the center of slaveholder ideology, and, likewise, a right to movement is essential to modern conceptualizations of freedom.[7] But in wanting to remain where they "belonged," among beloved kin and within their communities, free people of color yearned to be still. In free black enslavement and residency petitions, people were asking for the right *not* to move, because so much prior black movement—across the Atlantic and across the United States—had been enforced.

At the margins of the regime—the blurry line between slavery and freedom on the eve of war—there were personal and economic ties that bound people together, whether slave or free, black or white. Despite strenuous efforts by white southerners to create a biracial society in which blacks were slaves and whites were free, there remained middle grounds in between, where the enslaved, free blacks, and poorer whites continued to interact.[8] For every rare enslavement petition, there were surely many more households where free blacks worked under a more ad hoc system of informal bondage or servitude without recourse to the law. In the antebellum American South, rather than a singular slavery, there were many slaveries and a whole range of unequal relationships.

ACKNOWLEDGMENTS

There are many, many people who have assisted me in writing this book. First, I should like to thank my postdoctoral research assistant, Laura Sandy, who was funded by the Leverhulme Trust to undertake primary research for this project. Laura instinctively understood some of the difficulties involved in exploring the past when sources are scant, and, like me, she is drawn to this kind of history. Laura collated some fantastic materials; employment of this type provides an interesting way forward for young scholars who are seeking work and older ones who find themselves more restricted geographically. I also want to thank the Leverhulme Trust for investing some forty thousand pounds in this project and the University of Reading's Research Endowment Trust Fund, which granted me vital teaching relief to write this manuscript and enabled me to purchase microfilm editions of petitions relating to race and slavery. My own undergraduate and graduate students are now widely using these.

Colleagues on both sides of the Atlantic have made helpful suggestions about the overall conceptualization of my book and the individual arguments therein. Special thanks go to my PhD supervisor, Mike Tadman, who read the entire draft of this manuscript and made many useful suggestions about how it might be improved. A PhD supervisor is a supervisor for life! I am also grateful to the two anonymous readers at the University Press of Kentucky for their insightful comments, to Anne Dean Watkins for her thoughtful correspondence, and to Erin Holman for her fantastic copyediting. My colleagues in the Department of History at the University of Reading have waited patiently for this book's arrival, and my department chair, Jon Bell, remains a source of practical support and intellectual inspiration as well as a great friend. Other colleagues have also listened to various papers on this project at departmental seminars, including those at the Universities of Keele, Liverpool, Queen's University Belfast, Cambridge, Sussex, and Royal Holloway and the Rothermere

American Institute at Oxford University. I owe big "thank you"s to Laura Sandy (again!), Martin Crawford, Stephen Kenny, Catherine Clinton, Betty Wood, Richard Follett, John Kirk, Jay Sexton, and Richard Carwardine, plus anyone else who was involved in inviting me. Catherine Clinton deserves special mention for her help and support over the last few years. We are lucky to have her on this side of the pond.

I have also been able to give papers on "voluntary" enslavement at various academic conferences. Susan-Mary Grant and Diana Paton kindly invited me to present at a symposium on perspectives on gender and slavery at the University of Newcastle upon Tyne, where I was lucky to meet Camillia Cowling and learn all about her fantastic work. Camillia and I then presented together at the International Federation for Research in Women's History conference in Amsterdam. I am extremely grateful to my fellow panelists—Rachel Jean-Baptiste, Leslie Schwalm, Camillia Cowling, and Gloria Wekker—as well as the audience, for their insightful comments at this fantastic event organized by Francisca de Haan. Another great conference I was lucky enough to attend was entitled "Understanding the South, Understanding America: Citizenship, Nationalism, and Secession in the South and Beyond." Organized by Bill Link, it provided some welcome respite from British winter weather at the University of Florida, Gainesville, and my fellow participants made helpful comments about conceptualizing my project in terms of citizenship issues. I am grateful to my University of Manchester colleagues and friends David Brown and Brian Ward for inviting me, and for their continuing friendship, and also to Michael Bibler for encouraging me to be braver in my speculations. Bill Link has been extremely supportive of this project for some time, and I am grateful for his help and advice.

I should also like to thank other American historians with whom I have corresponded about this project. Susan O'Donovan made helpful suggestions about further reading, and I thank Bruce Baker for introducing us. Loren Schweninger shared his insights into petitioning, and John Wess Grant introduced me to "stranded families." David Gleeson of Northumbria University kindly introduced me to his graduate student while he was working in the States, and my thanks to David Dangerfield for sharing the petition of William Bass and participating in a conference as a fellow panelist. Within the UK, the supportive environment of the conference network has allowed for the interchange of many fruitful ideas. The annual British American Nineteenth Century Historians conference remains one of the academic and social highlights of my year, and I was pleased to be able to speak about the enslavement of women at the Liverpool conference in 2010. I always look forward to catching up with Adam Smith and benefiting from his wisdom and wit, and it has been a pleasure to introduce my own graduate students, Dan Hale and Mike Luff, to the organization.

George Lewis and James Campbell organized a terrific British Association for American Studies conference in Leicester, where I was grateful for the ability to present on voluntary enslavement. I should also like to thank Jay Kleinberg and Inge Dornan for allowing me to speak at the annual History of Women in the Americas conference at Brunel University. Finally, thanks to all my friends and colleagues who attend and present at the fabulous Institute of Historical Research seminars in American History at the University of London, where we are able to discuss American history in convivial surroundings over a nice glass of red wine. I also need to mention that an early version of my arguments about voluntary slavery appeared as "'She Is Dissatisfied with Her Present Condition': Requests for Voluntary Enslavement in the Antebellum American South," *Slavery and Abolition* 28, no. 3 (2007): 329–50.

Finally, I am very grateful for the continued support of my family and friends outside academia. I hope that, despite the time and effort I have had to devote to this project, I still put my own family first. My husband, Jamie Fahey, has yet again been subjected to the rigors of proofreading: my thanks to him for this and his continued love and support of my career. Both my grandmothers—Dolly James and Margaret West—passed away while I was finishing this manuscript, yet I know both would be proud of me for the finished result. My parents, Hilary and Christopher West, continue to offer me help and support—both practical and intellectual—for which I am very grateful. Along with my mother-in-law, Kathleen Kellett, they have also done more than their fair share of babysitting. My sons, Conor and Dominic, are a delightful, if rather exhausting, antidote to academic life. I hope that they, too, develop a lifelong passion for the study of the past, and I dedicate this book to them.

NOTES

Introduction

1. Hereafter, the word "voluntary" will not be placed in quotation marks; neither will "choice." The problematic nature of both words is considered throughout the work.

2. See the petition of Jane Moore (no. 7589), 11 January 1860, Sixth District Court of New Orleans, New Orleans Public Library (hereafter NOPL). See also Judith Kelleher Schafer, *Becoming Free, Remaining Free: Manumission and Enslavement in New Orleans, 1846–1862* (Baton Rouge: Louisiana State University Press, 2003), 158; 1860 census, New Orleans Ward 2, Orleans, Louisiana, roll M653_416, p. 518, image 200, Family History Library Film 803416. All census records accessed via ancestry.com.

3. "Possibly the most extraordinary legal right possessed by free negroes at any time during the continuation of slavery was the right to choose a master and go into voluntary bondage," wrote John Russell in 1969. See *The Free Negro in Virginia, 1619–1865* (New York: Dover, 1969), 108.

4. A good example of work on free people of color within a wide geographical context is Jane G. Landers, ed., *Against the Odds: Free Blacks in the Slave Societies of the Americas* (London: Frank Cass, 1996). I espoused my early ideas on this project in Emily West, "'She Is Dissatisfied with Her Present Condition': Requests for Voluntary Enslavement in the Antebellum American South," *Slavery and Abolition* 28, no. 3 (December 2007): 329–50.

5. Both authors were pioneers in the study of free people of color, expulsion, and enslavement, with the latter having been relatively neglected since their important works. Franklin's *The Free Negro in North Carolina, 1790–1860* first appeared in 1943, and Berlin's equally groundbreaking *Slaves without Masters: The Free Negro in the Antebellum South* was published in 1974. However, Berlin gives only scant attention to voluntary enslavement, situating it within the context of moves toward expulsion or forced enslavement in the 1850s. John Hope Franklin developed the topic in more depth within his book and a related article, although rather vaguely; he wrote only that "large" numbers of free blacks sought enslave-

ment in North Carolina before describing in more detail some of the individual cases, with little analysis of possible motivations. See John Hope Franklin, *The Free Negro in North Carolina, 1790–1860*, 3rd ed. (Chapel Hill: University of North Carolina Press, 1995), 218–19, and "The Enslavement of Free Negroes in North Carolina," *Journal of Negro History* 29, no. 4 (1944): 401–28. See also Ira Berlin, *Slaves without Masters: The Free Negro in the Antebellum South* (New York: Pantheon, 1974), 367.

6. Some of the earlier state-based research into voluntary slavery bears the taint of proslavery rhetoric. Andrew Forest Muir, writing in 1943 about Texas, described how "free negroes all over Texas took the opportunity of exchanging the dubious and unsatisfactory liberty of free people for the restriction and security of slavery." Yet Muir describes only one case of voluntary bondage—that of Bob Allen, who requested enslavement to William Thomas McNeil of Harris County. Moreover, I found fewer than ten individuals in Texas petitioning for enslavement, so the phenomenon was considerably less extensive than Muir suggests. See Andrew Forest Muir, "The Free Negro in Harris County, Texas," *Southwestern Historical Quarterly* 46, no. 3 (January 1943): 235.

7. For example, Thomas D. Morris has drawn attention to the complexity of motivations for enslavement in his detailed and nuanced book *Southern Slavery and the Law*, while Alvin O. Thompson writes briefly in *Flight to Freedom* about southern states' laws permitting free blacks to "re-enslave themselves." His phrase is slightly misleading because, as will be shown, few free blacks requesting bondage had previously been enslaved. Thomas D. Morris, *Southern Slavery and the Law, 1619–1860* (Chapel Hill: University of North Carolina Press, 1996), 35, and Alvin O. Thompson, *Flight to Freedom: African Runaways and Maroons in the Americas* (Kingston, Jamaica: University of the West Indies Press, 2006), 54.

8. Schafer, *Becoming Free, Remaining Free*, esp. 153–55. Schafer explores the phenomenon of voluntary enslavement in much more depth than H. E. Sterkx, who in *The Free Negro in Ante-Bellum Louisiana* (Rutherford, N.J.: Fairleigh Dickinson University Press, 1972) claimed just one free black person sought enslavement, when John Clifton chose Green Bumpass as his master (148–49). The original request appeared in *New Orleans Daily Delta*, 18 May 1860.

9. Schafer, *Becoming Free, Remaining Free*, 150.

10. Ibid. 162.

11. William A. Link, *Roots of Secession: Slavery and Politics in Antebellum Virginia* (Chapel Hill: University of North Carolina Press, 2003), 157–58. Link's study moves research into Virginian expulsion and enslavement forward from John H. Russell's 1969 work, *The Free Negro in Virginia*, which claimed that by September 1860, only seven "free negroes" had been sold within the state (109). Russell gives no names and cites only "House Documents, 1859–1861" in his reference. See also Gregg D. Kimball, *American City, Southern Place: A Cultural History of Antebellum Richmond* (Athens: University of Georgia Press, 2000), 211n63. This study found a total of thirty-five petitions for voluntary slavery within Virginia.

12. Laura Edwards, "Enslaved Women and the Law: Paradoxes of Subordination in the Post-Revolutionary Carolinas," *Slavery and Abolition* 26, no. 2 (August 2005): 307, 317–18. See also "Law, Domestic Violence, and the Limits of Patriarchal Authority in the Antebellum South," *Journal of Southern History* 65, no. 4 (November 1999): 733–70; and *The People and Their Peace: Legal Culture and the Transformation of Inequality in the Post-Revolutionary South* (Chapel Hill: University of North Carolina Press, 2009).

13. I am grateful to all participants at the conference "Understanding the South, Understanding America: Creating Citizenship in the Nineteenth Century South and Beyond," University of Florida, Gainesville, January 2009, for their helpful comments in conceptualizing this project in terms of citizenship issues.

14. See Ariela J. Gross, "Beyond Black and White: Cultural Approaches to Race and Slavery," *Columbia Law Review* 101, no. 3 (April 2001): 651–54; and François Furstenberg, *In the Name of the Father: Washington's Legacy, Slavery, and the Making of a Nation* (New York: Penguin, 2006), 194.

15. Gross, "Beyond Black and White," 643–44. Historiography on slavery and the law is now extensive. In addition to the key works by Edwards and Gross cited above, see Ariela J. Gross, *Double Character: Slavery and Mastery in the Antebellum Southern Courtroom* (Athens: University of Georgia Press, 2006); Peter Bardaglio, *Reconstructing the Household: Families, Sex, and the Law in the Nineteenth-Century South* (Chapel Hill: University of North Carolina Press, 1995); Paul Finkelman, ed., *Slavery and the Law* (Madison, Wisc.: Madison House, 1997) and his other works; Diane Miller Sommerville, *Race and Rape in the Nineteenth Century South* (Chapel Hill: University of North Carolina Press, 2004); Jon-Christian Suggs, *Whispered Consolations: Law and Narrative in African American Life* (Ann Arbor: University of Michigan Press, 2000).

16. Ira Berlin, "Southern Free People of Color in the Age of William Johnson," *Southern Quarterly* 43, no. 2 (2006): 10. This whole issue is entitled "Between Two Worlds: Free People of Color in Southern Cultural History" and contains many useful articles. For a succinct summary of the legal treatment of free people of color in the antebellum South, see David Brion Davis, *Inhuman Bondage: The Rise and Fall of Slavery in the New World* (New York: Oxford University Press, 2006), 181.

17. John Locke argued against the notion of voluntary slavery, writing that a man cannot by his own consent enslave himself to anyone. See Gary D. Glenn, "Inalienable Rights and Locke's Argument for Limited Government: Political Implications of a Right to Suicide," *Journal of Politics* 46, no. 1 (1984): 90–91. John Stuart Mill also opposed voluntary slavery contracts, writing: "The Principle of freedom cannot require that he should be free not to be free. It is not freedom to be allowed to alienate his freedom." See John Stuart Mill, *On Liberty*, ed. Gertrude Himmelfarb (1859; repr., Harmondsworth: Penguin, 1974), 173. See also David Archard, "Freedom Not to Be Free: The Case of the Slavery Contract in John Stuart Mill's *On Liberty*," *Philosophical Quarterly* 40 (October 1990): 453–65; Richard J. Arneson, "Mill versus Paternalism," *Ethics* 90, no. 4 (1980): 473, 487; Randy E.

Barnett, *The Structure of Liberty: Justice and the Rule of Law* (New York: Oxford University Press, 1998), 78–82; John Kleinig, "John Stuart Mill and Voluntary Slavery Contracts," *Politics* 18, no. 2 (1983): 76–83; Morris, *Southern Slavery and the Law*, 32–34; and Edmund S. Morgan, "Slavery and Freedom: The American Paradox," *Journal of American History* 59, no. 1 (1972): 5–29.

18. Historically, voluntary slavery has reflected different types of indentured servitude more accurately than the involuntary enslavement of Africans and their descendants. See Barnett, *Structure of Liberty*, 78. For a summary of voluntary slavery in the ancient world, see Stefano Fenoaltea, "Slavery and Supervision in Comparative Perspective: A Model," *Journal of Economic History* 44, no. 3 (1984): 659. Information about the types of slavery, including voluntary, existing in medieval and early modern Russia, is included in Richard Hellie, "Recent Soviet Historiography on Medieval and Early Modern Russian Slavery," *Russian Review* 35, no. 1 (1976): 11, 17–18. See also Morris, *Southern Slavery and the Law*, 33n82. A. E. M. Gibson writes of men who would submit themselves to bondage in West Africa as a means of avoiding fines in "Slavery in Western Africa," *Journal of the Royal African Society* 3, no. 9 (1903): 20–21, 40. Voluntary enslavement among sixteenth-century Native Brazilians is considered in Jose Eisenberg, "Cultural Encounters, Theoretical Adventures: The Jesuit Missions to the New World and the Justification of Voluntary Slavery," *History of Political Thought* 24, no. 3 (2003): 375–96.

19. See Stanley Engerman, "Slavery, Freedom, and Sen," *Feminist Economics* 9 (2003): 193; and "Some Considerations Relating to Property Rights in Man," *Journal of Economic History* 33, no. 1 (1973): 44n2. The controversial notion that children could voluntarily decide to become enslaved is considered in more depth in chapter 5.

20. See Mary Turner's introduction to *From Chattel Slaves to Wage Slaves: The Dynamics of Labour Bargaining in the Americas*, ed. Mary Turner (London: James Currey, 1995), 28.

21. See Frederick Cooper, Thomas C. Holt, and Rebecca J. Scott, *Beyond Slavery: Explorations of Race, Labor, and Citizenship in Postemancipation Societies* (Chapel Hill: University of North Carolina Press, 2000), 5. For more on the importance of belonging to a local place, see, Suggs, *Whispered Consolations*, 64–65.

22. See John Wess Grant, "Stranded Families: Free Colored Responses to Liberian Colonization and the Formation of Black Families in Nineteenth-Century Richmond, Virginia," in *The United States and West Africa: Interactions and Relations*, ed. Alusine Jalloh and Toyin Falola (Rochester, N.Y.: University of Rochester Press, 2008), 61–74. Other works that consider kinship and social ties among black people in the nineteenth-century South include Catherine Jones, "Ties That Bind, Bonds That Break: Children in the Reorganization of Households in Postemancipation Virginia," *Journal of Southern History* 76, no. 1 (2010): 71–106, esp. 105–6. Dylan Penningroth argues for a broader reconceptualization of enslaved

social ties in "'My People, My People': The Dynamics of Community in Southern Slavery," in *New Studies in the History of American Slavery*, ed. Edward E. Baptist and Stephanie M. H. Camp (Athens: University of Georgia Press, 2006), 166–76, esp. 170–71, and in his book *The Claims of Kinfolk: African American Property and Community in the Nineteenth-Century South* (Chapel Hill: University of North Carolina Press, 2003).

23. See Cooper, Holt, and Scott, *Beyond Slavery*, esp. 153. Rebecca J. Scott similarly frames her individual work in terms of "degrees of freedom." See *Degrees of Freedom: Louisiana and Cuba after Slavery* (Cambridge, Mass.: Belknap Press of Harvard University Press, 2005). See also Susan Eva O'Donovan's work on black women in the emancipation era in Southwest Georgia: *Becoming Free in the Cotton South* (Cambridge, Mass.: Harvard University Press, 2007); and Michael Craton, "Shuffling the Pack: The Transition from Slavery to Other Forms of Labor in the British Caribbean, ca. 1790–1890," *New West Indian Guide* 68, no. 12 (1994): 23–75. Craton here describes a continuum from slavery to freedom rather than an abrupt change. Dale Tomich similarly explores the reconstruction of labor relations and continuation of racial oppression in Martinique in *Through the Prism of Slavery: Labor, Capital, and World Economy* (New York: Rowman and Littlefield, 2004), chap. 9.

24. See Carl N. Degler, *Neither Black nor White: Slavery and Race Relations in Brazil and the United States* (New York: Macmillan, 1971), 83. More recent works on the construction, and problems, of "race" as an explanatory tool for historical phenomena include David Brion Davis, "Looking at Slavery from Broader Perspectives," *American Historical Review* 105, no. 2 (April 2000): 452–66, esp. 462–63; and *Inhuman Bondage*, chap. 7. See also François Furstenberg, "Beyond Freedom and Slavery: Autonomy, Virtue, and Resistance in Early American Political Discourse," *Journal of American History* 89, no. 4 (March 2003): 1279–94, esp. 1280–81; Barbara J. Fields, "Ideology and Race in American History," in *Region, Race, and Reconstruction: Essays in Honor of C. Vann Woodward*, ed. J. Morgan Kousser and James M. McPherson (New York: Oxford University Press, 1982), 143–77; and "Slavery, Race and Ideology in the United States of America," *New Left Review* 181 (May–June 1990): 114.

25. Furstenberg, *In the Name of the Father*, 202, 206.

26. For many white southerners, being a free person of color was a "worse fate" than enslavement to a white master. For more on proslavery thought in the Old South, see Elizabeth Fox-Genovese and Eugene Genovese, *The Mind of the Master Class: History and Faith in the Southern Slaveholders' Worldview* (New York: Cambridge University Press, 2005), 159.

27. Ibid., 70.

28. *Petersburg Daily Democrat*, 9 February 1858, quoted in Berlin, *Slaves without Masters*, 370n56.

29. As Eugene Genovese wrote: "The actual change in the circumstances of free Negro life [in the 1850s] probably was not great, but the insecurity and

fear induced by public discussion of proposed changes must have been intense." See *Roll, Jordan, Roll: The World the Slaves Made*, 3rd ed. (New York: Vintage, 1976), 399.

30. See Franklin, *Free Negro*, 221.

31. See Schafer, *Becoming Free, Remaining Free*, 153.

32. See Walter Johnson, "On Agency," *Journal of Social History* 37, no. 1 (Fall 2003): 113–24, esp. 116. Other works that have questioned the (over)use of the term "agency" among enslaved communities include Orlando Patterson, *Rituals of Blood: Consequences of Slavery in Two American Centuries* (New York: Basic Civitas, 1998), chap. 1; Peter Kolchin, *American Slavery, 1619–1877* (New York: Penguin, 1993), 148–49; Wilma Dunaway, *The African-American Family in Slavery and Emancipation* (Cambridge: Cambridge University Press, 2003), esp. the introduction; William Dusinberre, *Strategies for Survival: Recollections of Bondage in Antebellum Virginia* (Charlottesville: University of Virginia Press, 2009), esp. chap. 12; and Ben Schiller, "Selling Themselves: Slavery Survival and the Path of Least Resistance," *49th Parallel* 23 (Summer 2009): 1–23.

33. Edlie L. Wong, *Neither Fugitive nor Free: Atlantic Slavery, Freedom Suits, and the Legal Culture of Travel* (New York: New York University Press, 2009), 14.

34. For more on how the granting of "privilege" by masters contributed to enslaved individualism, see William Dusinberre, *Them Dark Days: Slavery in the American Rice Swamps* (New York: Oxford University Press, 1996), 348.

35. Rebecca J. Scott, "Exploring the Meaning of Freedom: Postemancipation Societies in Comparative Perspective," *Hispanic American Historical Review* 68, no. 3 (August 1988): 407–8.

36. See Marina Wikramanayake, *A World in Shadow: The Free Black in Antebellum South Carolina* (Columbia: University of South Carolina Press, 1973), 179–81.

37. See Schafer, *Becoming Free, Remaining Free*, 149; and Robert C. Reinders, "The Decline of the New Orleans Free Negro in the Decade before the Civil War," *Journal of Mississippi History* 24 (1962): 96.

38. Ruth Bogin, "Petitioning and the New Moral Economy of Post-Revolutionary America," *William and Mary Quarterly* 45, no. 3 (July 1988): 392.

39. See Edmund S. Morgan, *Inventing the People: The Rise of Popular Sovereignty in England and America* (New York: Norton, 1988), 230.

40. See Franz Kafka, *The Trial*, trans. Willa Muir and Edwin Muir (1925; repr., New York: Schocken, 1984), 189.

41. This book grows out of and extends some of the major findings of my earlier work on enslaved couples: that the family unit served as a refuge for oppressed people and, in the words of Larry Hudson, provided them with a "social space" to live their lives with a degree of independence. See Emily West, *Chains of Love: Slave Couples in Antebellum South Carolina* (Urbana: University of Illinois Press, 2004); and Larry E. Hudson Jr., "'All That Cash': Work and Status in the Slave Quarters," in *Working toward Freedom: Slave Society and Domestic Economy in the American South*, ed. Larry E. Hudson Jr. (Rochester, N.Y.: University of Rochester Press, 1994), 77–94.

42. Grant, "Stranded Families," 67. John D'Emilio and Estelle B. Freedman undertook pioneering work on the history of emotions in American history in *Intimate Matters: A History of Sexuality in America* (Chicago: University of Chicago Press, 1997). Ideas about affective communities have been espoused in Elizabeth Fox-Genovese, "Between Individualism and Fragmentation: American Culture and the New Literary Studies of Race and Gender," *American Quarterly* 42, no. 1 (1990): 24; and Jane Haggis and Margaret Allen, "Imperial Emotions: Affective Communities of Mission in British Protestant Women's Missionary Publications, c. 1880–1920," *Journal of Social History* 41, no. 3 (Spring 2008): 691–716. Feminist historians have devoted considerable scholarly attention to emotions across time and space. See Ann Stoler, "Tense and Tender Ties: The Politics of Comparison in North American History and (Post)Colonial Studies," *Journal of American History* 88, no. 3 (December 2001): 829–65, esp. 835, and, from a more theoretical perspective, William M. Reddy, *The Navigation of Feeling: A Framework for the History of Emotions* (Cambridge: Cambridge University Press, 2001). I am extremely grateful to Rachel Jean-Baptiste, Leslie Schwalm, Camillia Cowling, Gloria Wekker, and the audience for their insightful comments on this topic during the International Federation for Research in Women's History conference in Amsterdam, August 2010.

43. See Sharon Block, *Rape and Sexual Power in Early America* (Chapel Hill: University of North Carolina Press, 2006), 242–43.

44. Stephanie M. H. Camp, *Closer to Freedom: Enslaved Women and Everyday Resistance in the Plantation South* (Chapel Hill: University of North Carolina Press, 2004), 95. Michael Bibler has also inspired me to speculate about the past, for which I am very grateful.

45. Haggis and Allen, "Imperial Emotions," 692.

46. See Wilma King, "Out of Bounds: Emancipated and Enslaved Women in Antebellum America," in *Beyond Bondage: Free Women of Color in the Americas*, ed. David Barry Gaspar and Darlene Clark Hine (Urbana: University of Illinois Press, 2004), 128. Other useful articles on free women of color in the antebellum South include Mary Beth Corrigan, "'It's a Family Affair': Buying Freedom in the District of Columbia, 1850–1860," in Hudson, *Working toward Freedom*, 163–91; L. Virginia Gould, "Urban Slavery–Urban Freedom: The Manumission of Jacqueline Lemelle," in *More than Chattel: Black Women and Slavery in the Americas*, ed. David Barry Gaspar and Darlene Clark Hine (Bloomington: Indiana University Press, 1996), 298–314; and Henriette Dellille, "Free Women of Color and Catholicism in Antebellum New Orleans, 1727–1852," in Gaspar and Hine, *Beyond Bondage*, 271–85. Much of this research has concentrated on the lives of free black women within southern cities where records are more readily available.

47. I do not claim the U.S. census is unproblematic, and in particular, evidence prior to 1850 is scant and lacks detail. Yet, in tracing various individuals and their ownership of slaves from 1850 through 1870 using online census

materials, I aim to provide a framework for understanding more about the petitioners and their potential owners.

48. A listing of archives visited for this study is included in the bibliography. Some states' archives proved more fruitful than others. For example, Kentucky and Missouri have no surviving residency or enslavement requests, nor did they legislate on voluntary slavery. This research was facilitated by a Leverhulme Trust Research Grant of £39,043 awarded in 2007, through which the University of Reading was able to employ a postdoctoral researcher to visit archives of the southern states. I am immensely grateful to the Leverhulme Trust and to Laura Sandy for all her work here as well as her ongoing friendship. I am also grateful to the University of Reading for two Research Endowment Trust Fund awards. The first enabled the purchase of microfilmed petitions to southern legislatures, detailed below, while the second granted me research leave to complete my manuscript.

49. Around three thousand legislative petitions have been published on microfilm as a part of this project. See Loren Schweninger, Robert Shelton, and Charles Edward Smith, eds., *Race, Slavery, and Free Blacks*, ser. 1, *Petitions to Southern Legislatures, 1777–1867*, microfilm ed. (Bethesda, Md.: University Publications of America, 1999). 15,500 county court petitions are also available on microfilm. See Loren Schweninger and Marguerite Ross Howell, eds., *Race, Slavery, and Free Blacks: Petitions to Southern County Courts, 1775–1867*, pt. A, *Georgia* (1796–1867), *Florida* (1821–1867), *Alabama* (1821–1867) (Bethesda, Md.: University Publications of America, 2003); and Loren Schweninger, ed., *The Southern Debate over Slavery*, vol. 2, *Petitions to Southern County Courts, 1775–1867* (Urbana: University of Illinois Press, 2008). An edited collection of legislative petitions has also been published: Loren Schweninger, ed., *The Southern Debate over Slavery*, vol. 1, *Petitions to Southern Legislatures, 1778–1864* (Urbana: University of Illinois Press, 2001). Each petition collated by the Race and Slavery Petitions Project holds a unique Petition Analysis Record Number, or PAR. Hereafter, each petition will be referenced by its PAR. Information on the project can be found at http://library.uncg.edu/slavery. Other legislative petitions can also be consulted via this Web site. See also Loren Schweninger, "Slavery and Southern Violence: County Court Petitions and the South's Peculiar Institution," *Journal of Negro History* 85, nos. 12 (2000): 33–35. I am most grateful to Loren Schweninger for his help and advice on this project.

50. See Loren Schweninger, Robert Shelton, and Charles Edward Smith, eds., *A Guide to the Microfilm Edition of Race, Slavery, and Free Blacks*, ser. 1, *Petitions to Southern Legislatures, 1777–1867* (Bethesda, Md.: University Publications of America, 1999), xix.

51. Ibid., xi. A lack of surviving evidence for Washington, D.C., means it has not been included in this study.

52. For this reason I have not undertaken an extensive trawl through nineteenth-century southern newspapers looking for enslavement cases but have relied on accounts detailed in other records.

53. Where known, I have indicated the outcomes of petitions either in the text or endnotes.

54. Berlin, *Slaves without Masters,* 367.

55. Franklin, *Free Negro,* 220.

56. Franklin, "Enslavement of Free Negroes," 426.

57. See, for example, Percy Ann Martin (PAR 11286301), Emmarilla Jeffries (11086010), and Ann Archie (11086007). See also Franklin, "Enslavement of Free Negroes," 424.

58. Twenty-six residents of Sussex County, Virginia, petitioned the county court stating that three free people of color returning from Liberia would prefer "American slavery to Liberian freedom" (PAR 21685020). In 1861, W. G. Gore of Laurens District requested from the South Carolina State Legislature that William Jackson be enslaved to him. Ser. S165005, item 00079, Legislative Petitions, South Carolina Department of Archives and History, Columbia (hereafter SCDAH). On 31 January 1859, Charles Lamotte of the same county requested the enslavement of Lizzie Jones (PAR 11386005). See also ser. S165015, item 00055, Legislative Petitions, SCDAH. In 1859, W. P. Hill, of Greenwood, South Carolina, requested that Elizabeth Bug and her eleven-month-old child belong to him (PAR 11385902). See also ser. S165016, item 00054, Legislative Petitions, SCDAH. In North Carolina, C. A. Featherston of Gaston County requested the enslavement of a "negro boy" named Wyat, "about 35 years of age" (PAR 11286203). Franklin is skeptical about Featherston's motives. Quite rightly, he concludes that Wyat seems to have been virtually a slave prior to the petition and that Featherston, in requesting a "bona fide deed," seems mostly concerned with Wyat becoming his "legal property." Action was never taken in this case. See "Enslavement of Free Negroes," 424–25, and *Free Negro,* 220. Finally, Wilson Melton and John W. Sproles petitioned the Mississippi state legislature in 1859 requesting that Wesley Moore, a "free man of yellow complexion," be exempted from the bill designed to drive free people of color from the state. He was married to a slave belonging to one of the petitioners (PAR 11085915).

59. Franklin, "Enslavement of Free Negroes," 424.

1. Presumed Enslaved

The Code of the State of Georgia, 1863, pt. 2, title 1, chap. 1, art. 3. Of Slaves and Free Persons of Color, section 1, Of Slaves (no. 1608), p. 320, GA. See also W. McDowell Rogers, "Free Negro Legislation in Georgia before 1865," *Georgia Historical Quarterly* 16 (March 1932): 36; and Ralph B. Flanders, "The Free Negro in Ante-Bellum Georgia," *North Carolina Historical Review* 9 (July 1932): 263.

Editorial from the *Atlanta Daily Intelligencer,* 9 January 1860, quoted in U. B. Phillips, ed., *Plantation and Frontier, 1649–1863* (New York: Burt Franklin, 1910), 2:159–60.

1. See Peter Wallenstein, *Tell the Court I Love My Wife: Race, Marriage, and Law—An American History* (London: Palgrave Macmillan, 2002), 15–16.

2. Evelyn Nakano Glenn, *Unequal Freedom: How Race and Gender Shaped American Citizenship and Labor* (Cambridge, Mass.: Harvard University Press, 2002), 33. John Boles writes that in 1860 the free black population in the South stood at 261,918. This made up 6.2 percent of all blacks, "with the proportion in the upper South (12.8) eight times greater than in the Deep South." See *Black Southerners, 1619–1869* (Lexington: University Press of Kentucky, 1983), 135.

3. For more on these laws see, for example, Glenn, *Unequal Freedom*, 122–25; and Martha Hodes, "The Mercurial Nature and Abiding Power of Race: A Transnational Family Story," *American Historical Review* 108, no. 1 (February 2003): 84–118, esp. 85–89.

4. For more on these arguments, see Wikramanayake, *World in Shadow*, 155–57; and Peter J. Parish, *Slavery: History and Historians* (New York: Harper & Row, 1989), 107–9. Parish summarizes well the research on free people of color that has distinguished between the majority, who were poor, and the "mulatto elite" of the cities of the Deep South.

5. John Boles attributes a lack of legislation on enslavement—be this voluntary or compulsory—to the economic input of free people of color. See *Black Southerners*, 138. See also Michael P. Johnson and James L. Roark, "Strategies of Survival: Free Negro Families and the Problems of Slavery," in *In Joy and in Sorrow: Women, Family, and Marriage in the Victorian South, 1830–1900*, ed. Carol Bleser (New York: Oxford University Press, 1991), 90.

6. George Fitzhugh, "What Shall Be Done with the Free Negroes? Essays Written for the Fredricksburg Recorder," *Fredricksburg (Va.) Recorder*, 1851, 6, quoted in Johnson and Roark, "Strategies of Survival," 90n10.

7. See Berlin, *Slaves without Masters*, 368–70.

8. George Fitzhugh, *Sociology for the South: or, The Failure of Free Society* (Richmond: A. Morris, 1854), 264, quoted in Morris, *Southern Slavery and the Law*, 31. Drew Gilpin Faust defends the modern-day preoccupation with Fitzhugh, writing that although his views were extreme and unrepresentative, this extremity "meant he was able to articulate the unspoken—and even unrecognized—assumptions on which proslavery rested." See *The Ideology of Slavery: Proslavery Thought in the Antebellum South, 1830–1860* (Baton Rouge: Louisiana State University Press, 1981), 19.

9. For a concise summary of Cartwright's now outrageous claims, see Reinders, "Decline of the New Orleans Free Negro," 93–94.

10. Berlin, *Slaves without Masters*, 370–71.

11. For more on David Walker's 1829 *Appeal to the Colored Citizens of the World*, see Jason H. Silverman's entry in *Dictionary of Afro-American Slavery*, ed. Randall M. Miller and John David Smith (London: Praeger, 1997), 791–92; and Peter P. Hinks, *To Awaken My Afflicted Brethren: David Walker and the Problem of Antebellum Slave Resistance* (University Park: Pennsylvania State University Press, 1997).

12. Virginia Meacham Gould, introduction to *Chained to the Rock of Adversity: To Be Free, Black, and Female in the Old South*, ed. Virginia Meacham Gould (Athens: University of Georgia Press, 1998), xxx.

13. Walter Erlich, "Dred Scott Case," in Miller and Smith, *Dictionary of Afro-American Slavery*, 195–96.

14. See Michael P. Johnson and James L. Roark, *Black Masters: A Free Family of Color in the Old South* (New York: Norton, 1984), 165.

15. Berlin briefly considers voluntary enslavement in *Slaves without Masters*, 367.

16. Ira Berlin covered debates over enforced expulsion fairly extensively in the 1970s, but he did not address in any depth the linked—but ideologically separate issue—of permitting free people of color to choose bondage voluntarily. For more on humanitarian arguments against voluntary enslavement, see Franklin, *Free Negro*, 214–16.

17. Morris, *Southern Slavery and the Law*, 32. See also Wilbert E. Moore, "Slave Law and the Social Structure," *Journal of Negro History* 26, no. 2 (1941): 194n53; John Codman Hurd, *The Law of Freedom and Bondage in the United States* (Boston: Little, Brown & Co., 1858–1862), 2:12, 24, 94, 166, 174, 195, 199; Engerman, "Some Considerations Relating to Property Rights in Man," 44n2; Lewis Cecil Gray, *A History of Agriculture in the Southern United States to 1860* (Washington, D.C.: Carnegie Institution of Washington, 1933), 1:527n125. See also Schafer, *Becoming Free, Remaining Free*, 147–48.

18. "An Act to Prohibit the Emigration and Settlement of Free Negroes or Free Persons of Color, into This State," approved 20 January 1843, *Acts Passed at the Fourth Session of the General Assembly of Arkansas* (Little Rock: Eli Colby, 1843), 61–64, Arkansas History Commission and State Archives, Little Rock (hereafter AHCSA).

19. Ibid. Jonathan D. Martin explores the relationship between free people of color and hiring out in *Divided Mastery: Slave Hiring in the American South* (Cambridge, Mass.: Harvard University Press, 2004), 182–83.

20. "An Act to Amend an Act entitled 'An Act to Prohibit the Emigration and Settlement of Free Negroes or Free Persons of Color into This State, Approved 20th January 1843,'" approved 9 January 1845, *Acts, Memorials, and Resolutions Passed at the Fifth Session of the General Assembly of the State of Arkansas* (Little Rock: Borland and Farley, 1845), 99–100, AHCSA.

21. Any whites who broke this rule would be fined any amount between fifty and one hundred dollars. See "An Act to Prevent Slaves and Free Negroes from Being Employed in Retail Groceries or Dram Shops," approved 6 January 1853, *Acts Passed at the Ninth Session of the General Assembly of the State of Arkansas* (Arkadelphia: R. L. Pegues, 1853), 71–72, AHCSA.

22. Margaret Ross, "Mulattoes, Free Negroes Ordered to Leave Arkansas on Eve of War," *Little Rock Arkansas Gazette*, Sunday, 15 February 1959, 3E.

23. "An Act to Prohibit the Emigration of Free Negroes or Mulattoes into

This State and for Other Purposes," passed at Dover, 28 January 1811, vol. 1, pp. 410–12. *Laws of the State of Delaware on Slavery, Free Blacks, and Mulattos*, vols. 114, 1700–1874, comp. Robert C. Barnes and Judith M. Pfeiffer (Dover: Public Archives, 2002), 86–87, Delaware Public Archives, Dover (hereafter DPA).

24. "An Act to Prevent the Future Migration of Free Negroes or Mulattoes to This Territory, and for Other Purposes" (no. 32), approved 5 March 1842, *Acts and Resolutions of the Legislative Council of the Territory of Florida, Passed at Its Twentieth Session* (Tallahassee: C. E. Bartlett, 1842), 34–35, Florida State Archives, Tallahassee (hereafter FSA).

25. "An Act for the Better Regulation of Free Negroes in the Cities of Savannah and Augusta, and in the Towns of Washington and Lexington," approved 7 December 1807, Acts of the General Assembly of the State of Georgia, Passed in Milledgeville, at an Annual Session in November and December, 1807, vol. 1, p. 25, Georgia Archives, Morrow (hereafter GA). Watson Jennison has argued convincingly for a fluidity in Georgia's race relations at the turn of the nineteenth century, when the state began to codify a third racial tier. See "'The Privileges of Citizens': The Boundaries of Race in Early National Georgia," unpublished conference paper presented at the American Historical Association's annual conference, January 2005. I am grateful to Watson for discussing this issue with me at the conference entitled "Understanding the South, Understanding America: Creating Citizenship in the Nineteenth-Century South and Beyond," University of Florida, Gainesville, January 2009.

26. Rogers, "Free Negro Legislation in Georgia before 1865," 28–29.

27. "Short Report from the Committee on the State of the Republic," approved 29 December 1845, Acts of the State of Georgia, 1845: Resolutions Which Originated in the Senate, vol. 1, pp. 209–11, GA.

28. Annie Lee West Stahl, "The Free Negro in Ante-Bellum Louisiana," *Louisiana Historical Quarterly* 25 (April 1942): 330–33.

29. "An Act to Reduce into One, the Several Acts Concerning Slaves, Free Negroes, and Mulattoes," approved 18 June 1822, Laws Concerning Slavery and Free People of Color, Mississippi Statutes 1822, microfilm reel 4357, pp. 179–83, Mississippi Department of Archives and History, Jackson (hereafter MDAH).

30. Ibid., pp. 191–92.

31. Ibid., p. 198.

32. See Gross, *Double Character*, 65.

33. "An Act to Reduce into One, the Several Acts Concerning Slaves, Free Negroes, and Mulattoes," approved 18 June 1822, Laws Concerning Slavery and Free People of Color, Mississippi Statutes 1822, microfilm reel 4357, p. 188, MDAH.

34. Ibid., p. 200.

35. The Mississippi legislation may well speak to the significance of the 1822 Denmark Vesey conspiracy in Charleston, some distance away. Larry Koger argues in *Black Slaveowners: Free Black Masters in South Carolina, 1790–1860* (London:

McFarland, 1985) that Vesey's attempted insurrection was motivated by his frustration at the enslavement of his own wife and children (184–85). For more on Vesey and his marriages, see Douglas Egerton, *He Shall Go Free: The Lives of Denmark Vesey* (Madison, Wisc.: Madison House, 1999), 77–83. Drew Gilpin Faust has argued that from the 1830s onward, proslavery thought became less concerned about whether slavery was right and more about why it was right "and how its justice could best be demonstrated." See *Ideology of Slavery*, 5–6.

36. See Ronald Takaki, *Strangers from a Different Shore: A History of Asian Americans* (New York: Little, Brown, 1998), esp. pt. 2.

37. Gross, *Double Character*, 176n27.

38. "An Act to Amend the Several Acts of This State in Relation to Free Negroes and Mulattoes," approved 26 February 1842, *Laws of the State of Mississippi Passed at a Regular Biennial Session of the Legislature, Held in the City of Jackson in January and February 1842* (Jackson: C. M. Price & G. R. Fall, State Printers, 1842), 65–67, MDAH.

39. Ibid., 70–71.

40. Wong, *Neither Fugitive nor Free*, 143.

41. See Cynthia M. Kennedy, *Braided Relations, Entwined Lives: The Women of Charleston's Urban Slave Society* (Bloomington: Indiana University Press, 2005), 180.

42. "An Act to Restrain the Emancipation of Slaves, and to Prevent Free Persons of Color from Entering into This State; and for Other Purposes," approved 20 December 1820, and "An Act for the Better Regulation and Government of Free Negroes and Persons of Color; and for Other Purposes," approved 21 December 1822, *Statutes at Large of South Carolina*, ed. David J. McCord, vol. 7, *Containing the Acts Relating to Charleston Courts, Slaves, and Rivers* (Columbia: A. S. Johnson, 1840), 459–62, SCDAH.

43. See Thomas D. Russell, "Slave Auctions on the Courthouse Steps: Court Sales of Slaves in Antebellum South Carolina," in Finkelman, *Slavery and the Law*, 332–33; and Koger, *Black Slaveowners*, 181.

44. See Walter Edgar, *South Carolina, A History* (Columbia: University of South Carolina Press, 1998), 307, and West, *Chains of Love*, 140n87. Despite these laws, Marina Wikramanayake has argued, somewhat surprisingly, that compared to other states, South Carolina free blacks "enjoyed long legislative respite" until the 1850s. See *World in Shadow*, 166.

45. "An Ordinance and Decree to Prevent the Importation and Emigration of Free Negroes and Mulattoes into Texas," passed 5 January 1836, *The Laws of Texas, 1822–1897*, vol. 1, 121, accessed through Gammel's *Laws of Texas*: http://texinfo.library.unt.edu/lawsoftexas/default.htm. See also Harold Schoen, "The Free Negro in the Republic of Texas, IV," *Southwestern Historical Quarterly* 40, no. 3 (January 1937): 173.

46. "The Constitution of the Republic of Texas," 17 March 1836, *Laws of the Republic of Texas*, vol. 1, 19, accessed through Gammel's *Laws of Texas*, online at http://texinfo.library.unt.edu/lawsoftexas/default.htm.

47. "Joint Resolution for the Relief of Free Persons of Color," approved 5 June 1837, *Laws of the Republic of Texas*, vol. 1, 232, accessed through Gammel's *Laws of Texas*, online at http://texinfo.library.unt.edu/lawsoftexas/default.htm.

48. "An Act Concerning Free Persons of Color," approved 5 February 1840. *Laws of the Republic of Texas*, vol. 2, 151–53, accessed through Gammel's *Laws of Texas*, online at http://texinfo.library.unt.edu/lawsoftexas/default.htm.

49. "An Act for the Relief of Certain Free Persons of Color," approved 12 December 1840. *Laws of the Republic of Texas*, vol. 2, 85–86, accessed through Gammel's *Laws of Texas*, online at http://texinfo.library.unt.edu/lawsoftexas/default. htm. See also Harold Schoen, "Free Negro, IV," 196–97, and "The Free Negro in the Republic of Texas, V," *Southwestern Historical Quarterly* 40, no. 4 (April 1937): 273.

50. See Schoen, "Free Negro, V," 267–77.

51. Muir, "Free Negro in Harris County, Texas," 218.

52. Wallenstein, *Tell the Court I Love My Wife*, 21; Grant, "Stranded Families," 68.

53. Link, *Roots of Secession*, 153.

54. Ibid. See also June Purcell Guild, *Black Laws of Virginia: A Summary of the Legislative Acts of Virginia Concerning Negroes from the Earliest Times to the Present* (Richmond: Whittet and Shepperson, 1936), 98–99, 111, for examples of these individual requests.

55. On the legislative debates of 1831–32, see Faust, *Ideology of Slavery*, 8–9. She argues here that Thomas Dew "rejected the deductive principles of the Lockean contractual social theory" and "embraced the conservative organic view of social order that had been implicit in proslavery thought from its earliest beginnings." See also Erik S. Root, *All Honor to Jefferson? The Virginia Slavery Debates and the Positive Good Thesis* (Lanham, Md.: Lexington, 2008).

56. Guild, *Black Laws of Virginia*, 107.

57. Ibid., 109, 112.

58. Ibid., 117.

59. James Benson Sellers, *Slavery in Alabama* (Tuscaloosa: University of Alabama Press, 1950), 63–64. See also "An Act Permitting Free Negroes to Select a Master and Become Slaves," approved 25 February 1860, Session Laws of Alabama, 1859–1860, 63–64, Alabama Department of Archives and History, Montgomery (hereafter ADAH).

60. "An Act to Enable Ned Adkins and Other Free Persons of Color Therein Named to Become Slaves," approved 21 February 1860, Session Laws of Alabama, 1859–1860, 599–600, ADAH. At the same time William Patterson, "about" twenty-two years of age, was also allowed to become the slave of John W. Moore. None could be traced via relevant census schedules.

61. Quoted in Ruth B. Marr and Modeste Hargis, "The Voluntary Exile of Free Negroes of Pensacola," *Florida Historical Quarterly* 17, no. 1 (July 1938): 5.

62. See "An Act to Amend an Act Entitled an Act to Authorize Judges of Probate of the Several Counties in This State to Appoint Guardians for Free Negroes" (no. 20), approved 23 December 1856; and "An Act to Prevent trading with Free persons of Color in this State" (no. 21), approved 23 December 1856, both in *The Acts and Resolutions of the General Assembly of the State of Florida, Passed at Its Eighth Session* (Tallahassee: Office of the Floridian and Journal, James S. Jones, 1857), 27, FSA.

63. See Berlin, *Slaves without Masters,* 375, 379, and Hurd, *Law of Freedom and Bondage,* 195.

64. Quoted in Marr and Hargis, "Voluntary Exile of Free Negroes of Pensacola," 7.

65. "An Act to Levy and Collect a Tax for Each of the Political Years 1852 and 1863, and Thereafter until Repealed," Acts of the General Assembly of the State of Georgia, Passed in Milledgeville, at a Biennial Session in November, December, and January, 1851–1952, pt. 2, Public Laws, Tax, Title XXVII, 1851, vol. 1, p. 288, GA.

66. "An Act for the Relief of John Montgomery and William A. Lewis of Forsythe County; Nancy Going, Adaline Page, Thursday, Isabella de la Fayette, and Elmira, Free persons of Color, of the County of Columbia, and for Other purposes Therein Specified," approved 18 February 1854, Acts of the General Assembly of the State of Georgia, Passed in Milledgeville, at a Biennial Session in November, December, January, and February, 1853–54, pt. 2, Private and Local Laws, Relief, 1853, vol. 1, p. 533, GA.

67. "An Act to Prevent Free Persons of Color, Commonly Known as Free Negroes, from Being Brought or Coming into the State of Georgia," approved 17 December 1859. Acts of the General Assembly of the State of Georgia, Passed in Milledgeville, at an Annual Session in November and December, 1859, pt. 1, Public Laws, Title XXIII, Slaves and Free Persons of Color, 1859, vol. 1, pp. 68–70, GA.

68. Ibid.

69. Ibid.

70. The Code of the State of Georgia, 1863, pt. 2, title 1, chap. 1, art. 3. Of Slaves and Free Persons of Color, section 1, Of Slaves (no. 1608), p. 320, GA. See also Rogers, "Free Negro Legislation in Georgia before 1865," 36, and Flanders, "Free Negro in Ante-Bellum Georgia," 263.

71. Stahl, "Free Negro in Ante-Bellum Louisiana," 326.

72. Historian Robert Reinders has criticized historians' preoccupation with an overly romantic portrayal of "free negroes" in antebellum New Orleans, noting how their status steadily eroded over the 1850s. See "Decline of the New Orleans Free Negro," 88–91, 97.

73. For South Carolina legislation relating to free blacks' entry by water, see "An Act to Amend an Act more Effectually to Prevent Free Negroes and Other Persons of Color from Entering into This State, and for Other Purposes, Passed

19th December 1835," approved 20 December 1856, *The Statutes at Large of South Carolina* (Columbia: Republican Printing Company, 1875), 13:491–93, SCDAH.

74. See "An Act Relative to Free Persons of Color Coming into the State from Other States or Foreign Countries," approved 15 March 1859, *Acts Passed at the Fourth Legislature of the State of Louisiana, at Its Second Session, Held and Begun in the City of Baton Rouge* (Baton Rouge: J. M. Taylor, State Printer, 1859), 70–71, NOPL.

75. "An Act to Permit Free Persons of African Descent to Select Their Masters and Become Slaves for Life," approved 17 March 1859, *Acts Passed at the Fourth Legislature of the State of Louisiana, at Its Second Session, Held and Begun in the City of Baton Rouge* (Baton Rouge: J. M. Taylor, State Printer, 1859), 214–15, NOPL.

76. Ibid.

77. Ibid. See also Hurd, *Law of Freedom and Bondage*, 166.

78. See Barbara J. Fields, *Slavery and Freedom on the Middle Ground: Maryland during the Nineteenth Century* (New Haven: Yale University Press, 1985), chap. 4.

79. Legislation passed on 10 March 1860, Session Laws 1860, chap. 322, vol. 0588, pp. 484–85, Laws of Maryland, accessed via the archives of Maryland online: http:aomol.net/000001/0000588/html/am588–484.html.

80. Ibid.

81. Fields, *Slavery and Freedom on the Middle Ground*, 35.

82. Wikramanayake, *World in Shadow*, 168–69.

83. Historian Marina Wikramanayake claims most of the South Carolina petitioners were female and "encumbered with families and having no means of support," although, with four female and three male petitioners from South Carolina, I found gender profiles relatively equal (ibid., 183).

84. See Morris, *Southern Slavery and the Law*, 32. See also Moore, "Slave Law and the Social Structure," 194n53; Hurd, *Law of Freedom and Bondage*, 12, 24, 94, 166, 174, 195, 199; Engerman, "Some Considerations Relating to Property Rights in Man," 44n2; Gray, *History of Agriculture in the Southern United States*, 527n125.

85. Michael P. Johnson and James L. Roark, eds., *No Chariot Let Down: Charleston's Free People of Color on the Eve of the Civil War* (New York: Norton, 1984), 7. See also Koger, *Black Slaveowners*, 188–89.

86. *Charleston Mercury*, 24 November 1860, pt. D.

87. Johnson and Roark, *No Chariot Let Down*, 8.

88. See ibid., 43–44.

89. Entry for 26 May 1858, Hawkins County Chancery Court Minute Books, May 1856–May 1862, 185, Tennessee State Library and Archives, Nashville (hereafter TSLA). See also Jonathan M. Atkins, "Party Politics and the Debate over the Tennessee Free Negro Bill, 1859–1860," *Journal of Southern History* 71, no. 2 (2005): 252; James W. Patton, "The Progress of Emancipation in Tennessee, 1796–1860," *Journal of Negro History* 17, no. 1 (1932): 78; J. Merton England, "The Free Negro in Ante-Bellum Tennessee," *Journal of Southern History* 9, no. 1 (1943): 50.

90. See Hurd, *Law of Freedom and Bondage*, 94; and PAR 11286103.

91. See Johnson and Roark, *No Chariot Let Down*, 43–44, and Koger, *Black Slaveowners*, 166–68.

92. "Remarks of Hon. Wm. Ewing of Williamson County, Delivered in the House of Representatives, Monday, 5 December 1859, on the Second Reading of the Bill Introduced by the Committee on Free Negroes and Slave Population for the Expulsion of Free Persons of Color from this state," reported by W. H. Draper, microfilm 600036, pp. 1–2, TSLA.

93. "Speech of William Ewing, Esq. in the House of Representatives, 9 January 1860, on the Third Reading of the Bill for the Expulsion of Free Negroes from This State," reported by W. H. Draper, microfilm no. 600036, pp. 9, 11–12, TSLA.

94. These were Sarah Cheatham (PAR 21485839), James Johnson (PAR 21486104), and "Ben." See "Petition of Ben, Free Man of Color," 26 May 1858, Hawkins County Chancery Court Minute Books, May 1856–May 1862, 181–82, TSLA. All requested bondage from county courts rather than the Tennessee legislature itself. These petitions contradict the findings of historian Jonathan M. Atkins, who has claimed that "apparently no free black voluntarily submitted to slavery under the provision of the 1858 law." See "Party Politics," 253.

95. Hurd, *Law of Freedom and Bondage*, 199.

96. "An Act to Permit Free Persons of African Descent to Select Their Own Master and Become Slaves," approved 27 January 1858, General Laws of the Seventh Legislature of the State of Texas, *Laws of the Republic of Texas, 1822–1897*, vol. 4, 75–77, accessed through Gammel's *Laws of Texas*: http://texinfo.library.unt.edu/lawsoftexas/default.htm

97. Ibid.

98. Ibid.

99. Berlin, *Slaves without Masters*, 360–64, 371, and Russell, *Free Negro in Virginia*, 107–9.

100. Guild, *Black Laws of Virginia*, 119–20.

101. Hurd, *Law of Freedom and Bondage*, 12.

102. Guild, *Black Laws of Virginia*, 121.

103. "An Act Providing for the Voluntary Enslavement of Free Negroes of the Commonwealth," passed on 18 February 1856, chap. 46, pp. 37–38. See *Acts of the General Assembly of Virginia, 1855–1856* (Richmond: John Worrock, printer to the Senate, 1856), Library of Virginia, Richmond (hereafter LVA).

104. "An Act Providing for the Voluntary Enslavement of Free Negroes of the Commonwealth," passed on 18 February 1856, chap. 46, pp. 37–38. See *Acts of the General Assembly of Virginia, 1855–1856*, LVA.

105. See Berlin, *Slaves without Masters*, 360–64, 371, and Russell, *Free Negro in Virginia*, 107–9.

106. George Dunaway of Harrison County was forced into slavery for failing to leave Virginia. See Link, *Roots of Secession*, 157. See also Guild, *Black Laws of Virginia*, 119–20.

107. "An Act in Relation to Free Negroes and Slaves," passed at Dover, 5 March 5, 1851, vol. 10, pp. 591–93, *Laws of the State of Delaware on Slavery, Free Blacks, and Mulattos,* comp. Barnes and Pfeiffer, 136–38.

108. "An Act in Relation to Free Negroes and Mulattoes," passed at Dover, 18 March 1863, vol. 12, pp. 330–34, *Laws of the State of Delaware on Slavery, Free Blacks, and Mulattos,* comp. Barnes and Pfeiffer, 146.

109. See "An Act Concerning the Imprisonment of Free Negroes and Mulattoes for Debt," passed at Dover, 6 March 1861, vol. 12, pp. 151–53, *Laws of the State of Delaware on Slavery, Free Blacks, and Mulattos,* vols. 1–14, 1700–1874, comp. Barnes and Pfeiffer, 145–46; and "An Act Concerning the Binding out to Service of Free Negroes and Mulattoes," passed on 18 July 1861, Legislative Papers, General Assembly of Delaware (Petitions, Bills, Acts, Resolutions), RG1111.000, roll 062 (1759–1861), DPA.

110. Schafer, *Becoming Free, Remaining Free,* 147.

111. Loren Schweninger, *Black Property Owners in the South, 1790–1815* (Urbana: University of Illinois Press, 1990), 90.

112. Berlin, *Slaves without Masters,* 375, 379.

113. Franklin, *Free Negro,* 214–16. See also, "A Bill to Permit Free Persons of Color to Select Their Own Masters and Become Slaves," North Carolina Senate Bill No. 8, session 1860–1861, electronic edition accessed via the Documenting the American South project: http://docsouth.unc.edu/imls/bil18/bil18.html.

114. Franklin, *Free Negro,* 216, 220.

115. "An Act to Prohibit the Emancipation of Slaves" (no. 68), approved 2 February 1859, *Acts Passed at the Twelfth Session of the General Assembly of the State of Arkansas, 1858–1859* (Arkadelphia: R. L. Pegues, 1859), 69, AHCSA.

116. "An Act to Remove the Free Negroes and Mulattoes from this State" (no. 151), approved 12 February 1859, *Acts Passed at the Twelfth Session of the General Assembly of the State of Arkansas, 1858–1859,* 175–78, AHCSA.

117. See Hurd, *Law of Freedom and Bondage,* 174; and Berlin, *Slaves without Masters,* 373.

118. "An Act to Remove the Free Negroes and Mulattoes from This State" (no. 151), approved 12 February 1859, *Acts Passed at the Twelfth Session of the General Assembly of the State of Arkansas, 1858–1859,* 175–78, AHCSA.

119. "An Act to Amend the Eighth Section of an Act Approved 12 February 1859 Entitled 'An Act to Remove the Free Negroes and Mulattoes from This State'" (no. 62), approved 3 January 1861, Acts Passed at the Thirteenth Session of the General Assembly of the State of Arkansas, 1860–1861, *Acts of Arkansas,* 135–36, AHCSA. Billy D. Higgins has written that the law was repealed in 1863. See "The Origins and Fate of the Marion County Free Black Community," *Arkansas Historical Quarterly* 54 (Winter 1995): 440.

120. See Ross, "Mulattoes, Free Negroes Ordered to Leave Arkansas," 3E. Ross claims only 144 free blacks remained, all of whom were rather elderly; Ira

Berlin also cites this number. See *Slaves without Masters*, 373–74; and Morris, *Southern Slavery and the Law*, 30–31. Johnson and Roark also stress the significance of the State having the smallest "Afro-American population in the South, and most free Negroes left soon after the law passed." See *Black Masters*, 164–65.

121. Higgins, "Origins and Fate," 440.

122. I suspect there might be more surviving enslavement cases lurking within local courthouses; this is a topic in need of further exploration.

123. "An Act to Permit Certain Free Negroes and Mulattoes, Still in the State, to Remain until the First Day of January, 1863" (no. 99), approved 10 January 1861. Acts Passed at the Thirteenth Session of the General Assembly of the State of Arkansas, 1860–61, *Acts of Arkansas*, 206, AHSCA.

2. Free People of Color and Residency Requests

1. Petition of Julius and Lucinda, "To the Honorable Speaker and Members of the House of Delegates of the Commonwealth of Virginia," undated, Legislative Petitions, LVA.

2. The significance of "belonging" to a particular place is considered in more depth in chapter 4. See also Ben Schiller, "U.S. Slavery's Diaspora: Black Atlantic History at the Crossroads of 'Race,' Enslavement, and Colonisation," *Slavery and Abolition* 32, no. 2 (June 2011): 201; and Suggs, *Whispered Consolations*, 64–65.

3. These petitions were all accessed via the *Digital Library on American Slavery*, http://library.uncg.edu/slavery.

4. Parish, *Slavery*, 111.

5. For more on how law was "practiced and enacted" through performance, see Gross, "Beyond Black and White," esp. 650–53.

6. "Sheriff's Sale," Sheriff's Office, Newcastle County, Delaware, February 1838, NCC Court of General Sessions, microfilm RG2805.31, Court Papers, 1833–1838, DPA.

7. Cited in Morris, *Southern Slavery and the Law*, 33–34.

8. PAR 11386003 and Petition of 8 November 1860 (no. 00003), Legislative Petitions, SCDAH. Justine Birdie cannot be traced in the census.

9. Franklin, "Enslavement of Free Negroes," 419.

10. PAR 10182301.

11. PAR 11083008.

12. PAR 11483303.

13. Muir, "Free Negro in Harris County, Texas," 218

14. One free person of color in Texas at this time was Emily West. Muir writes she sought recourse to the law in her efforts to obtain passport to return to New York, having arrived in Texas in 1835, "Free Negro," 218. She is more famous in folklore as the "Yellow Rose of Texas," a story examined in exemplary detail by Trudier Harris. See "'The Yellow Rose of Texas': A Different Cultural View," *Callaloo* 20, no. 1 (Winter 1997): 8–19.

15. See PAR 11583702 and the 1860 census for Fort Bend, Texas, roll M653_1294, p. 360, image 211, Family History Library Film 805294. This seems an unusual household, where familial relationships could not clearly be traced. M. Clark also worked as a blacksmith, perhaps alongside Logan. Greenberry Logan's case is also described in Harold Schoen, "The Free Negro in the Republic of Texas, II," *Southwestern Historical Quarterly* 40, no. 1 (July 1936): 2.

16. PAR 11583807 and 11583802. Kavanaugh could not be traced using census evidence, and no outcome survives for his second petition.

17. PAR 11583806 and 11583808. Carter could not be traced in the census.

18. Historian Harold Schoen has argued that some white people held an economic interest in retaining free people of color within Texas because there was a scarcity of artisans. See "Free Negro, IV," 198–99.

19. PAR 11583809, 1158310, and 1158311. Edmund Carter could not be traced using the census. Of course, there is a chance the petitions have been mistranscribed either when they were initially written or at a later date and that these two men are actually one and the same.

20. PAR 11584002 and 11584015.

21. PAR 11584003 and 11584004. For more on the free people of color who requested residency in Texas, see Harold Schoen, "The Free Negro in the Republic of Texas, I," *Southwestern Historical Quarterly* 39, no. 4 (April 1936): 292–308.

22. As Ruthe Winegarten noted, most petitions requesting the right to remain in the Republic of Texas were ignored. See *Black Texas Women: 150 Years of Trial and Triumph* (Austin: University of Texas Press, 1995), 8.

23. PAR 11085903.

24. PAR 11085904.

25. PAR 11085922; and "Slave Inhabitants in the Town of Raymond, County of Hinds, State of Mississippi, Enumerated on the 24th July 1860," 165.

26. PAR 10183901.

27. PAR 11085906.

28. PAR 11085907.

29. PAR 11085908 and 11085910.

30. PAR 11085905.

31. PAR 11085912.

32. PAR 11089513.

33. PAR 11085911.

34. PAR 11085923 and 11085924.

35. PAR 11584005 and 11584104.

36. PAR 11681002, 11681121, and 11681301.

37. PAR 11681125.

38. PAR 11681511.

39. Petition of Julius and Lucinda, "To the Honorable Speaker and Members

of the House of Delegates of the Commonwealth of Virginia," undated, Legislative Petitions, LVA.

40. "An Act Making Appropriations for the Removal of Free Persons of Color, and for Other Purposes," *Acts of the General Assembly of Virginia Passed at the Extra and Regular Sessions, 1849 and 1850* (Richmond: William F. Ritchie, 1850), 7, LVA.

41. See Link, *Roots of Secession*, 155–57. As the colonization movement gathered momentum, petitions from white residents to various state assemblies illustrate the depth of feeling some had about the desirability of such an expulsion. For example, in 1850, seventy-seven individuals petitioned the North Carolina legislature writing that free black people encouraged a "spirit of discontent" among slaves. They suggested that "free negroes" be transported to Liberia and that the costs of this could be offset by using the proceeds from enslaving those who refused to leave (PAR 11285001). The Tennessee assembly also received two petitions in 1860, signed by ninety-two and eighty-one individuals respectively and similarly requesting the removal of free people of color to Liberia (PAR 11486601 and 11486005). In Virginia, there exist more than twenty petitions to the state legislature urging support for colonization. The majority of these were written in the early 1830s, when anxiety about the Nat Turner rebellion was still fresh in peoples' minds and removal to Liberia was seen as an alternative to the expulsion of free blacks to other states, especially in areas where the free black population was growing. See Berlin, *Slaves without Masters*, 355. For general information on the colonization movement and life in Liberia, see Edwin S. Redkey, "Colonization," and Tom W. Schick, "Liberia," both in Miller and Smith, *Dictionary of Afro-American Slavery*, 121–23, 400–402; and Schweninger, *Black Property Owners*, 93–94. For an excellent overview, see David Brion Davis, *Challenging the Boundaries of Slavery* (Cambridge, Mass.: Harvard University Press, 2003), 62–74, and Marie Tyler-McGraw, *An African Republic: Black and White Virginians in the Making of Liberia* (Chapel Hill: University of North Carolina Press, 2007). On the Liberian disease environment, see Tom W. Shick, *Behold the Promised Land: A History of Afro-American Settler Society in Nineteenth-Century Liberia*, 2nd ed. (Baltimore: Johns Hopkins University Press, 1980), 27–28. Letters from emigrants to Liberia are contained within Bell I. Wiley, ed., *Slaves No More: Letters from Liberia, 1833–1869* (Lexington: University Press of Kentucky, 1980).

42. See PAR 11683003.

43. PAR 11683602.

44. PAR 11683211.

45. PAR 11683207.

46. For example, see PAR 11683206, 11683208, 11683126, and 11683631.

47. PAR 11683121. See also 11683117, 11683113, 11683105, 11683102, 11683201, and 11683202 for similarly worded requests for expulsion to Liberia from white Virginians. Some petitions from other states are explored in chapter 4.

48. "An Act to Empower the Board of Police of Pike County to Remove the Lundy Free Negroes Living in Said County to Liberia," approved 10 February 1854. *Laws of the State of Mississippi, Passed at a Regular Session of the Mississippi Legislature Held in the City of Jackson* (Jackson: E. Barksdale, State Printer, 1852), 287–88, MDAH. Many thanks to the anonymous reader who coined the phrase "back to America."

49. 1850 census, Police District 2, Pike, Mississippi, roll M432_380, p. 17B, image 39.

50. 1850 census, Police District 1, Pike, Mississippi, roll M432_380, p. 19A, image 42. James Stallin appears as James Stalings on the slave schedules. See "Slave Inhabitants in the County of Pike, State of Mississippi, Enumerated on the 30th August 1850," 3.

51. See 1850 census, Police District 1, Pike, Mississippi, roll M432_380, p. 1B, image 7; and "Slave Inhabitants in the County of Pike, State of Mississippi, Enumerated on the 30th August 1850," 3.

52. See 1850 census, Police District 5, Pike, Mississippi, roll M432_380, p. 7B, image 19; and "Slave Inhabitants in the County of Pike, State of Mississippi, Enumerated on the 11th September 1850," 491.

53. 1850 census, Police District 1, Pike, Mississippi, roll M432_380, p. 2A, image 8; and "Slave Inhabitants in the County of Pike, Enumerated on the 29th August 1850," 530.

54. 1850 census, Police District 2, Pike, Mississippi, roll M432_380, p. 9A, image 22; and "Slave Inhabitants in the County of Pike, State of Mississippi, Enumerated on the 5th September 1850," 5.

55. 1850 census, Police District 5, Pike, Mississippi, roll M432_380, p. 7B, image 19; and "Slave Inhabitants in the County of Pike, State of Mississippi, Enumerated on the 11th September 1850," 491.

56. The 1850 Census, Police District 2, Pike, Mississippi, roll M432_380, p. 9A, image 22.

57. These members of the Lundy family can be seen on the 1860 census for Pike County, Mississippi, as follows: roll M653_589, p. 401, image 407; roll M653_589, p. 355, image 361; roll M653_589, p. 342, image 348; roll M653_589, p. 346, image 352, all in Family History Library Film 803589.

58. Wikramanayake, *World in Shadow,* 175–76.

59. See PAR 11384007; and Wikramanayake, *World in Shadow,* 177–78.

60. PAR 11384008. Jones could not be traced via the relevant censuses, although Loren Schweninger writes that his petitions were denied. See *Black Property Owners,* 94.

61. PAR 11681901.

62. PAR 11682002.

63. PAR 11682111.

64. PAR 11682109.

65. James D. Watkinson, "'Fit Objects of Charity': Community, Race, Faith,

and Welfare in Antebellum Lancaster County, Virginia, 1817–1860," *Journal of the Early Republic* 21, no. 1 (Spring 2001): 45.

66. This tells us something of the prevailing ideology, if not the reality of speculation in slaves in the South at this time. Speculators were frequently labeled as immoral or lower-class whites, and this developed into Lost Cause propaganda after the Civil War. See Michael Tadman, *Speculators and Slaves: Masters, Traders, and Slaves in the Old South*, 2nd ed. (Madison: University of Wisconsin Press, 1996), chap. 7, for more.

67. The three petitions can be accessed via PAR 11682708, 11682803, and 11683413.

68. See the 1850 census for St. Georges Parish, Accomack, Va., roll M432_932, p. 152B, image 311. Neither Henderson nor Joynes could be traced and may well have passed away by the date of the census.

69. PAR 11085925.

3. "Traditional" Motivations and White Perspectives on Voluntary Enslavement

1. Petition of Daniel Freeman to Become a Slave, undated, ser. S165015, item 2463, Legislative Petitions, SCDAH.

2. For more on how law was "practiced and enacted" through performance, see Gross, "Beyond Black and White," esp. 650–53.

3. "Slave Inhabitants in Orangeburg District, State of South Carolina, Enumerated on the 25th June 1860," 112.

4. 1860 census for Orangeburg, Orangeburg, South Carolina, roll M653_1224, p. 345, image 273, Family History Library Film 805224.

5. Franklin, *Free Negro*, 218n119. He writes that this case was cited in the *Greensborough Patriot* on 2 December 1854 and on 11 November 1859.

6. Cited in the *New Orleans Daily Picayune*, 7 February, 8 December 1852. Schafer reports these cases in *Becoming Free, Remaining Free*, where she writes how the paper "delighted" in printing such reports (150–51). Ridge could not be traced in census schedules, but a William Pennington who owned slaves appears on the 1860 census. Living in Pulaski County, he owned thirty-nine people. See "Slave Inhabitants in Campbell Township, County of Pulaski, State of Arkansas, Enumerated on the 29th day of July 1860," 6. It may well have been that Kent missed his family and wanted to return to them regardless of his status before the law.

7. PAR 21484847.

8. Cited in the *New Orleans Daily Picayune*, 15 January 1859, NOPL. None could be traced via census schedules.

9. Cited in the *New Orleans Daily Delta*, 18 May 1860. See Sterkx, *Free Negro in Ante-Bellum Louisiana*, 149n177. Sterkx wrote: "This is the only case the author could find [for the state of Louisiana] in which a free negro returned to slavery, under the act of 1859." Neither Clifton nor Bumpass could be found in census records.

10. *New Orleans Daily Delta*, 18 May 1860, cited in Schafer, *Becoming Free, Remaining Free*, 159–61.

11. *New Orleans Daily Picayune*, 15 September 1859, cited in Schafer, *Becoming Free, Remaining Free*, 157.

12. PAR 11286101. See also Franklin, "Enslavement of Free Negroes," 419. Bridgers could not be traced as a slaveholder, and Abisha Locus's request was not granted.

13. PAR 20586102. See also Morris, *Southern Slavery and the Law*, 35. Whether Alderman owned slaves is unknown.

14. Quoted in Winegarten, *Black Texas Women*, 11. Rachel, Anarcha, and George H. Thomas could not be traced via census records or slave schedules.

15. Franklin made this point in *Free Negro*, 218.

16. See Turner's introduction to *From Chattel Slaves to Wage Slaves*, 28.

17. PAR 20379505.

18. PAR 20379503.

19. PAR 20379516.

20. PAR 11085919.

21. "Slave Inhabitants in the County of Itawamba, State of Mississippi, Enumerated on the 29th June 1860," 475.

22. The 1860 census for New Orleans Ward 1, Orleans, Louisiana, roll M653_415, p. 180, image 300, Family History Library Film 803415. See also "Slave Inhabitants in the First District in the County of Orleans, State of Louisiana, Enumerated on the 19th June 1860," 214.

23. Petition of Henry Wilson and associated papers, 24 and 30 November 1860 (no. 13390), Records of the Fourth District Court of New Orleans, NOPL.

24. Schafer, *Becoming Free, Remaining Free*, 154.

25. Petition of Julia Elliot, 26 November 1861 (no. 15132), Records of the Fourth District Court of New Orleans, NOPL. Elliott is also mentioned in the *New Orleans Daily Picayune* on 8 May 1861, when she appeared before the First District Court and was charged with "being in the state contrary to laws." Judith Kelleher Schafer also details her enslavement request, arguing that the case became moot with the coming of war. See *Becoming Free, Remaining Free*, 155–56.

26. Petition of George Stephens, Free Man of Color, to Become a Slave, 1 February 1862 (no. 16624), Records of the Third District Court of New Orleans, NOPL. As early as 1855 he had been charged with residing in Louisiana illegally, though he had not left the state. See Schafer, *Becoming Free, Remaining Free*, 156. Neither George Stephens nor James Frank could be found in census records.

27. "An Act for the Relief of Thomas Crenshaw, a Free Man of Color, of Copiah County," approved 1 February 1860, *Laws of the State of Mississippi Passed at a Regular Session of the Mississippi Legislature Held in the City of Jackson, 1860* (Jackson: E. Barksdale, State Printer, 1860), 287–88. MDAH.

28. Minutes for 2 February 1860, Probate Court Minutes for Copiah County, Mississippi, 1859–1861, microfilm reel 8125, pp. 307–10, MDAH.

29. 1860 census, Copiah, Mississippi, roll M653_580, p. 949, image 465, Family History Library Film 803580. Crenshaw could not be found on the census, and McRae does not appear to have owned any slaves.

30. The historiography on relations among planters, yeomen, and non-slaveholding whites is extensive. For a solid introduction, see Mark M. Smith, *Debating Slavery: Economy and Society in the Antebellum American South* (Cambridge: Cambridge University Press, 1998), chap. 3. See also Jeff Forret, *Race Relations at the Margins: Slaves and Poor Whites in the Antebellum Southern Countryside* (Baton Rouge: Louisiana State University Press, 2006), 3–5; and David Brown, "Poor Whites, Herrenvolk Democracy, and the Value of Whiteness in the Old South," unpublished conference paper presented at Institute for Historical Research Seminar Series in American History, March 2010.

31. "An Act to Authorize Jane Miller, a Free Person of Color, to Sell Herself into Perpetual Slavery, 1862" (no. 101), Court Records for Clarke County, Ga., 95, GA.

32. 1850 census for Duprees, Clarke, Georgia, roll M432_65, p. 32B, image 349.

33. "An Act Permitting Charles Short and Others to Become Slaves, on Application to the Probate Court of Russell County," approved 23 February 1860, Session Laws of Alabama, 1859–1860, 662, ADAH.

34. See the 1850 census for Russell, Alabama, roll M432_14, p. 86, image 433; also the 1860 census for Beat 11, Russell, Alabama, roll M653_22, p. 1073, image 679, both in Family History Library Film 803022. Edwards's slave ownership in 1860 can be seen in the slave schedule for that year: "Slave Inhabitants in Beat 11 in the County of Russell, State of Alabama, Enumerated on the 19th July 1860" (55). The ages and genders of the Short family in the slave schedules match the profile of the "Edwards" family listed one decade earlier.

35. "An Act Permitting Charles Short and Others to Become Slaves, on Application to the Probate Court of Russell County," approved 23 February 1860, Session Laws of Alabama, 1859–1860, 662, ADAH.

36. PAR 20586112. Walter L. Cozzens was forty-five in 1860, married with one child. He appears to have had six slaves. See the 1860 census for Pensacola, Escambia, Florida, roll M653_106, p. 369, image 374, Family History Library Film 803106; and "Slave Inhabitants in the City of Pensacola, County of Escambia, State of Florida, Enumerated on the 6th June 1860," 6.

37. See Marr and Hargis, "Voluntary Exile of Free Negroes of Pensacola," 8; and the 1870 census for Pensacola, Escambia, Florida, roll M593_129, p. 632B, image 412, Family History Library Film 545628.

38. "An Act for the Relief of James Wall, a Free Man of Color," approved 11 February 1860, *Laws of the State of Mississippi Passed at a Regular Session of the Mississippi Legislature Held in the City of Jackson, 1860* (Jackson: E. Barksdale, State Printer,

1860), 243–44, MDAH. See also the 1860 census for Wilkinson, Mississippi, roll M653_594, p. 573, image 55, Family History Library Film 803594.

39. Petition of Joseph Thomas, Free Man of Color, 3 October 1859 (no. 13318), Records of the Fourth District Court of New Orleans, NOPL.

40. See the 1860 census for New Orleans Ward 7, Orleans, Louisiana, roll M653_419, p. 512, image 512, Family History Library Film 803419; and for New Orleans Ward 9, Orleans, Louisiana, roll M653_422, 721, image 89, Family History Library Film 803422.

41. Petition of William Gray, Free Man of Color, 1 October 1859 (no. 13320), Records of the Fourth District Court of New Orleans, NOPL.

42. I was reluctant to include potential owners who did not appear as slave-holders as non-slaveholders, since they could simply have been missed from the census by enumerators. Out of caution, I assumed their ownership of slaves was unknown. However, that some of these people were indeed "poor whites" who possessed no enslaved people serves only to strengthen my arguments about the aspirations of less wealthy whites to buy slaves.

43. Kolchin, *American Slavery*, 244.

44. Petition of Lewis Wilkinson, 8 October 1857, Records of the Circuit Court of Amelia County, Va., LVA. See also the 1860 census for District 2, Amelia, Va., roll M653_1332, p. 170, image 178, Family History Library Film 805332; and "Slave Inhabitants in District Number 2 in the County of Amelia, State of Virginia, Enumerated on the 25th June 1860," 12.

45. See the entries for the 12 August 1858 and 15 March 1859, Records of the Circuit Court of Prince Edward County, Va., LVA. None could be traced using census materials.

46. See the entries for December 1857, Records of the Circuit Court of Gloucester County, Va.; the entry for 16 August 1859, Records of Circuit Court of Prince Edward County, Va.; and the entry for 16 September, 1857, Records of the Circuit Court of Buckingham County, Va., all in LVA. None of these men or their potential owners could be traced in census schedules.

47. Entry for 5 August 1859, Records of the Circuit Court of Madison County, Va., LVA. See also "Slave Inhabitants in the County of Madison, State of Virginia, Enumerated on the 3rd August 1860," 23.

48. Entry for 13 March 1860, Records of the Circuit Court of Giles County, Va.; and Entry for 3 November 1860, Records of the Circuit Court of the City of Richmond, LVA. No further information could clearly be gleaned using census data for these cases.

49. Buying slaves for part cash, part credit was also common in local sales, which again conveys something of the promotion of slaveholding. See Tadman, *Speculators and Slaves*, 52–53.

50. Edmund S. Morgan considered the notion of petitions as "ventrilo-quism" in *Inventing the People*, 230.

4. Free People of Color and the Enslaved

1. Petition of Lucy Andrews, undated (no. 02811), Legislative Petitions, SCDAH.

2. Petition of Lucy Andrews, 26 January 1860 (no. 00017), Legislative Petitions, SCDAH.

3. See PAR 11386302, and also West, *Chains of Love*, 124–25; and Morris, *Southern Slavery and the Law*, 35.

4. See the 1860 Census, Lancaster, South Carolina, roll M653_1221, 209, image 422, Family History Library Film 805221. Lucy Andrews could not be traced thereafter.

5. "Slave Inhabitants in the County of Lancaster, State of South Carolina, Enumerated on the 3rd October 1850," 687.

6. In "The Fragile Nature of Freedom: Free Women of Color in the U.S. South," in Gaspar and Hine, *Beyond Bondage*, Loren Schweninger claims Andrews's petition was rejected (115, 118).

7. For more on the complexity of relationships between free people of color and the enslaved, see John Hope Franklin and Loren Schweninger, *In Search of the Promised Land: A Slave Family in the Old South* (New York: Oxford University Press, 2006), 254.

8. Schiller, "U.S. Slavery's Diaspora," 201. For more on the importance of belonging to a local place, see, Suggs, *Whispered Consolations*, 64–65.

9. For more on the meanings attached to slavery and freedom in a historiographical context, see Cooper, Holt, and Scott, *Beyond Slavery*, 5–11. They note that the "meanings of freedom must be sought in a whole sequence of particular historical and social contexts" (9). The present work seeks to further such notions through my exploration of such meanings in the rare context of voluntary slavery requests.

10. For more on ties of affection between enslaved spouses, see West, *Chains of Love*, especially the introduction, and Rebecca Fraser, *Courtship and Love among the Enslaved in North Carolina* (Jackson: University Press of Mississippi, 2007). John Wess Grant has studied black families that straddled slavery and freedom in antebellum Richmond in "Stranded Families," 61–74.

11. See Koger, *Black Slaveowners*, for more on free blacks who bought their loved ones (69). Koger argues that the slave conspirator Denmark Vesey was motivated by his increasing sense of frustration at the bondage of his wife and children (184–85). See also Egerton, *He Shall Go Free*, 77–83. Koger also takes into account black slaveholding that was more exploitative in nature. See especially "Black Masters: The Misunderstood Slaveowners," *Southern Quarterly* 43, no. 2 (2006): 52–73, esp. 53–54; and also Michael P. Johnson and James L. Roark, who argue that the evidence for benevolent black slaveholding has been exaggerated. Instead, free people of color often bought slaves as a ploy to separate themselves from the mass of enslaved African Americans. See "Strategies of Survival," 94–101.

12. Wallenstein, *Tell the Court I Love My Wife*, 21.

13. PAR 11681208. Unfortunately, no outcome survives for this case.

14. Petition of Lucinda, 27 March 1813, Legislative Petitions, LVA. See also PAR 11681303. The case is also detailed in Loren Schweninger, "Fragile Nature of Freedom," 106, 116–17; and in *Plantation and Frontier, 1649–1863*, vol. 2, ed. U. B. Philips (New York: Burt Franklin, 1910), 161–62. Philips has transcribed the date of this petition as 1815. No outcome survives.

15. For more on cross-plantation marriages among the enslaved, see West, *Chains of Love*, chap. 3

16. PAR 11683910. See also the petition of Lizzie Purdie, circa 28 January 1839, Legislative Petitions, LVA.

17. PAR 11683701.

18. *New Orleans Daily Picayune*, 22 September 1850. No other records could be found for this case.

19. PAR 21685020.

20. *Expedition by the Liberia Packet, May 1848* (Washington, D.C.: American Colonization Society, C. Alexander, printer, 1848), *African Repository and Colonial Journal* (1825–1849), vol. 24, pt. 5 (May 1848), 153–55. I am grateful to Marie Tyler-McGraw for giving this information to my research assistant, Laura Sandy.

21. Petition of Willis and Andrew, circa 1854, Legislative Petitions, LVA.

22. See Guild, *Black Laws of Virginia*, 119.

23. See the 1850 census for Lunenburg, Va., roll M432_958, p. 53A, image 111.

24. See Guild, *Black Laws of Virginia*, 120; the 1850 census for Culpeper, Va., roll M432_941, p. 269A, image 116; and "Slave Inhabitants in the County of Culpeper, State of Virginia, Enumerated on the 22nd October 1850," 969.

25. On 17 January 1856, the act was read for a second time and ordered to be read for a third time. See the *Acts of the Senate of the Commonwealth of Virginia* (Richmond: John Worrock, 1855), no. 198. An act was passed on 31 January 1856. See the entry for 1 February 1856, *Acts of the Senate of the Commonwealth of Virginia*. See also "An Act Providing for the Voluntary Enslavement of Thomas Grayson, a Free Person of Color of the County of Culpeper," passed on 31 January 1856, *Acts of the General Assembly of Virginia*, 1855–1856, chap. 432, p. 278, all in LVA.

26. "An Act Providing for the Voluntary Enslavement of Simon and Martha, His Wife, and Judy and Margaret, Daughters of the Same, Free Persons of Color of the County of Southampton," passed on 26 February 1856, *Acts of the General Assembly of Virginia*, 1855–1856, chap. 433, p. 278, LVA.

27. See "Slave Inhabitants in the Nottaway Parish in the County of Southampton, State of Virginia, Enumerated on the 23rd September 1850," 456; and "Slave Inhabitants in the East Side of Nottaway River, County of Southampton, State of Virginia, Enumerated on the 25th July 1860," 5.

28. "An Act Providing for the Voluntary Enslavement of Lewis Williamson, a

Free Person of Color of the County of Southampton," passed on 4 January 1856, *Acts of the General Assembly of Virginia, 1855–1856,* chap, 434, p. 279, LVA.

29. "Slave Inhabitants in the East Side of Nottaway River, County of Southampton, State of Virginia, Enumerated on the 1st September 1860," 21.

30. See the entry for 15 April 1857, Records of the Circuit Court of Lancaster County, LVA; and "Slave Inhabitants in the Eastern District of the County of Lancaster, State of Virginia, 16th July 1860," 19.

31. See the entry for 14 April 1860, Records of the Circuit Court of Rockbridge County, LVA; and "Slave Inhabitants in the Fourth District, County of Rockbridge, State of Virginia, Enumerated on the 27th June 1860," 31.

32. See the entry for 4 February 1860, Records of the Circuit Court of Pulaski County, LVA; and "Slave Inhabitants in the Western District in the County of Pulaski, State of Virginia, 29th June 1860," 71. No outcome survives for this case.

33. See PAR 11686102; 1860 census for Staunton, Augusta, Va., roll M653_1333, p. 786, image 266, Family History Library Film 805333; and "Slave Inhabitants in Staunton District Number 1, County of Augusta, State of Virginia, Enumerated on the 20th June 1860," 11.

34. "An Act to Enable Ned Adkins and Other Free Persons of Color Therein Named to Become Slaves," approved on 21 February 1860, Session Laws of Alabama, 1859–1860, 599–600, ADAH.

35. See "Slave Inhabitants in the Southern Division, County of Coosa, State of Alabama, Enumerated on the 27th June 1860," 11, for Thomas Williams's slaves. Those belonging to H. H. Ware can be seen in "Slave Inhabitants in Selma, in the County of Dallas, State of Alabama, Enumerated on the 8th July 1860," 68. For Inda Ware, see the 1860 census for Selma, Dallas, Alabama, roll M653_8, p. 811, image 315, Family History Library Film 803008. For Cealy Adkins, see the 1870 census for Township 18, Elmore, Alabama, roll M593_15, p. 62A, image 314, Family History Library Film 545514.

36. PAR 20186011. See also the petition of James Fagin, 24 December 1860, minutes of the Probate Court, Book N, local government microfilm 50 (hereafter LGM), microfilm reel 13, pp. 14–15, Lowndes County Probate Records, ADAH.

37. See the 1850 census for Lowndes, Alabama, roll M432_8, p. 172A, image 562; the 1860 census for the Northern Division, Lowndes, Alabama, roll M653_14, p. 535, image 53, both in Family History Library Film 803014; "Slave Inhabitants in the Northern Division, County of Lowndes, State of Alabama, Enumerated on the 16th August 1860," 133; and "Slave Inhabitants in the Southern Division, County of Lowndes, State of Alabama, Enumerated on the 9th August 1860," 150.

38. See the 1870 census, Township 16 Range, Montgomery, Alabama, roll M593_34, p. 292B, image 587, Family History Library Film 545533.

39. See the petition of John Williams, 1860, Madison County Probate Records, 1860–1862, 109–10, ADAH; and "Slave Inhabitants in the North Western Division, County of Madison, State of Alabama, Enumerated on 9th June 1860," 12.

40. See "An Act to Authorize Lewis Wetherspoon, and Cora, Free Negroes, to Become Slaves" (no. 606), approved on 10 February 1860, Session Laws of Alabama, 1859–1860, 674–75, ADAH; and "Slave Inhabitants in the Eastern Division, County of Pike, State of Alabama, Enumerated on 17th September 1860," 47.

41. Minutes for 11 March 1861 and 25 March 1861, Pike County Probate Judge Minutes, 1858–1862, microfilm LGM 045, vol. F, reel 2, pp. 617, 625, ADAH. Nat Gunter, Jonathan Jones, and Billy Jones could not be traced.

42. See the 1860 census for Troy, Pike, Alabama, roll M653_21, p. 218, image 218, Family History Library Film 803021; and "Slave Inhabitants in Troy, in the County of Pike, State of Alabama, Enumerated on the 27th June 1860," 11.

43. See the petitions of Samuel Cobler and associated paperwork, 18 May, 1, 15 June, and 20 August 1861, Minutes of Pike County Probate Court, 1858–62, LGM 045, microfilm vol. F, reel 2, pp. 644, 651, 657, 672, ADAH.

44. See the 1860 census for Troy, Pike, Alabama, roll M653_21, p. 210, image 210, Family History Library Film 803021; and "Slave Inhabitants in Troy, County of Pike, State of Alabama, Enumerated on the 25th June 1960," 9. Neither Sam Cobler nor Wyatt Hogan could be traced.

45. The latest enslavement request found was made in 1864, when John Sexton petitioned in Georgia. The case is detailed later in this chapter.

46. Minutes of 2 June 1863, Chambers County Probate Minutes, vol. 9, 1861–1864, 463, ADAH.

47. See the 1860 census for the Northern Division, Chambers, Alabama, roll M653_4, p. 865, image 587, Family History Library Film 803004; and "Slave Inhabitants in the Northern Division of Chambers County, State of Alabama, Enumerated on the 24th September 1860," 56. George and Susan could not be traced in the 1870 census.

48. Minutes of 13 June 1863, Chambers County Probate Minutes, vol. 9, 1861–1864, 473–74, ADAH.

49. The 1860 census, Lafayette, Chambers, Alabama, roll M653_4, p.722, image 444, Family History Library Film 803004.

50. Minutes of 13 June 1863, Chambers County Probate Minutes, vol. 9, 1861–1864, 474–75, ADAH.

51. Entry for 17 May 1860, microfilm roll misc. 39, Circuit Court Record Book "Z" (Civil), pp. 1–639, May 1859–July 1863, Pulaski County, Ark., 281, AHCSA. A fuller consideration of the financial value of free people of color is considered in the previous chapter.

52. See the 1850 census for Vaugine, Jefferson, Ark., roll M432_27, p. 75A,

image 154. Evidence on Yell's ownership of slaves can be seen via "Slave Inhabitants in Campbell Township in the County of Pulaski, State of Arkansas, Enumerated on the 27th July 1860," 7.

53. A notable exception is Forret, *Race Relations at the Margins*.

54. The 1870 census, Campbell, Pulaski, Ark., roll M593_62, 94B, image 189, Family History Library Film 545561.

55. Entry for 6 May 1861, microfilm roll misc. 39, Circuit Court Record Book "Z" (Civil), pages 1–639, May 1859–July 1863, Pulaski County, Ark., 444, AHSCA.

56. See "Slave Inhabitants in the City of Little Rock, County of Pulaski, State of Arkansas, Enumerated on the 6th June 1860," 5. Mary Brock could not be traced.

57. Entry for 6 May 1861, microfilm roll misc. 39, Circuit Court Record Book "Z" (Civil), pages 1–639, May 1859–July 1863, Pulaski County, Ark., 443–44, AHSCA.

58. "Slave Inhabitants in Big Rock Township, County of Pulaski, State of Arkansas, Enumerated on the 4th July 1860," 12. Elizabeth Keatts could not be traced.

59. Circuit Court Record, May 1860, Phillips County Circuit Court Minutes, 392–93, AHCSA; "Slave Inhabitants in St. Francis Township, County of Phillips, State of Arkansas, Enumerated on the 15th August 1860," 76.

60. Minutes for May 1860, Phillips County Circuit Court Record, May 1860, Phillips County Circuit Court Records, 388–89, AHCSA; and "Slave Inhabitants in St. Francis Township in the County of Phillips, State of Arkansas, Enumerated on the 17th August 1860," 84.

61. Entry for 13 November 1862, Lafayette County Circuit Court Minutes, 1852–1869, book 5, p. 111, AHCSA.

62. "Slave Inhabitants in La Grange Township in the County of Lafayette, State of Arkansas, Enumerated on the 6th June 1860," 4; and the 1860 census for La Grange, Lafayette, Ark., roll M653_45, p. 11, image 11, Family History Library Film 803045.

63. *Slaves without Masters* is, of course, the title of Berlin's seminal 1974 work.

64. Petition of Jane "To the Hon. James M. Baker Judge of Said Court," Circuit Court of Florida, Suwannee Circuit, Suwannee County to wit Spring term 1860, minute 1, Petitions to the Current Court of Suwannee, Fla., no. 71, Suwannee County Courthouse. Historian Craig Buettinger has researched this case and believes Jane's husband, George, was enslaved to Mary Rowland. I am grateful to him for passing on a transcript of this document to my research assistant, Laura Sandy, and for his helpful correspondence with me over this case. See also the 1860 census for Suwannee, Florida, roll M653_109, 787, image 257, Family History Library Film 803109; and "Slave Inhabitants in the County of Suwannee, State of Florida, Enumerated on the 22nd of August 1860," 6.

65. Interview with Samuel Smalls, conducted by Martin D. Richardson, *WPA*

Slave Narrative Project, vol. 3, *Florida Narratives,* ed. George P. Rawick (Westport, Conn.: Greenwood, 1972), 300–302.

66. Ulrich B. Philips, *Georgia Local Archives: Reprinted from the Annual Report of the American Historical Association for the Year 1904* (Washington, D.C.: GPO, 1905), 577.

67. Michael Tadman has estimated the average price paid by traders for a prime male field hand in 1859–60 (the nearest year I could obtain for a comparison) to be 805 dollars. Admittedly, the war would have affected average prices. See *Speculators and Slaves,* 285. Steven Deyle also considers the complexities of calculating slave prices in *Carry Me Back: The Domestic Slave Trade in American Life* (New York: Oxford University Press, 2005), 56–60.

68. The 1860 census, Habersham, Georgia, roll M653_125, p. 841, image 391, Family History Library Film 803125. Unfortunately, no members of the Sexton family could be traced into the postwar era.

69. PAR 11085921.

70. "Perrit" was a laborer living with a white family. See the 1860 census for Kemper, Mississippi, roll M653_584, p. 883, image 305, Family History Library Film 803584. See also "Slave Inhabitants in the County of Kemper, State of Mississippi, Enumerated on the 24th July 1860," 34. Since Hale does not seem to have owned any male slaves, Perrot's request may have been unsuccessful.

71. See PAR 1105915; the 1860 census for Dark Corner Beat, Holmes, Mississippi, roll M653_582, p. 803, image 335, Family History Library Film 803582; and "Slave Inhabitants in Dark Corner, County of Holmes, State of Mississippi, Enumerated on the 24th August 1860," 62. Sproles could not be traced as a slave owner himself, but there were several Sproles in Dark Corner who owned slaves. Wesley Moore could not be traced.

72. "Robert Grayham" of Lafayette County owned eighteen slaves in 1860, some of whom were presumably Joe Bird's family. See "Slave Inhabitants in the County of Lafayette, State of Mississippi, Enumerated on the 7th of July 1860," 4.

73. PAR 11085918; and "Slave Inhabitants in the County of Hinds, State of Mississippi, Enumerated on the 12th July 1860," 46.

74. PAR 11085917; and "Slave Inhabitants in the Northern Division, County of Tippah, State of Mississippi, Enumerated on the 21st July 1860," 11.

75. PAR 11086010. None could be traced in the census.

76. PAR 11085920. This case is elusive—certainly one might find a suggestion of a homosexual relationship in the apparently intimate relationship of these two men. Homosexuality has existed across time and space, even if documentary evidence is lacking. See Patterson, *Rituals of Blood,* 289n70.

77. "An Act of the Relief of William Webster, a Free Man of Color," approved 20 January 1860, *Laws of the State of Mississippi, Passed at a Regular Session of the Mississippi Legislature Held in the City of Jackson, November 1860* (Jackson: E. Barksdale, State Printer, 1860), 259–60, MDAH. See also the 1860 census (where "Atheral" is mistakenly transcribed as "Alfred"), Tallahatchie, Mississippi, roll M653_591,

416, image 422, Family History Library Film 803591; and "Slave Inhabitants in the County of Tallahatchie, State of Mississippi, Enumerated on the 19th, 21st, and 22nd July 1860," 33.

78. PAR 11286203. Franklin writes that action was never taken in this case. See *Free Negro*, 220; "Enslavement of Free Negroes," 424–25; the 1860 census, Gaston, North Carolina, roll M653_898, p. 88, image 92, Family History Library Film 803898; and "Slave Inhabitants in the County of Gaston, State of North Carolina, Enumerated on the 18th July 1860," 10.

79. Franklin, *Free Negro*, 219. He also writes that this request was indefinitely postponed by the senate. See "Enslavement of Free Negroes," 418. The number of slaves owned by Marsh is unknown.

80. PAR 11286301. I am extremely grateful to Christopher Meekins, correspondence archivist at the Office of Archives and History, Raleigh, North Carolina, for providing me with a copy of the original petition, "Request of Percy Ann Martin," Legislative Petitions, 1863. This seems to be the "Peggy Ann Morton" of Davidson County who sought enslavement to Henderson Adams, as cited in Franklin, *Free Negro*, 220. He writes that her petition was denied. Adams owned eight slaves in 1860. See "Slave Inhabitants in the Northern Division, County of Davidson, State of North Carolina, Enumerated on the 14th August 1860," 17.

81. See Franklin, *Free Negro*, 220; and "Slave Inhabitants in District Seven, County of Northampton, State of North Carolina, Enumerated on the 18th Day of June 1860," 35. Neither woman could be found on the 1860 census.

82. Franklin, *Free Negro*, 220; and "Enslavement of Free Negroes," 416. Hartley's ownership of slaves can be seen in "Slave Inhabitants in Beaver Creek District, County of Jones, State of North Carolina, Enumerated on the 20th August 1860," 41.

83. PAR 11385902; and Petition of Elizabeth Bug, undated [1859] (no.00054), Legislative Petitions, SCDAH.

84. The 1860 census for Abbeville, South Carolina, roll M653_1212, p. 55, image 110, Family History Library Film 805212. See also "Slave Inhabitants in the County of Abbeville, State of South Carolina, Enumerated on the 19th July 1860," 50.

85. Neither woman can be traced in the census. Only the petition of Elizabeth Jane Bug seeking enslavement to William P. Hill appears in the Race and Slavery Petitions Project website. In *World in Shadow*, Marina Wikramanayake mentions both cases but cites the former as "Elizabeth Jane Berg, 1859" (183).

86. Petition of Elizabeth Bug, undated (no. 05738–01), Legislative Petitions, SCDAH.

87. "Report Rejecting the Petition from Elizabeth Bug, a Free Person of Color, Asking That She and Her Three Small Children Be Made the Slaves of A. B. Dean," 7 December 1859, ser. S165005, item 00390, Legislative Petitions, SCDAH. Unfortunately, A. B. Dean cannot clearly be traced in either census as there are two men with that name in Edgefield County.

88. "Petition of William Jackson, Free Boy of Color, Asking Leave to Go into Slavery," 23 November 1861 (no. 00079), Legislative Petitions, SCDAH. See also "Slave Inhabitants in the County of Laurens, State of South Carolina, Enumerated on the 2nd August 1860," 140.

89. "Petition of William Bass, a Free Person of Color, Praying to Become a Slave," 14 December 1859, quoted in Philips, *Plantation and Frontier*, 163–64. The outcome of this case is not stated.

90. See David Dangerfield, "Plain Folk of Color: Rural Free People of Color on the Antebellum Charleston District" (MA thesis, 2009, Graduate School of the College of Charleston and the Citadel), 64–65. My thanks to the author for alerting me to this case, which is also cited in Johnson and Roark, *Black Masters*, 165–66, and Paul Heinnegg, *Free African Americans of North Carolina and Virginia*, 3rd ed. (Baltimore: Genealogical Publishing, 1997), 26.

91. "Slave Inhabitants in the County of Marlboro, State of South Carolina, Enumerated on the [no date inserted], 1860," 70. Pledger lived alongside his wife, son, and their overseer, Nicholas Smith, and although William Bass could not be traced, census records show several free people of color with the surname "Bass" in Marlboro County. Some free people of color named Bass petitioned the Marlboro District court in the 1850s in regard to appointing guardians. See, for example, PAR 21385840, 21386111, 21386112, and 21386206. In 1859 someone named William Bass requested of the County Court that Benjamin Mc-Gilvray become his guardian, though it is unknown whether this was the same William Bass; see PAR 21385941.

92. PAR 21486104; and "Slave Inhabitants in the Second District 1, County of Washington, State of Tennessee, Enumerated on the [no date inserted], 1860," 2. In this case, the request was granted.

93. "Petition of Ben, Free Man of Color," 26 May 1858, Hawkins County Chancery Court Minute Books, May 1856–May 1862, 181–82, TSLA.

94. PAR 21585808.

95. See the 1860 census for San Augustine, San Augustine, Texas, roll M653_1304, p. 343, image 317, Family History Library Film 805304.

96. See PAR 21586008; "Slave Inhabitants in Precinct Number 3 in the County of Polk, State of Texas, Enumerated on the 13th August 1860," 29; and the 1870 census for Houston Ward 3, Harris, Texas, roll M593_1589, p. 569B, image 440, Family History Library Film 553088.

5. Expulsion, Enslavement, and Ties across the Color Line

1. Petition of Lucy Boomer to the Legislature of Virginia, 21 December 1833, Sundry Petitions of the County of Lunenberg, LVA.

2. Will of John Winn, 29 April 1819, filed with a copy of the petition of Lucy Boomer, Sundry Petitions of the County of Lunenberg, LVA.

3. Counterpetitions of the family of John Winn, undated, filed with a copy

of the petition of Lucy Boomer, Sundry Petitions of the County of Lunenberg, LVA.

4. Affidavit of Charlotte Winn, 25 January 1834, Sundry Petitions of the County of Lunenberg, LVA.

5. For more on poisoning by enslaved women, see Elizabeth Fox-Genovese, "Strategies and Forms of Resistance: Focus on Slave Women in the United States," in In Resistance: Studies in African, Caribbean, and Afro-American History, ed. Gary Y. Okihiro (Amherst: University of Massachusetts Press, 1986), 143–65, esp. 155–56.

6. Affidavit of Charleen Winn, 21 January 1834, Sundry Petitions of the County of Lunenberg, LVA.

7. Affidavit of Sophia Winn, 21 January 1834, Sundry Petitions of the County of Lunenberg, LVA.

8. Affidavit of James Winn, 21 January 1834, Sundry Petitions of the County of Lunenberg, LVA.

9. Affidavit of Edward Winn, 29 December 1834, Sundry Petitions of the County of Lunenberg, LVA.

10. Affidavit of Richard May, 28 July 1834, Sundry Petitions of the County of Lunenberg, LVA.

11. Affidavit of David Tirrell, 15 December 1834, Sundry Petitions of the County of Lunenberg, LVA.

12. Petition of Lucy Boomer to the General Assembly of Virginia, 16 December 1835, Sundry Petitions of the County of Lunenberg, LVA. For more on the notion of "performance" in legal documentation, see Gross, "Beyond Black and White," esp. 650–53.

13. Lucy Boomer's petitions were categorized here under "residency" as her primary motive: she did not want to leave.

14. PAR 11386005. Lamotte petitioned the South Carolina Assembly on 31 January 1859, and the request was approved on 7 December 1859. See ser. S165015, item 00055, and ser. S165005, item 00100, both in Legislative Petitions, SCDAH. He cannot clearly be traced on the census.

15. See Suzanne Lebsock, The Free Women of Petersburg: Status and Culture in a Southern Town, 1784–1860 (New York: Norton, 1984), 87–111.

16. Johnson and Roark, "Strategies of Survival," 92.

17. In this study, twelve women requested enslavement for themselves and their children. The other six cases are detailed in chapter 4, as these were women requesting enslavement to remain with black (enslaved or free) family members.

18. PAR 11286103. Kissiah, from Pasquotank County, North Carolina, was twenty-three years old and requested enslavement to Dr. H. P. Ritter. Franklin writes that her plea was "laid on the table of the House and not taken up again." See Free Negro, 220, and "Enslavement of Free Negroes," 417–18. Ritter, a medical doctor, appears to have owned no slaves. See the 1860 census, Elizabeth City,

Pasquotank, North Carolina, roll M653_909, p. 324, image 18, Family History Library Film 803909. Kissiah Trueblood could not be found on the census.

19. Evidence about Margaret's free status is questionable, and one of her children (Adam Tunno was their father) was legally emancipated. She exemplifies much about the lives of women whose status was somewhere between slave and free. See Amrita Chakrabati Myers, "The Bettingall-Tunno Family and the Free Black Women of Antebellum Charleston: A Freedom Both Contingent and Constrained," South Carolina Women, vol. 1, Their Life and Times, ed. Marjorie J. Spruill, Valinda W. Littlefield, and Joan M. Johnson (Athens: University of Georgia Press, 2009), 146–49.

20. See Camellia Cowling, "Defining Freedom: Women of Color and the Ending of Slavery in Havana and Rio de Janeiro, 1870–1888," unpublished conference paper presented at the International Federation for Research in Women's History conference in Amsterdam, August 2010. See also her "Negotiating Freedom: Women of Colour and the Transition to Free Labour in Cuba, 1870–1886," Slavery and Abolition 26, no. 3 (December 2005): 377–91.

21. Wong, Neither Fugitive nor Free, 9.

22. For more on the sexual assault of black women by white men in the antebellum era, see Susan Brownmiller, Against Our Will: Men, Women, and Rape (Harmondsworth: Penguin, 1975), 160; Angela Davies's pioneering article, "Reflections on the Black Woman's Role in the Community of Slaves," Black Scholar 3, no. 4 (1971): 2–15; Darlene Clark Hine, "Rape and the Inner Lives of Black Women in the Middle West: Preliminary Thoughts on the Culture of Dissemblance," Signs 14 (Summer 1989): 912–20; West, Chains of Love, 126–31.

23. See the 1860 census, North Western District, Wake, North Carolina, roll M653_916, p. 210, image 214, Family History Library Film 803916.

24. This was in 1861. This petition was laid before the House Committee on Propositions and Grievances, which decided the enslavement of the child should not extend beyond the age of twenty-one. See Franklin, "Enslavement of Free Negroes," 421. See also the 1860 census, Southern Division, Wake, North Carolina, roll M653_916, p. 75, image 79, Family History Library Film 803916.

25. This was in 1861. See PAR 11286202. The petition was referred to a House Judiciary Committee for consideration and was not brought again to the floor. See Franklin, "Enslavement of Free Negroes," 425; and 1860 census, Southern Division, Wake, North Carolina, roll M653_916, p. 88, image 92, Family History Library Film 803916.

26. PAR 11086007. See "Slave Inhabitants in the County of Marshall, State of Mississippi, Enumerated on the 9th August 1860," 34.

27. Franklin, Free Negro, 220; and "Enslavement of Free Negroes," 416. See also the 1860 census, Trenton, Jones, North Carolina, roll M653_903, p. 497, image 444, Family History Library Film 803903.

28. PAR 21586103. Unfortunately, none could be traced via the census;

however, a man named Aaron Burleson was summoned in relation to this case in October 1861. The owner of thirty slaves, Burleson, also of Travis County, apparently became the owner of a free black woman named Rachel Grumbles, although I could not decipher whether the two Rachels were actually the same person. See Winegarten, *Black Texas Women*, 12.

29. Petition of Mary Walker, Free Woman of Color (no. 13319), 1 October 1859, Fourth District Court of New Orleans, NOPL. The case is also cited in Schafer, *Becoming Free, Remaining Free*, 156–57.

30. See Franklin, *Free Negro*, 219; and "Enslavement of Free Negroes," 415. I am grateful to an anonymous reader for drawing my attention to the parallel language of the petitions and marriage vows. See also the 1860 census, District 9, Martin, North Carolina, roll M653_905, p. 446, image 297, Family History Library Film 803905.

31. "Slave Inhabitants in District Number Nine, County of Martin, State of North Carolina, Enumerated on the 26th day of September 1860," 48.

32. PAR 21286106. Apparently the bill passed in the North Carolina House but failed in the Senate. See Franklin, "Enslavement of Free Negroes," 422–23.

33. See "Slave Inhabitants in the North Division, County of Guilford, State of North Carolina, Enumerated on the 11th July 1860," 9, and "Enumerated on the 25th July 1860," 16.

34. See Franklin, *Free Negro*, 219. However, the senate refused this. See Franklin, "Enslavement of Free Negroes," 416. See also the 1860 census, Franklinton, Franklin, North Carolina, roll M653_897, p. 432, image 297, Family History Library Film 803897. Perry could not be traced using census evidence.

35. See Franklin, "Enslavement of Free Negroes," 416; and PAR 1286102. See also the 1860 census, District 4, Martin, North Carolina, roll M653_905, p. 392, image 193, Family History Library Film 803905. As Spruill was the owner of twenty-nine enslaved people, Eliza may have been tied to his broader enslaved community. See "Slave Inhabitants in District Number Four, County of Martin, State of North Carolina, Enumerated on the 11th July 1860," 14.

36. Alexander Jones could not be traced on the census, and it is unknown whether he owned any slaves. The senate indefinitely postponed Chavis's case. See Franklin, "Enslavement of Free Negroes," 418.

37. Petition of Judy Cullins, 25 August 1858, Records of the Powhatan Circuit Court, LVA. See also "Slave Inhabitants in My District in the County of Powhatan, State of Virginia, Enumerated on the 22nd June 1860," 40. Scott was a married lawyer. See 1860 census, "My District," Powhatan, Va., roll M653_1371, 818, image 215, Family History Library Film 805371.

38. Petition of Lavinia Napper, 13 September 1859, Records of the Circuit Court of Fauquier County, Va., LVA. See also "Slave Inhabitants in the South West Revenue District of Fauquier County, State of Virginia, Enumerated 17th July 1860," 16. Smith was married with two young children. See 1860 census, South

West Revenue District, Fauquier, Va., roll M653_1344, p. 189, image 191, Family History Library Film 805344.

39. This article, accessed via the Valley of the Shadow project (www.valley.lib.virginia.edu), originally appeared in the *Lexington Gazette*. The case is also cited in William Link's *Roots of Secession*, 158.

40. Saville appears on the 1860 census with his family but does not appear on the slave schedules. See the 1860 census, District 4, Rockbridge, Va., roll M653_1378, p. 114, image 118, Family History Library Film 805378.

41. Petition of Mary Elizabeth, 13 September 1860, Records of the Circuit Court of Rockbridge County, Va., LVA.

42. Register of Free Negroes, Fauquier County, 1817–1865, 107, LVA.

43. Petition of Fanny Gillison, 15 September 1860, Records of the Circuit Court of Fauquier County, LVA. See also "Slave Inhabitants in the Southwestern Revenue District, County of Fauquier, State of Virginia, Enumerated on the 2nd Day of October 1860," 60.

44. Petition of Elizabeth Jones (no. 13900), 22 December 1859, Third District Court of New Orleans, NOPL. See also Schafer, *Becoming Free, Remaining Free*. She writes that "presumably the transaction went through" (157). Neither Jones nor Musselman could be traced in the census.

45. Petition of Emilia Stone (no. 13245), 7 September 1859, Fifth District Court of New Orleans, NOPL. See also the 1860 census, New Orleans Ward 11, Orleans, Louisiana, roll M653_420, p. 872, image 300, Family History Library Film 803420.

46. See Schafer, *Becoming Free, Remaining Free*, 157–58; and the 1860 census, New Orleans Ward 11, Orleans, Louisiana, roll M653_420, 977, image 405, Family History Library Film 803420; and "Slave Inhabitants of the 11th District, City of New Orleans, in the County of Orleans, State of Louisiana, Enumerated on the 12th day of July 1860," 299. In this study, I have assumed Emilia and Amelia are the same person.

47. *New Orleans Daily Picayune*, 30 July 1861.

48. Petition of Mary Ann Randolph, 5 October 1860, Montgomery County Probate Court Records, 1860, 578, ADAH.

49. "Slave Inhabitants in the First District of the County of Montgomery, State of Alabama, Enumerated on the 28th June 1860," 39.

50. "An Act to Enable Lucy Green, of Coosa County, and Cora, of Chambers County, Free Women of Color, to Become Slaves, and to Repeal the Fifth Section of an Act, Approved 10th February 1860," approved 24 February 1860, Session Laws of Alabama, 1859–1860, 623–25, ADAH. See also "Slave Inhabitants in the Second Sub Division, County of Coosa, State of Alabama, Enumerated on the 27th June 1860," 16. Neither Lucy Green nor Daniel Crawford could be traced using census evidence.

51. "An Act to Authorize Elmira Matthews, a Free Person of Color, to Sell Herself into Perpetual Slavery," Acts of the General Assembly of the State of Geor-

gia, passed in Milledgeville, at an annual session in November and December, 186, pt. 2, Private and Local Laws, Title XV, Slaves and Free Persons of Color, 1861, vol. 1, p. 121, sequential number 129, law number 130, GA.

52. See the 1860 census, Greene, Georgia, roll: M653_125, p. 488, image 38, Family History Library Film 803125.

53. "Slave Inhabitants in the County of Greene, State of Georgia, Enumerated on the 2nd August, 1860," 35. This is the only person named Doherty who appears in the electronic census as owning slaves in the state.

54. PAR 11086003. A man named "C. Bolls" appears in Hinds County as owning nine slaves in 1860. See "Slave Inhabitants in the County of Hinds, State of Mississippi, Enumerated on the 13th September 1860," 246. No more information about either Roseanna or Calvin Bolls could be found.

55. Cited in Philips, *Plantation and Frontier*, 162. None could clearly be traced using census evidence.

56. PAR 21485839 and the 1860 census, District 1, Williamson, Tennessee, roll M653_1279, p. 122, image 250, Family History Library Film 80527.

57. PAR 21585818 and the 1860 census for Mason, Texas, roll M653_1300, p. 486, image 397, Family History Library Film 805300.

58. These were James Fagin and Ned Atkins, whose cases are detailed in chapter 4.

59. On the alleged closeness of the relationships between female slaves and white mistresses, see Catherine Clinton, *The Plantation Mistress: Woman's World in the Old South* (New York: Pantheon, 1982), 187; Marli F. Weiner, *Mistresses and Slaves: Plantation Women in South Carolina, 1830–1880* (Urbana: University of Illinois Press, 1998), 76–80, 93–96; Anne Firor Scott, *The Southern Lady: From Pedestal to Politics, 1830–1930*, 2nd ed.(Charlottesville: University of Virginia Press, 1995), 51. In contrast, Elizabeth Fox-Genovese and Thavolia Glymph highlight the gulf that race created across the color line. See Fox-Genovese, *Within the Plantation Household: Black and White Women of the Old South* (Chapel Hill: University of North Carolina Press, 1988), 338; and Glymph, *Out of the House of Bondage: The Transformation of the Plantation Household* (Cambridge: Cambridge University Press, 2008), 123, where she refers to mistresses as "co-masters."

60. PAR 10185701.

61. For the purpose of tabulation, both Lucy Boomer and Narcissa Daniel have been placed in the "residency" category here.

62. Of course, Lucy Boomer's residency request also involved intimate interracial liaisons, but this did not provide the primary motivation for her petitioning. Her familial ties assumed utmost importance.

63. Petition of Flora Jones, 3 December 1852, to the Virginia General Assembly, Mss2 J7155al, LVA. None of the individuals involved could be found using the census.

64. Detailed in *Charlotte (Va.) Western Democrat*, 11 January 1859. Cited in

Franklin, *Free Negro*, 219. See also Morris, *Southern Slavery and the Law*, 35n92. Ben Schiller has argued Emily Hooper immigrated to Liberia with her father. See "U.S. Slavery's Diaspora," 202–3.

65. See the 1850 census, District 1, Orange, North Carolina, roll M432_639, 163B, image 321. Information on Sally Mallett's ownership of slaves can be found in "Slave Inhabitants in the First District, County of Orange, State of North Carolina, Enumerated on the 16th July 1850" (no page number), and "Slave Inhabitants in the First District, County of Orange, State of North Carolina, Enumerated on the 4th June 1860," 4.

66. See the petition of Ann Barney (no. 13526), 27 October 1859, and reports dated 26 December 1859 and 24 February 1860, Fourth District Court of New Orleans, NOPL. None could be traced via the census.

67. Petition of Mary W. Green, 22 October 1859 (no. 13353), Fourth District Court of New Orleans, NOPL. None could be traced using census evidence.

68. "An Act for the Benefit of Ann Mataw, a Free Woman of Color," approved 11 February 1860, *Laws of the State of Mississippi, Passed at a Regular Session of the Mississippi Legislature Held in the City of Jackson, November 1859* (Jackson: E. Barkdale, State Printer, 1860), 252–53, MDAH.

69. Elizabeth also possessed a ten-year-old boy. See "Slave Inhabitants in the City of Jackson, in the County of Hinds, State of Mississippi, Enumerated on the 15th June 1860," 14. See also the 1860 census, Jackson, Hinds, Mississippi, roll M653–582, p. 517, image 49, Family History Library Film 803582.

70. PAR 20186037.

71. Elizabeth Witter was twenty-five in 1860. See the 1860 census, Lafayette, Chambers, Alabama, roll M653_4, p. 718, image 440, Family History Library Film 803004.

72. Minutes for 17 February 1860, Chambers County Probate Court Minutes, vol. 8, 1859–1861, 261, ADAH.

73. The 1860 census, Southern Division, Chambers, Alabama, roll M653_4, p. 999, image 723, Family History Library Film 803004.

74. See the Minutes for 25 February 1860, Chambers County Probate Court Minutes, vol. 8, 1859–1861, 276; "An Act to Authorize Lewis Wetherspoon, and Cora, Free Negroes, to Become Slaves" (no. 606), approved 10 February 1860, *Session Laws of Alabama*, 159–60, 674–75; and "An Act to Enable Lucy Green, of Coosa County, and Cora, of Chambers County, Free Women of Color, to Become Slaves, and to Repeal the Fifth Section of an Act Approved 10th February 1860," approved 24 February 1860, *Session Laws of Alabama*, 1859–1860, 623–25, ADAH.

75. Minutes for 25 February 1860, Chambers County Probate Court Minutes, vol. 8, 1859–1861, 276, ADAH.

76. Petition of Cora Bellama, 23 February 1861, Minutes of the Probate Court of Russell County, Alabama, reel 14, 1861–1864, 348–49, ADAH.

77. The 1860 census, Southern Division, Chambers, Alabama, roll M653_4,

p. 1000, image 724, Family History Library Film 803004. Unfortunately, J. M. Kennedy could not clearly be traced as a slaveholder.

78. The 1850 census, Talladega, Alabama, roll M432_15, p. 485, image 453.

79. Minutes for 16 February 1860, Chambers County Probate Court Minutes, vol. 8, 1859–1861, 261, ADAH.

80. Minutes for 10 February 1861, Chambers County Probate Court Minutes, vol. 8, 1859–1861, 613–15, ADAH.

81. The 1860 census, Southern Division, Chambers, Alabama, roll M653_4, p. 963, image 687, Family History Library Film 803004. See also the minutes for 9 February 1861, Chambers County Probate Court Minutes, vol. 8, 1859–1861, 615–16, ADAH.

82. Minutes for 29 January 1861, Chambers County Probate Court Minutes, vol. 8, 1859–1861, 615, ADAH.

83. Minutes for 9 February 1861, Chambers County Probate Court Minutes, vol. 8, 1859–1861, 615–18, ADAH.

84. See the minutes for 19 February 1861, Chambers County Probate Court Minutes, vol. 8, 1859–1861, 643–44, and the minutes for 25 February 1861, Chambers County Probate Court Minutes, vol. 8, 1859–1861, 645–52, ADAH.

85. The 1860 census, Southern Division, Chambers, Alabama, roll M653_4, p. 944, image 668, Family History Library Film 803004. See also "Slave Inhabitants in the Southern Division, County of Chambers, State of Alabama, Enumerated on the 27th July 1860," 44.

86. Barbara J. Fields provides an excellent summary of apprenticeship in Maryland in *Slavery and Freedom on the Middle Ground*; see esp. 35. In Delaware, too, many free people of color labored under an apprentice system that seemed to legitimize a category between slave and free. Condemned to perpetual impoverishment, some permitted their children to work for a master or mistress in return for their keep until the ages of eighteen for females and twenty-one for males. For more on the apprentice system in Delaware, see Randy L. Goss, "The 'Art and Mystery' of Delaware's Apprentice Indentures," *Delaware History* 31, no. 4 (Fall–Winter 2006–2007): 251–84.

87. Petition of Mary Brown, 21 September 1852, Baltimore County Register of Wills (Petitions and Orders), MSA SC 4239–18–7, reel 11020, Schweninger Collection, MSA. Unfortunately, neither could be traced via relevant census data.

88. Petition of Eliza Cullison, 29 July 1856, Baltimore County Register of Wills (Petitions and Orders), MSA SC 4239–18–40, reel 11020, Schweninger Collection, MSA. Whether Eliza was able to pay for the costs of the case is unknown.

Conclusion

1. Caroline Lee Hentz, *The Planter's Northern Bride* (Philadelphia: T. B. Peterson and Brothers, 1854), online at http://www.docsouth.unc.edu/southlit/hentz/hentz.html. My thanks to Michael Bibler, who directed me to this source.

2. Michael Tadman disproved this benevolent view of slaveholders in his groundbreaking book, *Speculators and Slaves*.

3. For more on the "habits and rituals" of race, see Fields, *Slavery and Freedom on the Middle Ground*, 206. A concise introduction to the ideology behind the Lost Cause is included in Nina Silber, *The Romance of Reunion: Northerners and the South, 1865–1900* (Chapel Hill: University of North Carolina Press, 1993), especially the introduction.

4. O. Nigel Bolland, "Proto-Proletarians? Slave Wages in the Americas, between Slave Labour and Free Labour," in Turner, *From Chattel Slaves to Wage Slaves*, 143. For more on enslaved workers' attempts to secure subsistence, see Turner's introduction to the same volume and also her chapter "Chattel Slaves into Wage Slaves: A Jamaican Case Study," 28, 33–47.

5. Parish, *Slavery*, 111. See also Peter J. Parish, "The Edges of Slavery in the Old South: Or, Do Exceptions Prove Rules?" *Slavery and Abolition* 4, no. 1 (1983): 106–25.

6. See Camp, *Closer to Freedom*, 95.

7. Ibid., 13; and Wong, *Neither Fugitive nor Free*, 242–43.

8. The historian Jeff Forret has recently argued that relationships (and power relations) between the enslaved and poor whites were often more complex and less hostile than has hitherto been recognized. Free people of color should be added into this analysis as well. See *Race Relations at the Margins*, 3–5

BIBLIOGRAPHY

Primary Sources

General

U.S. Census for 1850, 1860, and 1870, plus slave schedules for 1850 and 1860, all accessed via www.ancestry.com.

Schweninger, Loren, ed. *The Southern Debate over Slavery.* Vol. 1, *Petitions to Southern Legislatures, 1778–1864.* Urbana: University of Illinois Press, 2001.

———. *The Southern Debate over Slavery.* Vol. 2, *Petitions to Southern County Courts, 1775–1867.* Urbana: University of Illinois Press, 2008.

Schweninger, Loren, and Marguerite Ross Howell, eds. *Race, Slavery, and Free Blacks: Petitions to Southern County Courts, 1775–1867.* Part A, *Georgia (1796–1867), Florida (1821–1867), Alabama (1821–1867).* Bethesda, Md.: University Publications of America, 2003.

Schweninger, Loren, Robert Shelton, and Charles Edward Smith, eds. *Race, Slavery, and Free Blacks.* Ser. 1, *Petitions to Southern Legislatures, 1777–1867.* Microfilm edition. Bethesda, Md.: University Publications of America, 1999.

———. *A Guide to the Microfilm Edition of Race, Slavery, and Free Blacks.* Ser. 1, *Petitions to Southern Legislatures, 1777–1867.* Bethesda, Md.: University Publications of America, 1999.

Petitions for Enslavement. Race and Slavery Petitions Project. Digital Library on American Slavery, http://library.uncg.edu/slavery.

Alabama Department of Archives and History, Montgomery (ADAH)

"An Act to Authorize Lewis Wetherspoon, and Cora, Free Negroes, to Become Slaves" (no. 606), approved on 10 February 1860. Session Laws of Alabama, 1859–1860, 674–75.

Minutes for 29 January, 9, 10, 16, 17, 19, and 25 February 1860. Chambers County Probate Court Minutes. Vol. 8, 1859–1861, 613–18, 645–52.

"An Act to Enable Ned Adkins and Other Free Persons of Color Therein Named to Become Slaves," approved 21 February 1860. Session Laws of Alabama, 1859–1860, 599–600.

"An Act Permitting Charles Short and Others to Become Slaves, on Application to the Probate Court of Russell County," approved 23 February 1860. Session Laws of Alabama, 1859–1860, 662.

"An Act to Enable Lucy Green, of Coosa County, and Cora, of Chambers County, Free Women of Color, to Become Slaves, and to Repeal the Fifth Section of an Act, Approved 10 February 1860," approved 24 February 1860. Session Laws of Alabama, 1859–1860, 623–25.

"An act Permitting Free Negroes to Select a Master and Become Slaves," approved 25 February 1860. Session Laws of Alabama, 1859–1860, 63–64.

Petition of Mary Ann Randolph, 5 October 1860. Montgomery County Probate Court Records, 1860, 578.

Petition of James Fagin, 24 December 1860. Minutes of the Probate Court, Book N. Local Government Minutes 50, microfilm reel 13, pp. 14–15. Lowndes County Probate Records.

Petition of John Williams, 1860. Madison County Probate Records, 1860–1862, 109–10.

Petition of Cora Bellama, 23 February 1861. Minutes of the Probate Court of Russell County, Alabama, reel 14, 1861–1864, 348–49.

Minutes for 11 and 25 March 1861. Pike County Probate Judge Minutes, 1858–1862. Microfilm, Local Government Minutes 045. Vol. F, reel 2, pp. 617, 625.

Petitions of Samuel Cobler and associated paperwork. 18 May 1861, 1, 15 June, and 20 August 1861.

Minutes of Pike County Probate Court, 1858–1862. Microfilm, Local Government Minutes 045. Vol. F, reel 2, pp. 644, 651, 657, 672.

Minutes of 2 and 13 June 1863. Chambers County Probate Minutes. Vol. 9, 1861–1864, 463, 473–74.

Arkansas History Commission and State Archives, Little Rock (AHCSA)

"An Act to Prohibit the Emigration and Settlement of Free Negroes or Free Persons of Color, into This State," approved 20 January 1843. *Acts Passed at the Fourth Session of the General Assembly of Arkansas,* 61–64. Little Rock: Eli Colby, 1843.

"An Act to Amend an Act Entitled 'An Act to Prohibit the Emigration and Settlement of Free Negroes or Free Persons of Color into This State, approved 20th January 1843,'" approved 9 January 1845. *Acts, Memorials, and Resolutions Passed at the Fifth Session of the General Assembly of the State of Arkansas,* 99–100. Little Rock: Borland and Farley, 1845.

"An Act to Prevent Slaves and Free Negroes from Being Employed in Retail Groceries or Dram Shops," approved 6 January 1853. *Acts Passed at the Ninth Session of the General Assembly of the State of Arkansas,* 71–72. Arkadelphia: R. L. Pegues, 1853.

"An Act to Prohibit the Emancipation of Slaves" (no. 68), approved 2 February 1859. *Acts Passed at the Twelfth Session of the General Assembly of the State of Arkansas, 1858–1859,* 69. Arkadelphia: R. L. Pegues, 1859.

"An Act to Remove the Free Negroes and Mulattoes from This State" (no. 151), approved 12 February 1859. *Acts Passed at the Twelfth Session of the General Assembly of the State of Arkansas, 1858–1859, 175–78.* Arkadelphia: R. L. Pegues, 1859.

Entry for 17 May 1860. Microfilm Roll Misc. 39. Circuit Court Record Book "Z" (Civil), pp. 1–639, May 1859–July 1863. Pulaski County, Ark., 281.

Minutes for May 1860. Phillips County Circuit Court Records, 388–39, 392–93.

"An Act to Amend the Eighth Section of an Act Approved 12 February 1859 Entitled 'An Act to Remove the Free Negroes and Mulattoes from This State'" (no. 62), approved 3 January 1861. *Acts Passed at the Thirteenth Session of the General Assembly of the State of Arkansas, 1860–1861, 135–36.* Arkadelphia: R. L. Pegues, 1861.

"An Act to Permit Certain Free Negroes and Mulattoes, Still in the State, to Remain until the First Day of January, 1863" (no. 99), approved 10 January 1861. *Acts Passed at the Thirteenth Session of the General Assembly of the State of Arkansas, 1860–61, 206.* Arkadelphia: R. L. Pegues, 1861.

Entry for 6 May 1861. Microfilm Roll Misc. 39. Circuit Court Record Book "Z" (Civil), pp. 1–639, May 1859–July 1863. Pulaski County, Ark., 443–44.

Entry for 13 November 1862. Lafayette County Circuit Court Minutes, 1852–1869. Book 5, p. 111.

Delaware Public Archives, Dover (DPA)

"An Act to Prohibit the Emigration of Free Negroes or Mulattoes into This State and for Other Purposes," passed at Dover, 28 January 1811. Vol. 1, 410–12. *Laws of the State of Delaware on Slavery, Free Blacks, and Mulattos.* Vols. 114, 1700–1874. Comp. Robert C. Barnes and Judith M. Pfeiffer, 8687. Dover: Public Archives, 2002.

"Sheriff's Sale." Sheriff's Office, Newcastle County, Delaware. February 1838, Newcastle County Court of General Sessions. Microfilm RG2805.31, Court Papers, 1833–1838.

"An Act in Relation to Free Negroes and Slaves," passed at Dover, 5 March 1851. Vol. 10, 591–93, *Laws of the State of Delaware on Slavery, Free Blacks, and Mulattoes.* Vols. 1–14, 1700–1874. Comp. Robert C. Barnes and Judith M. Pfeiffer, 136–38. Dover: Public Archives, 2002.

"An Act Concerning the Imprisonment of Free Negroes and Mulattoes for Debt," passed at Dover, 6 March 1861. Vol. 12, 151–53, *Laws of the State of Delaware on Slavery, Free Blacks, and Mulattoes.* Vols. 1–14, 1700–1874. Comp. Robert C. Barnes and Judith M. Pfeiffer, 145–56. Dover: Public Archives, 2002.

"An Act Concerning the Binding out to Service of Free Negroes and Mulattoes," passed on 18 July 1861. Legislative Papers, General Assembly of Delaware (Petitions, Bills, Acts, Resolutions), RG1111.000, Roll 062 (1759–1861).

"An Act in Relation to Free Negroes and Mulattoes," passed at Dover, 18 March 1863. Vol. 12, 330–34, *Laws of the State of Delaware on Slavery, Free Blacks, and Mulattoes,*

Vols. 1–14, 1700–1874. Comp. Robert C. Barnes and Judith M. Pfeiffer, 146. Dover: Public Archives, 2002.

Florida State Archives, Tallahassee (FSA)

"An Act to Prevent the Future Migration of Free Negroes or Mulattoes to This Territory, and for Other Purposes" (no. 32), approved 5 March 1842. *Acts and Resolutions of the Legislative Council of the Territory of Florida, Passed at Its Twentieth Session.* Tallahassee: C. E. Bartlett, 1842.

"An Act to Amend an Act Entitled an Act to Authorize Judges of Probate of the Several Counties in This State to Appoint Guardians for Free Negroes" (no. 20), approved 23 December 1856. *The Acts and Resolutions of the General Assembly of the State of Florida, Passed at Its Eighth Session,* 27. Tallahassee: Office of the Floridian and Journal, James S. Jones, 1857.

"An Act to Prevent Trading with Free Persons of Color in This State" (no. 21), approved 23 December 1856. *The Acts and Resolutions of the General Assembly of the State of Florida, Passed at Its Eighth Session,* 27. Tallahassee: Office of the Floridian and Journal, James S. Jones, 1857.

Other Florida Primary Sources

Petition of Jane "To the Hon. James M. Baker Judge of Said Court." Circuit Court of Florida, Suwannee Circuit, Suwannee County to wit Spring term 1860, minute 1. Petitions to the Current Court of Suwannee, Fla., no. 71, Suwannee County Courthouse.

Interview with Samuel Smalls, conducted by Martin D. Richardson. *WPA Slave Narrative Project.* Vol. 3: *Florida Narratives,* ed. George P. Rawick, 300–302. Westport, Conn.: Greenwood, 1972.

Georgia Archives, Morrow (GA)

"An Act for the Better Regulation of Free Negroes in the Cities of Savannah and Augusta, and in the Towns of Washington and Lexington," approved 7 December 1807. Vol. 1, p. 25, Acts of the General Assembly of the State of Georgia, Passed in Milledgeville, at an Annual Session in November and December, 1807.

"Short Report from the Committee on the State of the Republic," approved 29 December 1845. Vol. 1, p. 209–11. Acts of the State of Georgia, 1845: Resolutions which Originated in the Senate.

"An Act to Levy and Collect a Tax for Each of the Political Years 1852 and 1853, and Thereafter Until Repealed." Vol. 1, p. 288, Acts of the General Assembly of the State of Georgia, Passed in Milledgeville, at a Biennial Session in November, December, and January, 1851–1852. Part 2, Public Laws, Tax. Title XXVII. 1851.

"An Act for the Relief of John Montgomery and William A. Lewis of Forsythe

County; Nancy Going, Adaline Page, Thursday, Isabella de la Fayette, and Elmira, Free Persons of Color, of the County of Columbia, and for Other Purposes Therein Specified," approved 18 February 1854. Vol. 1, p. 533, Acts of
the General Assembly of the State of Georgia, Passed in Milledgeville, at a Biennial Session in November, December, January, and February, 1853–1854.
Part 2, Private and Local Laws, Relief. 1853.

"An Act to Prevent Free Persons of Color, Commonly Known as Free Negroes, from
Being Brought or Coming into the State of Georgia," approved 17 December
1859. Vol. 1, pp. 68–70, Acts of the General Assembly of the State of Georgia, Passed in Milledgeville, at an Annual Session in November and December,
1859. Part 1, Public Laws. Title XXIII. Slaves and Free Persons of Color, 1859,

"An Act to Authorize Elmira Matthews, a Free Person of Color, to Sell Herself
into Perpetual Slavery." Vol. 1, p. 121, Acts of the General Assembly of the
State of Georgia, Passed in Milledgeville, at an Annual Session in November
and December, 1861. Part 2, Private and Local Laws, Title XV. Slaves and Free
Persons of Color. 1861. Number 129, Law number 130.

"An Act to Authorize Jane Miller, a Free Person of Color, to Sell Herself into Perpetual Slavery, 1862" (no. 101), Court Records for Clarke County, Ga., 95.

The Code of the State of Georgia, 1863. Part 2, Title 1, Chap. 1, Art. 3, Of Slaves
and Free Persons of Color. Section 1, Of Slaves (no. 1608), p. 320.

Phillips, Ulrich B. *Georgia Local Archives: Reprinted from the Annual Report of the American
Historical Association for the Year 1904*. Washington, D.C.: GPO, 1905.

Louisiana: New Orleans Public Library (NOPL)

"An Act Relative to Free Persons of Color Coming into the State from Other
States or Foreign Countries," approved 15 March 1859. *Acts Passed at the Fourth
Legislature of the State of Louisiana, at Its Second Session, Held and Begun in the City of Baton
Rouge*, 70–71. Baton Rouge: J. M. Taylor, State Printer, 1859.

"An Act to Permit Free Persons of African Descent to Select Their Masters and
Become Slaves for Life," approved 17 March 1859. *Acts Passed at the Fourth Legislature of the State of Louisiana, at Its Second Session, Held and Begun in the City of Baton Rouge*,
214–15. Baton Rouge: J. M. Taylor, State Printer, 1859.

Petition of Emilia Stone, 7 September 1859 (no. 13245). Records of the Fifth
District Court of New Orleans.

Petition of Mary Walker, Free Woman of Color, 1 October 1859 (no. 13319).
Records of the Fourth District Court of New Orleans.

Petition of William Gray, Free Man of Color, 1 October 1859 (no. 13320). Records of the Fourth District Court of New Orleans.

Petition of Joseph Thomas, Free Man of Color, 3 October 1859 (no. 13318).
Records of the Fourth District Court of New Orleans.

Petition of Mary W. Green, 22 October 1859 (no. 13353). Records of the Fourth
District Court of New Orleans.

Petition of Ann Barney, 27 October 1859, and reports dated 26 December 1859 and 24 February 1860 (no. 13526). Records of the Fourth District Court of New Orleans.

Petition of Elizabeth Jones, 22 December 1859 (no. 13900). Records of the Third District Court of New Orleans.

Petition of Jane Moore, 11 January 1860 (no. 7589). Records of the Sixth District Court of New Orleans.

Petition of Henry Wilson and associated papers, 24 and 30 November 1860 (no. 13390). Records of the Fourth District Court of New Orleans.

Petition of Julia Elliot, 26 November 1861 (no. 15132). Records of the Fourth District Court of New Orleans.

Petition of George Stephens, Free Man of Color, to Become a Slave, 1 February 1862 (no. 16624). Records of the Third District Court of New Orleans.

Maryland State Archives, Annapolis (MSA)

Petition of Mary Brown, 21 September 1852. Baltimore County Register of Wills (Petitions and Orders), MSA SC 4239–18–7, reel 11020. Schweninger Collection.

Petition of Eliza Cullison, 29 July 1856. Baltimore County Register of Wills (Petitions and Orders), MSA SC 4239–18–40, reel 11020. Schweninger Collection.

Other Maryland Primary Sources

Legislation passed on 10 March 1860. Session Laws 1860, Chap. 322, Vol. 0588, pp. 484–85, Laws of Maryland, accessed via the archives of Maryland online: http:aomol.net/000001/0000588/html/am588–484.html

Mississippi Department of Archives and History (MDAH)

"An Act to Reduce into One, the Several Acts Concerning Slaves, Free Negroes, and Mulattoes," approved 18 June 1822. Laws Concerning Slavery and Free People of Color, Mississippi Statutes 1822, microfilm reel 4357, pp. 179–83.

"An Act to Amend the Several Acts of This State in Relation to Free Negroes and Mulattoes," approved 26 February 1842. *Laws of the State of Mississippi Passed at a Regular Biennial Session of the Legislature, Held in the City of Jackson in January and February 1842*, 65–67. Jackson: C. M. Price & G. R. Fall, State Printers, 1842.

"An Act to Empower the Board of Police of Pike County to Remove the Lundy Free Negroes Living in Said County to Liberia," approved 10 February 1854. *Laws of the State of Mississippi, Passed at a Regular Session of the Mississippi Legislature Held in the City of Jackson*, 287–88. Jackson: E. Barksdale, State Printer, 1852.

"An Act of the Relief of William Webster, a Free Man of Color," approved 20 January 1860. *Laws of the State of Mississippi, Passed at a Regular Session of the Mississippi Legislature Held in the City of Jackson, November 1860*, 259–60. Jackson: E. Barksdale, State Printer, 1860.

"An Act for the Relief of Thomas Crenshaw, a Free Man of Color, of Copiah County," approved 1 February 1860. *Laws of the State of Mississippi Passed at a Regular Session of the Mississippi Legislature Held in the City of Jackson, 1860, 287–88.* Jackson: E. Barksdale, State Printer, 1860.

Minutes for 2 February 1860. Probate Court Minutes for Copiah County, Mississippi, 1859–1861. Microfilm reel 8125, pp. 307–10.

"An Act for the Relief of James Wall, a Free Man of Color," and "An Act for the Benefit of Ann Mataw," approved 11 February 1860. *Laws of the State of Mississippi Passed at a Regular Session of the Mississippi Legislature Held in the City of Jackson, 1860,* 252–53. Jackson: E. Barksdale, State Printer, 1860.

North Carolina Office of Archives and History, Raleigh (NCOAH)

"Request of Percy Ann Martin." Legislative Petitions, 1863.

Other North Carolina Primary Sources

"A Bill to Permit Free Persons of Color to Select Their Own Masters and Become Slaves," North Carolina Senate Bill, No 8, Session 1860–1861. Electronic edition: http://docsouth.unc.edu/imls/bi118/bi118.html.

South Carolina Department of Archives and History, Columbia (SCDAH)

"An Act to Restrain the Emancipation of Slaves, and to Prevent Free Persons of Color from Entering into This State; and for Other Purposes," approved 20 December 1820. "An Act for the Better Regulation and Government of Free Negroes and Persons of Color; and for Other Purposes," approved 21 December 1822. Both in *Statutes at Large of South Carolina.* Ed. by David J. McCord. Vol. 7, *Containing the Acts Relating to Charleston Courts, Slaves, and Rivers,* 459–62. Columbia: A. S. Johnson, 1840.

"An Act to Amend an Act more Effectually to Prevent Free Negroes and Other Persons of Color from Entering into This State, and for Other Purposes," passed 19 December 1835, approved 20 December 1856. *Statutes at Large of South Carolina.* Vol. 13. Columbia: Republican Printing Company 1875.

Petition of Charles Lamotte and Associated Approval, 31 January 1859. Ser. S165015, Item 00055, and Ser. S165005, Item 00100, Legislative Petitions.

"Report Rejecting the Petition from Elizabeth Bug, a Free Person of Color, Asking That She and Her Three Small Children Be Made the Slaves of A. B. Dean," 7 December 1859. Ser. S165005, Item 00390, Legislative Petitions.

Petition of Elizabeth Bug, undated [1859] (no. 00054), Legislative Petitions.

Petition of W. P. Hill, undated [1859], Ser. S165016, Item 00054. Legislative Petitions.

Petition of Lucy Andrews, 26 January 1860 (no. 00017). Legislative Petitions.

Petition of William Jackson, Free Boy of Color, Asking Leave to Go into Slavery, 23 November 1861 (no. 00079). Ser. S165005, Item 00079. Legislative Petitions.

Petition of Daniel Freeman to Become a Slave, undated. Ser. S165015, Item 2463. Legislative Petitions.

Petition of Lucy Andrews, undated (no. 02811). Legislative Petitions.

Tennessee Library and State Archives, Nashville (TLSA)

"Petition of Ben, Free Man of Color," 26 May 1858. Hawkins County Chancery Court Minute Books, May 1856–May 1862, 181–82.

"Remarks of Hon. Wm. Ewing of Williamson County, delivered in the House of Representatives, Monday, 5 December 1859, on the Second Reading of the Bill Introduced by the Committee on Free Negroes and Slave Population for the Expulsion of Free Persons of Color from This State." Reported by W. H. Draper. Microfilm no. 600036, pp.1–2.

"Speech of William Ewing, Esq. in the House of Representatives, 9 January 1860, on the Third Reading of the Bill for the Expulsion of Free Negroes from This State." Reported by W. H. Draper. Microfilm no. 600036, pp. 9, 11–12.

Texas: Gammel's *Laws of Texas*

All accessed via http://texinfo.library.unt.edu/lawsoftexas/default.htm.

"An Ordinance and Decree to Prevent the Importation and Emigration of Free Negroes and Mulattoes into Texas," passed 5 January 1836. *The Laws of Texas, 1822–1897.* Vol. 1, 121.

"The Constitution of the Republic of Texas," 17 March 1836. *Laws of the Republic of Texas, 1822–1897.* Vol. 1, 19.

"Joint Resolution for the Relief of Free Persons of Color," approved 5 June 1837. *Laws of the Republic of Texas, 1822–1897.* Vol. 1, 232.

"An Act Concerning Free Persons of Color," approved 5 February 1840. *Laws of the Republic of Texas, 1822–1897.* Vol 2, 151–53.

"An Act for the Relief of Certain Free Persons of Color," approved 12 December 1840. *Laws of the Republic of Texas, 1822–1897.* Vol. 2, 85–86.

"An Act to Permit Free Persons of African Descent to Select Their Own Master and Become Slaves," approved 27 January 1858. General Laws of the Seventh Legislature of the State of Texas. *Laws of the Republic of Texas, 1822–1897.* Vol, 4, 75–77.

Virginia: Library of Virginia, Richmond (LVA)

Petition of Lucinda, 27 March 1813, Legislative Petitions.

Petition of Lucy Boomer to the Legislature of Virginia, 21 December 1833. Sundry Petitions of the County of Lunenberg, Va.

Affidavit of Charleen Winn, 21 January 1834. Sundry Petitions of the County of Lunenberg, Va.

Affidavit of James Winn, 21 January 1834. Sundry Petitions of the County of Lunenberg, Va.

Affidavit of Sophia Winn, 21 January 1834. Sundry Petitions of the County of Lunenberg, Va.

Affidavit of Charlotte Winn, 25 January 1834. Sundry Petitions of the County of Lunenberg, Va.

Affidavit of David Tirrell, 15 December 1834. Sundry Petitions of the County of Lunenberg, Va.

Affidavit of Edward Winn, 29 December 1834. Sundry Petitions of the County of Lunenberg, Va.

Affidavit of Richard May, 28 July 1834. Sundry Petitions of the County of Lunenberg, Va.

Petition of Lucy Boomer to the General Assembly of Virginia, 16 December 1835. Sundry Petitions of the County of Lunenberg, Virginia.

Petition of Lizzie Purdie, circa 28 January 1839. Legislative Petitions.

"An Act Making Appropriations for the Removal of Free Persons of Color, and for Other Purposes." *Acts of the General Assembly of Virginia Passed at the Extra and Regular Sessions, 1849 and 1850*, p. 7. Richmond: William F. Ritchie, 1850.

Petition of Flora Jones, 3 December 1852 to the Virginia General Assembly, Mss2 J7155al. Legislative Petitions.

Petition of Willis and Andrew, circa 1854. Legislative Petitions.

Acts of the Senate of the Commonwealth of Virginia. Richmond: John Worrock, 1855.

"An Act Providing for the Voluntary Enslavement of Lewis Williamson, a Free Person of Color of the County of Southampton," passed on 4 January 1856. *Acts of the General Assembly of Virginia, 1855–1856*, Chap. 434, p. 279. Richmond: John Worrock, printer to the Senate, 1856.

An Act Providing for the Voluntary Enslavement of Free Negroes of the Commonwealth," passed 18 February 1856. *Acts of the General Assembly of Virginia, 1855–1856*, Chap. 46, pp. 7–38. Richmond: John Worrock, printer to the Senate, 1856.

"An Act Providing for the Voluntary Enslavement of Thomas Grayson, a Free Person of Color of the County of Culpeper," passed 31 January 1856. *Acts of the General Assembly of Virginia, 1855–1856*, Chap. 432, p. 278. Richmond: John Worrock, printer to the Senate, 1856.

"An Act Providing for the Voluntary Enslavement of Simon and Martha, his Wife, and Judy and Margaret, Daughters of the Same, Free Persons of Color of the County of Southampton," passed 26 February 1856. *Acts of the General Assembly of Virginia, 1855–1856*, Chap. 433, p. 278. Richmond: John Worrock, printer to the Senate, 1856.

Entry for 15 April 1857. Records of the Circuit Court of Lancaster County, Va.

Entry for 16 September 1857. Records of the Circuit Court of Buckingham County, Va.

Petition of Lewis Wilkinson, 8 October 1857. Records of the Circuit Court of Amelia County, Va.

Entries for December 1857. Records of the Circuit Court of Gloucester County, Va.

Entry for 12 August 1858. Records of the Circuit Court of Prince Edward County, Va.

Petition of Judy Cullins, 25 August 1858. Records of the Powhatan Circuit Court, Va.

Entry for 15 March 1859. Records of the Circuit Court of Prince Edward County, Va.

Entry for 5 August 1859. Records of the Circuit Court of Madison County, Va.

Entry for 16 August 1859. Records of Circuit Court of Prince Edward County, Va.

Petition of Lavinia Napper, 13 September 1859. Records of the Circuit Court of Fauquier County, Va.

Entry for 4 February 1860. Records of the Circuit Court of Pulaski County, Va.

Entry for 13 March 1860. Records of the Circuit Court of Giles County, Va.

Entry for 14 April 1860. Records of the Circuit Court of Rockbridge County, Va.

Petition of Mary Elizabeth, 13 September 1860. Records of the Circuit Court of Rockbridge County, Va.

Petition of Fanny Gillison, 15 September 1860. Records of the Circuit Court of Fauquier County, Va.

Entry for 3 November 1860. Records of the Circuit Court of the City of Richmond, Va.

Register of Free Negroes. Fauquier County, 1817–1865.

Petition of Julius and Lucinda, "To the Honorable Speaker and Members of the House of Delegates of the Commonwealth of Virginia," undated. Legislative Petitions.

Miscellaneous Primary Sources

The Valley of the Shadow project: www.valley.lib.virginia.edu.

Expedition by the Liberia Packet, May 1848. Washington, D.C.: American Colonization Society, C. Alexander, printer, 1848; African Repository and Colonial Journal (1825–1849).

Caroline Lee Hentz, The Planter's Northern Bride (Philadelphia: T. B. Peterson and Brothers, 1854), online at http://www.docsouth.unc.edu/southlit/hentz/hentz.html.

Newspapers

Charleston Mercury
New Orleans Daily Picayune

Secondary Sources

Archard, David. "Freedom Not to Be Free: The Case of the Slavery Contract in J. S. Mill's On Liberty." Philosophical Quarterly 40 (1990): 453–65.

Arneson, Richard J. "Mill versus Paternalism." *Ethics* 90, no. 4 (1980): 470–89.

Atkins, Jonathan M. "Party Politics and the Debate over the Tennessee Free Negro Bill, 1859–1860." *Journal of Southern History* 71, no. 2 (2005): 245–78.

Baptist, Edward E., and Stephanie M. H. Camp, eds. *New Studies in the History of American Slavery.* Athens: University of Georgia Press, 2006.

Bardaglio, Peter. *Reconstructing the Household: Families, Sex, and the Law in the Nineteenth-Century South.* Chapel Hill: University of North Carolina Press, 1995.

Barnett, Randy E. *The Structure of Liberty: Justice and the Rule of Law.* New York: Oxford University Press, 1998.

Berlin, Ira. *Slaves without Masters: The Free Negro in the Antebellum South.* New York: Pantheon, 1974.

———. "Southern Free People of Color in the Age of William Johnson." *Southern Quarterly* 43, no. 2 (2006): 9–17.

Bleser, Carol. ed. *In Joy and in Sorrow: Women, Family, and Marriage in the Victorian South, 1830–1900.* New York: Oxford University Press, 1991.

Block, Sharon, *Rape and Sexual Power in Early America.* Chapel Hill: University of North Carolina Press, 2006.

Bogin, Ruth "Petitioning and the New Moral Economy of Post-Revolutionary America." *William and Mary Quarterly* 45, no. 3 (July 1988): 392–425.

Boles, John. *Black Southerners, 1619–1869.* Lexington: University Press of Kentucky, 1983.

Brown, David. "Poor Whites, Herrenvolk Democracy, and the Value of Whiteness in the Old South." Unpublished conference paper presented at Institute for Historical Research Seminar Series in American History, March 2010.

Brownmiller, Susan. *Against Our Will: Men, Women, and Rape.* Harmondsworth: Penguin, 1975.

Camp, Stephanie M. H. *Closer to Freedom: Enslaved Women and Everyday Resistance in the Plantation South.* Chapel Hill: University of North Carolina Press, 2004.

Clinton, Catherine. *The Plantation Mistress: Woman's World in the Old South.* New York: Pantheon, 1982.

Cooper, Frederick, Thomas C. Holt, and Rebecca J. Scott. *Beyond Slavery: Explorations of Race, Labor, and Citizenship in Postemancipation Societies.* Chapel Hill: University of North Carolina Press, 2000.

Cowling, Camellia, "Defining Freedom: Women of Color and the Ending of Slavery in Havana and Rio de Janeiro, 1870–1888." Unpublished conference paper presented at the International Federation for Research in Women's History conference in Amsterdam, August 2010.

———. "Negotiating Freedom: Women of Colour and the Transition to Free Labour in Cuba, 1870–1886." *Slavery and Abolition* 26, no. 3 (December 2005): 377–91.

Craton, Michael. "Shuffling the Pack: The Transition from Slavery to Other Forms of Labor in the British Caribbean, ca. 1790–1890." *New West Indian Guide* 68, no. 12 (1994): 23–75.

Dangerfield, David. "Plain Folk of Color: Rural Free People of Color on the Antebellum Charleston District." MA thesis, Graduate School of the College of Charleston and the Citadel, 2009.

Davies, Angela. "Reflections on the Black Woman's Role in the Community of Slaves." *Black Scholar* 3, no. 4 (1971): 2–15.

Davis, David Brion. *Challenging the Boundaries of Slavery.* Cambridge, Mass.: Harvard University Press, 2003.

———. *Inhuman Bondage: The Rise and Fall of Slavery in the New World.* New York: Oxford University Press, 2006.

———. "Looking at Slavery from Broader Perspectives." *American Historical Review* 105, no. 2 (April 2000): 452–66.

Degler, Carl N. *Neither Black nor White: Slavery and Race Relations in Brazil and the United States.* New York: Macmillan, 1971.

D'Emilio, John, and Estelle B. Freedman. *Intimate Matters: A History of Sexuality in America.* Chicago: University of Chicago Press, 1997.

Deyle, Steven. *Carry Me Back: The Domestic Slave Trade in American Life.* Oxford: Oxford University Press, 2005.

Dunaway, Wilma. *The African-American Family in Slavery and Emancipation.* Cambridge: Cambridge University Press, 2003.

Dusinberre, William. *Strategies for Survival: Recollections of Bondage in Antebellum Virginia.* Charlottesville: University of Virginia Press, 2009.

———. *Them Dark Days: Slavery in the American Rice Swamps.* New York: Oxford University Press, 1996.

Edgar, Walter. *South Carolina, A History.* Columbia: University of South Carolina Press, 1998.

Edwards, Laura. "Enslaved Women and the Law: Paradoxes of Subordination in the Post-Revolutionary Carolinas." *Slavery and Abolition* 26, no. 2 (August 2005): 305–23.

———. "Law, Domestic Violence, and the Limits of Patriarchal Authority in the Antebellum South." *Journal of Southern History* 65, no. 4 (November 1999): 733–70.

———. *The People and Their Peace: Legal Culture and the Transformation of Inequality in the Post-Revolutionary South.* Chapel Hill: University of North Carolina Press, 2009.

Egerton, Douglas. *He Shall Go Free: The Lives of Denmark Vesey.* Madison, Wisc.: Madison House, 1999.

Eisenberg, Jose. "Cultural Encounters, Theoretical Adventures: The Jesuit Missions to the New World and the Justification of Voluntary Slavery." *History of Political Thought* 24, no. 3 (2003): 375–96.

Engerman, Stanley. "Slavery, Freedom, and Sen." *Feminist Economics* 9 (2003): 185–211.

———. "Some Considerations Relating to Property Rights in Man." *Journal of Economic History* 33, no. 1 (1973): 43–65.

England, J. Merton. "The Free Negro in Ante-Bellum Tennessee." *Journal of Southern History* 9, no. 1 (1943): 37–58.

Faust, Drew Gilpin. *The Ideology of Slavery: Proslavery Thought in the Antebellum South, 1830–1860.* Baton Rouge: Louisiana State University Press, 1981.

Fenoaltea, Stefano. "Slavery and Supervision in Comparative Perspective: A Model." *Journal of Economic History* 44, no. 3 (1984): 635–68.

Fields, Barbara J. *Slavery and Freedom on the Middle Ground: Maryland during the Nineteenth Century.* New Haven: Yale University Press, 1985.

———. "Slavery, Race, and Ideology in the United States of America." *New Left Review* 181 (May–June 1990): 95–118.

Finkelman, Paul, ed. *Slavery and the Law.* Madison, Wisc.: Madison House, 1997.

Flanders, Ralph B. "The Free Negro in Ante-Bellum Georgia." *North Carolina Historical Review* 9 (July 1932): 250–72.

Forret, Jeff. *Race Relations at the Margins: Slaves and Poor Whites in the Antebellum Southern Countryside.* Baton Rouge: Louisiana State University Press, 2006.

Fox-Genovese, Elizabeth. "Between Individualism and Fragmentation: American Culture and the New Literary Studies of Race and Gender." *American Quarterly* 42, no. 1 (1990): 7–34.

———. *Within the Plantation Household: Black and White Women of the Old South.* Chapel Hill: University of North Carolina Press, 1988.

Fox-Genovese, Elizabeth, and Eugene Genovese. *The Mind of the Master Class: History and Faith in the Southern Slaveholders' Worldview.* New York: Cambridge University Press, 2005.

Franklin, John Hope. "The Enslavement of Free Negroes in North Carolina." *Journal of Negro History* 29, no. 4 (1944): 401–28.

———. *The Free Negro in North Carolina, 1790–1860.* 3rd ed. Chapel Hill: University of North Carolina Press, 1995.

Franklin, John Hope, and Loren Schweninger. *In Search of the Promised Land: A Slave Family in the Old South.* New York: Oxford University Press, 2006.

Fraser, Rebecca. *Courtship and Love among the Enslaved in North Carolina.* Jackson: University Press of Mississippi, 2007.

Furstenberg, François. "Beyond Freedom and Slavery: Autonomy, Virtue, and Resistance in Early American Political Discourse." *Journal of American History* 89, no. 4 (March 2003): 1279–94.

———. *In the Name of the Father: Washington's Legacy, Slavery, and the Making of a Nation.* New York: Penguin, 2006.

Gaspar, David Barry, and Darlene Clark Hine, eds. *Beyond Bondage: Free Women of Color in the Americas.* Urbana: University of Illinois Press 2004.

———. *More than Chattel: Black Women and Slavery in the Americas.* Bloomington: Indiana University Press, 1996.

Gibson, A. E. M. "Slavery in Western Africa." *Journal of the Royal African Society* 3, no. 9 (1903): 17–52.

Glenn, Evelyn Nakano. *Unequal Freedom: How Race and Gender Shaped American Citizenship and Labor.* Cambridge, Mass.: Harvard University Press, 2002.

Glenn, Gary D. "Inalienable Rights and Locke's Argument for Limited Government: Political Implications of a Right to Suicide." *Journal of Politics* 46, no. 1 (1984): 80–105.

Glymph, Thavolia. *Out of the House of Bondage: The Transformation of the Plantation Household.* Cambridge: Cambridge University Press, 2008.

Goss, Randy L. "The 'Art and Mystery' of Delaware's Apprentice Indentures." *Delaware History* 31, no. 4 (Fall–Winter 2006–2007): 251–84.

Gould, Virginia Meacham, ed. *Chained to the Rock of Adversity: To Be Free, Black, and Female in the Old South.* Athens: University of Georgia Press, 1998.

Gray, Lewis Cecil. *A History of Agriculture in the Southern United States to 1860.* Vol. 1. Washington, D.C.: Carnegie Institution of Washington, 1933.

Gross, Ariela J. "Beyond Black and White: Cultural Approaches to Race and Slavery." *Columbia Law Review* 101, no. 3 (April 2001): 640–90.

———. *Double Character: Slavery and Mastery in the Antebellum Southern Courtroom.* Athens: University of Georgia Press, 2006.

Guild, June Purcell. *Black Laws of Virginia: A Summary of the Legislative Acts of Virginia Concerning Negroes from the Earliest Times to the Present.* Richmond, Va.: Whittet and Shepperson, 1936.

Haggis, Jane, and Margaret Allen. "Imperial Emotions: Affective Communities of Mission in British Protestant Women's Missionary Publications, c. 1880–1920." *Journal of Social History* 41, no. 3 (Spring 2008): 691–716.

Harris, Trudier. "'The Yellow Rose of Texas': A Different Cultural View." *Callaloo* 20, no. 1 (Winter 1997): 8–19.

Heinnegg, Paul. *Free African Americans of North Carolina and Virginia.* 3rd ed. Baltimore: Genealogical Publishing, 1997.

Hellie, Richard. "Recent Soviet Historiography on Medieval and Early Modern Russian Slavery." *Russian Review* 35, no. 1 (1976): 1–32.

Higgins, Billy D. "The Origins and Fate of the Marion County Free Black Community." *Arkansas Historical Quarterly* 54 (Winter 1995): 427–43.

Hine, Darlene Clark. "Rape and the Inner Lives of Black Women in the Middle West: Preliminary Thoughts on the Culture of Dissemblance." *Signs* 14 (Summer 1989): 912–20.

Hinks, Peter P. *To Awaken My Afflicted Brethren: David Walker and the Problem of Antebellum Slave Resistance.* University Park: Pennsylvania State University Press, 1997.

Hodes, Martha. "The Mercurial Nature and Abiding Power of Race: A Transnational Family Story." *American Historical Review* 108, no. 1 (February 2003): 84–118.

Hudson, Larry E., Jr., ed. *Working toward Freedom: Slave Society and Domestic Economy in the American South.* Rochester, N.Y.: University of Rochester Press, 1994.

Hurd, John Codman. *The Law of Freedom and Bondage in the United States.* Vol. 2. Boston: Little, Brown & Co., 1858–1862.

Jalloh, Alusine, and Toyin Falola, eds. *The United States and West Africa: Interactions and Relations*. Rochester, N.Y.: University of Rochester Press, 2008.

Jennison, Watson. "'The Privileges of Citizens': The Boundaries of Race in Early National Georgia." Unpublished conference paper presented at the American Historical Association's annual conference, January 2005.

Johnson, Michael P., and James L. Roark. *Black Masters: A Free Family of Color in the Old South*. New York: Norton, 1984.

———, eds. *No Chariot Let Down: Charleston's Free People of Color on the Eve of the Civil War*. New York: Norton, 1984.

Johnson, Walter. "On Agency." *Journal of Social History* 37, no. 1 (Fall 2003): 113–24.

Jones, Catherine. "Ties That Bind, Bonds That Break: Children in the Reorganization of Households in Postemancipation Virginia." *Journal of Southern History* 76, no. 1 (2010): 71–106.

Kafka, Franz. *The Trial*. Trans. Willa Muir and Edwin Muir. 1925. Repr., New York: Schocken, 1984.

Kennedy, Cynthia M. *Braided Relations, Entwined Lives: The Women of Charleston's Urban Slave Society*. Bloomington: Indiana University Press, 2005.

Kimball, Gregg D. *American City, Southern Place: A Cultural History of Antebellum Richmond*. Athens: University of Georgia Press, 2000.

Kleinig, John. "John Stuart Mill and Voluntary Slavery Contracts." *Politics* 18, no. 2 (1983): 76–83.

Koger, Larry. "Black Masters: The Misunderstood Slaveowners." *Southern Quarterly* 43, no. 2 (2006): 52–73.

———. *Black Slaveowners: Free Black Masters in South Carolina, 1790–1860*. London: McFarland, 1985.

Kolchin, Peter. *American Slavery, 1619–1877*. New York: Penguin, 1993.

Kousser, J. Morgan, and James M. McPherson, eds. *Region, Race, and Reconstruction: Essays in Honor of C. Vann Woodward*. New York: Oxford University Press, 1982.

Landers, Jane G., ed. *Against the Odds: Free Blacks in the Slave Societies of the Americas*. London: Frank Cass, 1996.

Lebsock, Susanne. *The Free Women of Petersburg: Status and Culture in a Southern Town, 1784–1860*. New York: Norton, 1984.

Link, William A. *Roots of Secession: Slavery and Politics in Antebellum Virginia*. Chapel Hill: University of North Carolina Press, 2003.

Marr, Ruth B., and Modeste Hargis. "The Voluntary Exile of Free Negroes of Pensacola." *Florida Historical Quarterly* 17, no. 1 (July 1938): 4–20.

Martin, Jonathan D. *Divided Mastery: Slave Hiring in the American South*. Cambridge, Mass.: Harvard University Press 2004.

Mill, John Stuart. *On Liberty*. Ed. Gertrude Himmelfarb. 1859. Repr., Harmondsworth: Penguin, 1974.

Miller, Randall M., and John David Smith, eds. *Dictionary of Afro-American Slavery*. London: Praeger, 1997.

Moore, Wilbert E. "Slave Law and the Social Structure." *Journal of Negro History* 26, no. 2 (1941): 171–202.

Morgan, Edmund S. *Inventing the People: The Rise of Popular Sovereignty in England and America.* New York: Norton, 1988.

———. "Slavery and Freedom: The American Paradox." *Journal of American History* 59, no. 1 (1972): 5–29.

Morris, Thomas D. *Southern Slavery and the Law, 1619–1860.* Chapel Hill: University of North Carolina Press, 1996.

Muir, Andrew Forest. "The Free Negro in Harris County, Texas." *Southwestern Historical Quarterly* 46, no. 3 (January 1943): 214–37.

O'Donovan, Susan Eva. *Becoming Free in the Cotton South.* Cambridge, Mass.: Harvard University Press, 2007.

Okihiro, Gary Y., ed. *In Resistance: Studies in African, Caribbean, and Afro-American History.* Amherst: University of Massachusetts Press, 1986.

Parish, Peter J. "The Edges of Slavery in the Old South: Or, Do Exceptions Prove Rules?" *Slavery and Abolition* 4, no. 1 (1983): 106–25.

———. *Slavery: History and Historians.* New York: Harper & Row, 1989.

Patterson, Orlando. *Rituals of Blood: Consequences of Slavery in Two American Centuries.* New York: Basic Civitas, 1998.

Patton, James W. "The Progress of Emancipation in Tennessee, 1796–1860." *Journal of Negro History* 17, no. 1 (1932): 67–102.

Penningroth, Dylan. *The Claims of Kinfolk: African American Property and Community in the Nineteenth-Century South.* Chapel Hill: University of North Carolina Press, 2003.

Phillips, U. B., ed. *Plantation and Frontier, 1649–1863.* Vol. 2. New York: Burt Franklin, 1910.

Reddy, William M. *The Navigation of Feeling: A Framework for the History of Emotions.* Cambridge: Cambridge University Press, 2001.

Reinders, Robert C. "The Decline of the New Orleans Free Negro in the Decade before the Civil War." *Journal of Mississippi History* 24 (1962): 8–98.

Rogers, W. McDowell. "Free Negro Legislation in Georgia before 1865." *Georgia Historical Quarterly* 17 (March 1932): 27–37.

Root, Erik S. *All Honor to Jefferson? The Virginia Slavery Debates and the Positive Good Thesis.* Lanham, Md.: Lexington, 2008.

Ross, Margaret. "Mulattoes, Free Negroes Ordered to Leave Arkansas on Eve of War." *Little Rock Arkansas Gazette,* 15 February 1959, 3E.

Russell, John H. *The Free Negro in Virginia, 1619–1865.* New York: Dover, 1969.

Schafer, Judith Kelleher. *Becoming Free, Remaining Free: Manumission and Enslavement in New Orleans, 1846–1862.* Baton Rouge: Louisiana State University Press, 2003.

Schiller, Ben. "Selling Themselves: Slavery Survival and the Path of Least Resistance." *49th Parallel* 23 (Summer 2009): 1–23.

———. "U.S. Slavery's Diaspora: Black Atlantic History at the Crossroads of 'Race,' Enslavement, and Colonisation." *Slavery and Abolition* 32, no. 2 (June 2011): 199–212.

Schoen, Harold. "The Free Negro in the Republic of Texas, I." *Southwestern Historical Quarterly* 39, no. 4 (April 1936): 292–308.

———. "The Free Negro in the Republic of Texas, II." *Southwestern Historical Quarterly* 40, no. 1 (July 1936): 26–34.

———. "The Free Negro in the Republic of Texas, III." *Southwestern Historical Quarterly* 40, no. 2 (October 1936): 85–113.

———. "The Free Negro in the Republic of Texas, IV." *Southwestern Historical Quarterly* 40, no. 3 (January 1937): 169–99.

———. "The Free Negro in the Republic of Texas, V." *Southwestern Historical Quarterly* 40, no. 4 (April 1937): 267–89.

Schweninger, Loren. *Black Property Owners in the South, 1790–1815*. Urbana: University of Illinois Press, 1990.

———. "Slavery and Southern Violence: County Court Petitions and the South's Peculiar Institution." *Journal of Negro History* 85, no. 12 (2000): 33–35.

Scott, Anne Firor. *The Southern Lady: From Pedestal to Politics, 1830–1930*, 2nd ed. Charlottesville: University of Virginia Press, 1995.

Scott, Rebecca J. *Degrees of Freedom: Louisiana and Cuba after Slavery*. Cambridge, Mass.: Belknap Press of Harvard University Press, 2005.

———. "Exploring the Meaning of Freedom: Postemancipation Societies in Comparative Perspective." *Hispanic American Historical Review* 68, no. 3 (August 1988): 407–28.

Sellers, James Benson. *Slavery in Alabama*. Tuscaloosa: University of Alabama Press, 1950.

Shick, Tom W. *Behold the Promised Land: A History of Afro-American Settler Society in Nineteenth-Century Liberia*. 2nd ed. Baltimore: Johns Hopkins University Press, 1980.

Silber, Nina. *The Romance of Reunion: Northerners and the South, 1865–1900*. Chapel Hill: University of North Carolina Press, 1993.

Smith, Mark M. *Debating Slavery: Economy and Society in the Antebellum American South*. Cambridge: Cambridge University Press, 1998.

Sommerville, Diane Miller. *Race and Rape in the Nineteenth Century South*. Chapel Hill: University of North Carolina Press, 2004.

Spruill, Marjorie J., Valinda W. Littlefield, and Joan M. Johnson, eds. *South Carolina Women*. Vol. 1, *Their Life and Times*. Athens: University of Georgia Press, 2009.

Stahl, Annie Lee West. "The Free Negro in Ante-Bellum Louisiana." *Louisiana Historical Quarterly* 25 (April 1942): 3.

Sterkx, H. E. *The Free Negro in Ante-Bellum Louisiana*. Rutherford, N.J.: Fairleigh Dickinson University Press, 1972.

Stoler, Ann. "Tense and Tender Ties: The Politics of Comparison in North American History and (Post)Colonial Studies." *Journal of American History* 88, no. 3 (December 2001): 829–65.

Suggs, Jon-Christian. *Whispered Consolations: Law and Narrative in African American Life*. Ann Arbor: University of Michigan Press, 2000.

Tadman, Michael. *Speculators and Slaves: Masters, Traders, and Slaves in the Old South.* 2nd ed. Madison: University of Wisconsin Press, 1996.

Takaki, Ronald. *Strangers from a Different Shore: A History of Asian Americans.* New York: Little, Brown, 1998.

Thompson, Alvin O. *Flight to Freedom: African Runaways and Maroons in the Americas.* Kingston, Jamaica: University of the West Indies Press, 2006.

Turner, Mary, ed. *From Chattel Slaves to Wage Slaves: The Dynamics of Labour Bargaining in the Americas.* London: James Currey, 1995.

Tyler-McGraw, Marie. *An African Republic: Black and White Virginians in the Making of Liberia.* Chapel Hill: University of North Carolina Press, 2007.

Wallenstein, Peter. *Tell the Court I Love My Wife: Race, Marriage, and Law—An American History.* London: Palgrave Macmillan, 2002.

Watkinson, James D. "'Fit Objects of Charity': Community, Race, Faith, and Welfare in Antebellum Lancaster County, Virginia, 1817–1860." *Journal of the Early Republic* 21, no. 1 (Spring 2001): 41–70.

Weiner, Marli F. *Mistresses and Slaves: Plantation Women in South Carolina, 1830–1880.* Urbana: University of Illinois Press, 1998.

West, Emily. *Chains of Love: Slave Couples in Antebellum South Carolina.* Urbana: University of Illinois Press, 2004.

———. "'She Is Dissatisfied with Her Present Condition': Requests for Voluntary Enslavement in the Antebellum American South." *Slavery and Abolition* 28, no. 3 (December 2007): 329–50.

Wikramanayake, Marina. *A World in Shadow: The Free Black in Antebellum South Carolina.* Columbia: University of South Carolina Press, 1973.

Wiley, Bell I., ed. *Slaves No More: Letters from Liberia, 1833–1869.* Lexington: University Press of Kentucky, 1980.

Winegarten, Ruthe. *Black Texas Women: 150 Years of Trial and Triumph.* Austin: University of Texas Press, 1995.

Wong, Edlie L. *Neither Fugitive nor Free: Atlantic Slavery, Freedom Suits, and the Legal Culture of Travel.* New York: New York University Press, 2009.

INDEX

Abingdon Democrat, 140
Adams, Henderson, 117, 193n80
Adams, Lucien, 137
Adams, Recorder, 138
Adams, William W., 110–11
Adkins, Cealy, 105
Adkins, Ned, 105
African American history: argument for multiple sources/approaches, 12; as nonlinear narrative, 11–12
African colonization. *See* colonization movement
"agency," 8–9
Alabama: enslavement and expulsion laws in the 1850s, 35–36; enslavement petitions, 86–87, 88, 105–9, 138–39, 145–50; residency requests, 57, 62, 142; voluntary slavery legislation, 39
Alderman, Sidney S., 80
Allen, Bob, 162n6
Allen, William C., 148, 149
American Colonization Society, 6, 66
Andrews, Lucy, 93–95, 118
Appeal (Walker), 25
apprentice system, 150, 201n86
Archie, Ann, 133–34
Arkansas: enslavement petitions, 50, 111–12; expulsion of free people of color, 47, 48–50; forced enslavement in, 83, 109–11;

restrictive legislation before the 1850s, 27–28
Atkins, Jonathan M., 177n94

Ball, Atheral, 116
Barland, Esther, 16, 57
Barney, Ann, 144–45
Barrett, John B., 148, 149–50
Barrett, Oliver S., 148, 149
Barrett, William, 81
Bass, William, 97, 120, 194n91
Baxter, John M., 56
Beason, Peter, 100–101
Becoming Free, Remaining Free (Schafer), 3, 137
Bellenger/Belanny, Alick, 148–49
Bellenger/Belanny, Cora, 145–48
Bellenger/Belanny, Henry, 148–49
Bellenger/Belanny, Lavinia, 148–49
Bellenger/Belanny, Prince, 148
Bellenger/Belanny family, 145–50
"belonging": as a choice in voluntary enslavement, 8, 9, 10; importance to free people of color, 6; residency requests and, 53–54, 57, 70, 74
Berlin, Ira, 2, 4, 16, 161n5, 171n16
Bettingall, Margaret, 132, 196n19
Bickley, Elizabeth, 140
Bird, Joe, 115
Birdie, Justine, 56

black women: sexual exploitation by white men, 22, 129, 130, 131–32. *See also* enslaved women; free black women; single free black women

Blake, William, 57

Block, Sharon, 12

Bogin, Ruth, 9–10

Bolland, O. Nigel, 154

Bolls, Calvin, 140

bondage: defined in enslavement petitions, 75. *See also* enslavement

Booker, James, 91

Boomer, Lucy, 16, 123–29, 130, 142, 199n62

Bowen, John D., 134

Bowen, William A., 136, 137

Bowser, David, 56

Bradford, C. M., 81–82

Bradshaw, Willis, 102–3

Bridgers, D. H., 80

Bright, Florida, 88

Brock, Mary, 110–11

Brockman, George, 150

Brooks, Jesse, 81

Brown, James, 125, 127

Brown, John, 25

Brown, Martha, 91

Brown, Mary, 150

Brown, William, 55

Bug, Elizabeth Jane, 118–19, 169n58, 193n85

Bumpass, Green L., 78, 162n8

Burleson, Aaron, 197n28

Butler, James, 64–65

Cain, Nancy, 101

Caldwell, Andrew H., 133–34

Caldwell, Ann, 63–64

Cameron, Margaret, 63

Camp, Stephanie, 12

Carter, Edward, 60

Carter, Emanuel, 59–60

Cartwright, Samuel, 24

Cash, Howard, 74

Chapman, Jeptha and Thadeus, 91

Charleston (SC), 42

Charleston Mercury, 42

Chavers, Elizabeth, 133

Chavis, Cynthia, 136

Cheatham, Sarah, 140–41

Chevis, A. L., 62

Claibourne, Lucy, 72–73

Clark, John, 135

Clifton, John, 78, 162n8

Cobler, Samuel, 107–8

Coleman, Sidney J., 36

Collier family, 101

colonization movement, 66–71, 181n41

Cooper, Frederick, 6

court costs, 80–81, 82, 83

Cozzens, Walter L., 88, 185n36

Craig, James T., 115

Crawford, Daniel, 139

Crenshaw, Thomas, 83–84

Crosswell, William, 106

Cullins, John, 136

Cullins, Judy, 136

Cullison, Eliza and Frances, 150–51

Currie, Armistead, 103

Dabney, A., 61

Dabney, Julius and Lucinda, 53–54, 66

Daily Delta, 78

Dangerfield, David, 120

Daniel, Alen, 142

Daniel, Narcissa, 16, 142

Davis, Elizabeth, 108

Davis, George, 108

Davis, Presley, 107

Davis, Samuel, 107

Davis, Susan, 108–9

Davis, W. F., 108

Deam, Robert, 109–10, 111

Dean, A. B., 118–19

Delaware: apprentice system in, 201n86; enslavement petitions, 80–81; indenture cases, 55; restrictive legislation before the 1850s, 28; restrictive legislation in the 1850s, 47

Denmark Vesey conspiracy, 25, 172–73n35, 187n11

Dennis, Thomas, 81

Dickens, Ann Johnson, 144–45

Dickens, Samuel B., 144

Dickinson, Julia, 117

Dodd, Mark, 111–12

Dodds, Hannah, 77–78

Dodds, James, 77–78

Doherty, Charlotte, 140

Doherty, John J., 139–40

Doswell, David, 101

Doswell, Willis and Andrew, 101–2

Douglass, Thomas, 106

Dred Scott v. Sanford, 25

Dunaway, George, 177n106

Duncan, Henry H., 94

Earhart, Agnes, 63, 64

Earhart, John Jefferson, 78

Easley, Charles, 146

"economic" motherhood, 132–33

economic motivations: in the framing of residency requests by white southerners, 57–58, 59–60, 61, 62–63, 64, 74; for voluntary enslavement, 5, 80–81

Edwards, Laura, 4

Edwards, Young, 86–87, 88

Elizabeth, Mary, 136

Elliot, Julia, 82–83, 184n25

Ellis, James W., 90, 91

emancipation laws: in Arkansas, 48; in Louisiana, 38; in Maryland, 40; in Mississippi, 29, 31; in South Carolina, 31

enforced enslavement: in Arkansas, 83, 109–11; in Georgia, 37–38; in Mississippi, 30–31; in South Carolina, 31; in Texas, 32; in Virginia, 34, 177n106. See also enslavement and expulsion laws

enslaved couples: motivation for enslavement petitions and voluntary enslavement, 88, 95, 96, 97, 98–99; paradoxes of slavery in the antebellum South, 10. See also spousal relationships

enslaved women: Laura Edwards on, 3–4; interracial liaisons and, 22; monetary value of, 91; paradoxes of slavery in the antebellum South, 10; restrictive legislation in Mississippi, 29. See also black women; free black women; single free black women

enslavement: cases of blacks between freedom and enslavement, 71–74; proslavery views of, 22, 23, 24; "traditional" motivations for, 80–84. See also enforced enslavement; slavery; voluntary enslavement

enslavement and expulsion laws: proslavery ideology and the rise of, 22–26; question of effective implementation, 51; request for exemption from in Mississippi, 169n58; in the 1850s, 35–51

enslavement petitions: "agency" and, 8–9; ages of petitioners, 16–17; analysis of, 13–19; from Arkansas, 50; authorship, 18–19; the choice to "belong" and, 8, 9, 10; context of southern oppression of blacks, 7; decades with the greatest

enslavement petitions (*cont.*)
number of, 17, 23; discussion of
the discourses within, 122; effect
of white family ties on, 142–43;
emotional ties across the slave-free
divide and, 93–97; of entire free
black families, 86–87, 88, 102–3,
116, 117–18; expression of free
black initiative and, 3, 4, 5–6,
8–9, 79, 154, 156; family ties and
(*see* family ties and enslavement
petitions); financial transactions
and, 90–92, 113–14; framed in
terms of petitioner's ill health,
81–82; framed to escape legal
difficulties, 82–84; framing in
terms of proslavery ideology, 75;
gender differences, 15; historical
significance of, 154–55, 156;
historiographical context, 2–4;
invoking a guardianship system,
150; involving interracial intimate
relationships, 127–29 (*see also*
interracial intimate relationships);
involving white southern women,
141–52; Liberian emigrants
and, 96, 101, 143–44, 169n58;
motivations for (*see* motivations
for enslavement petitions and
voluntary enslavement); notions
of the right to movement
and, 9, 156; outcomes, 16;
parallels to residency requests,
74; as proslavery propaganda,
77–80; reasons historians are
uncomfortable about using,
154; requests by free black men
for enslavement to women,
105–6; socioeconomic profiles
of potential slave owners, 84–90;
southern legal context and, 4,
18; ties between black and white
households, 145–50; trickery
and cajolery of white southerners
in, 8, 10, 87, 155–56; unease of
white southerners with, 79, 83
Ewing, William, 42, 43
expulsion: in Arkansas, 47, 48–50;
attempted in Florida and Missouri,
48; "traditional" explanations, 76.
See also enslavement and expulsion
laws
Expulsion Act of 1859 (AR), 48–49

Fagin, Caroline, 106
Fagin, James, 106, 107
family: importance to free people
of color, 6, 11; motivation for
residency requests and, 57, 58,
61, 64–65, 70, 74; "stranded"
families, 6; ties between black
and white households, 145–50;
white family ties and enslavement
petitions, 142–43. *See also* free
black families; kinship
family ties and enslavement petitions:
cases in Alabama, 105–9; cases in
Arkansas, 109–12; cases in Florida,
112–13; cases in Georgia, 113–14;
cases in Mississippi, 114–16; cases
in North Carolina, 116–18; cases
in South Carolina, 93–95, 118–20;
cases in Tennessee, 120–21; cases
in Texas, 121–22; cases in Virginia,
97–105; enslavement petitions
of entire families, 86–87, 88,
102–3, 116, 117–18; family ties
as motivation for enslavement
petitions, 2, 3, 5–6, 8, 10–11, 74,
95–97, 155; Liberian emigrants
and, 96
Faust, Drew Gilpin, 170n8, 173n35
Featherston, C. A., 117, 169n58
Ferguson, Daniel, 55

Filmore, Billard, 81
Fitch, Walker, 104–5
Fitzhugh, George, 24, 170n8
Florence, John E., 89, 90
Florida: attempt to expel free people
   of color from, 48; enslavement
   and expulsion laws in the 1850s,
   36, 43–44; enslavement petitions,
   80, 88, 112–13; restrictive
   legislation before the 1850s,
   28; socioeconomic profiles of
   potential slave owners, 88
Fort, Lewis B., 112
Frank, James P., 83
Franklin, John Hope, 2, 18, 77,
   161–62n5
free black children: de facto slavery
   and, 68, 69–70; enslavement
   legislation in Alabama, 39–40;
   enslavement legislation in Florida,
   43; enslavement legislation in
   Louisiana, 39–40; enslavement
   legislation in Texas, 43, 44–45;
   enslavement legislation in Virginia,
   45–46; enslavement petitions
   in South Carolina, 118–19;
   enslavement petitions of single
   free black women and, 131–34;
   family formations and, 68–70
free black families: enslavement
   petitions, 86–87, 88, 102–3,
   116, 117–18; family formations,
   68–70; residency requests, 100;
   women as heads of households,
   131. See also family; kinship
free black men: family ties and
   voluntary enslavement, 11;
   gender profile of enslavement
   and residency requests, 15;
   implications of voluntary
   enslavement, 13; requests for
   enslavement to women, 105–6

free black orphans: enslavement
   legislation in Texas, 44–45
free black women: coercion by
   white men into voluntary
   enslavement, 155–56;
   "economic" motherhood,
   132–33; expulsion or enslavement
   related to interracial intimate
   relationships, 123–33; family ties
   and voluntary enslavement, 11;
   framing of residency requests on
   maternal roles, 63–64; gender
   profile of enslavement and
   residency requests, 15; as heads
   of households, 131; implications
   of voluntary enslavement, 13;
   indenture cases, 55–56; monetary
   value as slaves, 91. See also black
   women; enslaved women; single
   free black women
freedom: cases of blacks between
   freedom and slavery, 71–74;
   meaning and experience of
   "freedom" and "slavery" for free
   people of color, 9, 34, 70–71
Freeman, Daniel, 75–76
free people of color: "agency,"
   8–9; apprentice systems, 150,
   201n86; cases between freedom
   and enslavement, 71–74;
   conceptualizations of race and
   racial exploitation, 6; de facto
   slavery, 68, 69–70; Dred Scott
   decision and, 25; emotional ties
   across the slave-free divide and,
   93–97; enforced enslavement
   (see enforced enslavement);
   enslavement and expulsion laws
   in the 1850s, 35–51; enslavement
   petitions (see enslavement
   petitions); expulsion and, 47,
   48–50, 76; importance of

free people of color (*cont.*)
family and kinship to, 6, 11;
indentured servitude requests,
54, 55–56; interracial intimate
relationships and (*see* interracial
intimate relationships); meaning
and experience of "freedom"
and "slavery" for, 9, 34, 70–71;
monetary value as new voluntary
slaves, 90–92, 113–14, 192n67;
motivations for voluntary
enslavement (*see* motivations
for enslavement petitions and
voluntary enslavement); notions
of "home" and "belonging,"
6; perspectives on migration to
Liberia, 67; perspectives on the
choice of slave owners, 152;
population in the South, 22,
170n2; residency requests (*see*
residency requests); restrictive
southern legislation, 22–35;
"right" to enter enslavement, 2;
routes to freedom, 22; southern
legal system and, 4
Fuller, William H., 113–14
Furstenberg, François, 4, 6

Garnes family, 117–18
gender: differences in enslavement
petitions, 15; differences in
implications of voluntary
enslavement for, 11
Georgia: enslavement and expulsion
laws in the 1850s, 36–38;
enslavement petitions, 85–86,
113–14, 139–40; restrictive
legislation before the 1850s,
28; socioeconomic profiles of
potential slave owners, 85–86
Gillison, Fanny, 136–37
Gore, W. G., 119–20, 169n58

Gowan, Florida, 88
Gowan, George, 88
Goyens, William, 60
Graham, Benjamin, 133
Graham, Robert, 115
Grant, John Wess, 6
Gray, William, 89–90
Grayson, Thomas, 102, 103
Green, Lewis, 111
Green, Lucy, 139
Green, Mary W., 145
Gross, Ariela, 4
Grumbles, Rachel, 197n28
guardianship system, 150, 201n86
Gunnell, John James Henry, 142–43
Gunter, Nat, 106–7

Hailey, Charles, 114
Hall, Addison, 103
Hamilton, Rachel, 134
Harman, Frank, 104
Harman, Michael G., 104–5
Harpers Ferry raid, 25
Hartley, Joseph A., 117
Haslip, Eliza Ann, 145
Haslip, Jacob, 145
Hassel, Eliza, 136, 197n35
heads of households, 131
health. *See* ill health
Henderson, Littleton, 73
Higgins, Billy D., 49
Hill, Edward, 63
Hill, William P., 118, 169n58
Hinton, Sidney A., 133
Hoe, William H., 98
Hogan, Wyatt, 107, 108
Holiday, J. G., 117
Holmes, Edward, 58
Holt, Thomas C., 6
homosexuality, 192n76
Hooper, Emily, 16, 143–44, 152
Hope, Judith, 71–72

Hope, Tenar, 71, 72
Humphrey bill (NC), 48
Hunter, John, 62
Husk, Zelia and Emily, 64

ill health: as a motivation for
    voluntary enslavement, 81–82
indentured servitude, 40, 54, 55–56
"Inquisition": in Mississippi, 30–31
interracial intimate relationships:
    coercion of black women into
    voluntary enslavement and,
    155–56; enslavement petitions
    involving white women, 141–52;
    expulsion or enslavement of black
    women and, 123–33; motivation
    for enslavement petitions of
    single free black women, 123–33;
    residency and enslavement
    requests in Virginia and, 123–29;
    residency requests involving, 142;
    single free black women seeking
    enslavement to white men, 134–
    41; single women with children
    seeking enslavement by white
    men, 133–34; Virginia law on, 22.
    See also sexual exploitation

Jackson, Ann, 141
Jackson, Francis, 55
Jackson, William, 115, 119–20, 169n58
Jeffries, Emmarilla, 115–16
Jessops, Isaac, 81
Johnson, James, 120–21
Johnson, Michael P., 42
Johnson, Walter, 8
Jones, Alexander, 136
Jones, Billy, 106–7
Jones, Elizabeth, 137, 198n44
Jones, Flora, 142–43
Jones, Jehu, Jr., 70–71
Jones, Jonathan, 106

Jones, Lizzie, 130–31, 169n58
Joynes, John G., 73

Kafka, Franz, 10
Kavanaugh, Nelson, 59
Keatts, Elizabeth, 111
Keatts, James B., 111
Kennedy, J. M., 147
Kentucky: restrictive legislation in the
    1850s, 47–48
kinship: importance to free people
    of color, 6; motivation for
    enslavement petitions and voluntary
    enslavement, 2, 3, 8, 11, 74, 93–97.
    See also family; free black families
Koger, Larry, 96
Kolchin, Peter, 90
Kyger, David, 103

Lackie, John D., 82
Lamkin, John T., 69
Lamotte, Charles O., 130–31,
    169n58, 195n14
law. See southern legal system
Lebsock, Suzanne, 131
Lee, Joseph, 103–4
legal trial narratives, 4
Lemar, Alfred G., 146
Lemar, George, 146, 147
Lemar, Samuel R., 146
Lemar family, 146–48
Lewis, Susan, 117
Lewis, W. C., 141
Lewis, William, 62
Liberian colonization movement,
    66–71, 181n41
Liberian emigrants: enslavement
    petitions and voluntary
    enslavement, 96, 101, 169n58;
    free black women seeking
    enslavement to white women,
    143–44

Lindsey, James J., 81
Link, William, 3, 66
Litterall, Benjamin F., 78
Lockard, A. J., 107
Locke, John, 163n17
Locus, Abisha, 80, 184n12
Logan, Greenberry and Caroline, 59
Louisiana: enslavement and expulsion
    laws in the 1850s, 38–40;
    enslavement petitions, 1–2,
    134, 137–38; indenture cases,
    55; restrictive legislation before
    the 1850s, 28–29. See also New
    Orleans
Lundy family, 68–70
Lynch, Celia, 135, 139

Mallett, Sally, 143–44
Marsh, William, 117
Marshall, Charles, 151
Marter, Robert, 108–9
Martin, Edward D., 122
Martin, Percy Ann, 117
Maryland: enslavement and expulsion
    laws in the 1850s, 40–41;
    enslavement petitions, 150–51
Mataw, Ann, 145
Matthews, Elmira, 139–40
Matthews, Mary, 98, 99
May, Richard, 125, 126–27
McComas, William, 91
McDaniel, Morris and Elvin, 134
McGilvray, Benjamin, 194n91
McNeil, William Thomas, 162n6
McRae, D. W., 84
Meese, Elliott H., 108–9
Melton, Wilson, 114–15, 169n58
Memminger, Gustavus, 42–43
Mill, John Stuart, 163n17
Miller, James, 121
Miller, Jane, 85–86
Miller, William, 103, 121, 136

Millsaps, Jackson, 84
Mississippi: cases of blacks between
    freedom and enslavement, 74;
    enslavement petitions, 81, 83–84,
    88–89, 114–16, 133–34, 140,
    145; family formations within
    free black households, 68–70;
    "the Inquisition," 30–31; Liberian
    colonization movement, 67–70;
    request for exemption from
    expulsion, 169n58; residency
    requests, 57, 61–64; restrictive
    legislation before the 1850s,
    29–31; restrictive legislation in
    the 1850s, 48; socioeconomic
    profiles of potential slave owners,
    88–89
Missouri: attempt to expel free people
    of color from, 48; restrictive
    legislation before the 1850s, 31
"mixed race" persons, 22
Montgomery, John, 37
Moore, Edward, 42
Moore, Jane, 1–2, 137
Moore, John W., 174n60
Moore, Wesley, 114–15, 169n58
"moral" slavery, 7
Morgan, Edmund, 10
Morgan, Mary, 84
Morris, Thomas D., 162n7
Morton, Peggy Ann, 193n80
Moss, Tarleton, 36
motherhood: enslavement petitions
    of single free black women and,
    131–33
motivations for enslavement petitions
    and voluntary enslavement:
    categories of, 17–18; discussion
    of, 4–13, 155, 156; economic, 5,
    80–81; of enslaved couples, 88,
    95, 96, 97, 98–99; family ties
    (see family ties and enslavement

petitions); ill health, 81–82; interracial intimate relationships, 123–33 (*see also* interracial intimate relationships); kinship, 2, 3, 8, 11, 74, 93–97; Liberian emigrants, 101; problematic nature of "choosing" slavery, 4–5; romantic love, 96, 98–99; seeking to escape legal difficulties, 82–84; spousal relationships, 88, 95, 96, 97, 98–99; "traditional," 76, 80–84

Muir, Andrew Forest, 58–59, 162n6

"mulatto elite," 23

Murphree, James K., 107, 108

Murrow, John B., 75–76

Musselman, John W., 137

Myers, Amrita Chakrabati, 132

Napper, Lavinia, 136

Native American displacement, 48

Nat Turner rebellion, 25, 66

Naturalization Act of 1790, 25

Nelson, Joseph, 61–62

New Orleans (LA): enslavement petitions, 1–2, 77, 81–83, 89–90, 134, 137–38, 144–45; Louisiana enslavement and expulsion laws in the 1850s, 38; proslavery coverage of enslavement petitions by newspapers in, 77, 78–79; socioeconomic profiles of potential slave owners, 89–90

New Orleans Daily Picayune, 77, 78–79, 100–101, 138

newspapers. *See* southern newspapers

Nicholson, George, 69

"nominal slavery," 96

North Carolina: colonization debate in, 181n41; debate on enslavement legislation in, 48;

enslavement petitions, 80, 116–18, 133, 134, 135–36, 143–44, 169n58; indenture cases, 56

Osborne, John, 65

Outten, Jim, 73–74

Owens, Anthony, 104

Oxendine, Bryant, 37

paper certification: use of to define racial difference, 30

Parish, Peter J., 155, 170n4

Patterson, Nelson, 117

Patterson, William, 174n60

Pennington, William, 77, 183n6

Perrot, Johan, 114, 192n70

Perry, Leonidas, 135–36

Pfeltz, Mary Ann, 150

Pillow, Gideon J., 111–12

Planter's Northern Bride, The, 153–54

Pledger, Philip W., 120, 194n91

Pope, John H., 137

press. *See* southern newspapers

proslavery ideology: enslavement petitions as propaganda for, 77–80; expressed in state-based research into voluntary slavery, 162n6; framing enslavement petitions in terms of, 75; racial views, 22; rise of restrictive southern legislation and, 22–26; views of enslavement, 22, 23, 24; views of voluntary enslavement, 153–54; voluntary enslavement legislation and, 22

Purdie, Eliza, 99, 101

Purdie, Thomas, 99

Purdom, Elizabeth G., 145, 200n69

Quin, Daniel, 69

Quin, H. Murry, 69

Quin, Peter H., 69

race: black southerners'
    conceptualization of, 6; paradoxes
    in the antebellum South, 10; use
    of paper certification in defining
    racial difference, 30; views of
    proslavery advocates, 22; white
    southerners' conceptualization
    of, 6
Race and Slavery Petitions Project, 13
race-based rebellions: Denmark Vesey
    conspiracy, 15, 172–73n35,
    187n11; Nat Turner rebellion,
    25, 66; proslavery views of
    enslavement and, 24–25
Ragsdale, Milley, 102
Randolph, James D., 138–39
Randolph, Mary Ann, 138–39
Ransom, Ellen, 135–36
rape, 129. See also sexual exploitation
Reed, Henry, 80
Reese, Ann, 106
Reese, George, 106
Reese, Perry, 106, 107
residency licenses, 31
residency requests: analysis of,
    13–19, 55; authorship, 18–19;
    cases between freedom and
    enslavement, 71–74; the choice
    to "belong" and, 53–54, 57, 70,
    74; colonization and, 66–71;
    context of southern oppression
    of blacks, 7; decades of most
    requests, 17, 55, 57; differences
    between whites and blacks in the
    framing of, 54, 57–65; discussion
    of motivations for, 4–13, 56–57;
    family ties as motivations for, 57,
    58, 61, 64–65, 70, 74; framing
    in economic terms by white
    southerners, 57–58, 59–60,
    61, 62–63, 64, 74; framing in
    terms of maternal roles for black

women, 63–64; framing in terms
    of "respectability," 60–64; by
    free black families, 100; gender
    differences, 15; geographic
    distribution, 55; involving
    interracial intimate relationships,
    123–27, 142; outcomes, 16;
    parallels to enslavement petitions,
    74
"respectability": framing of residency
    requests in terms of, 60–64
Ritter, Henry, 131, 195n18
Roark, James L., 42
romantic love: interracial, 130;
    motivation for enslavement
    petitions and voluntary
    enslavement, 96, 98–99
Roots of Secession (Link), 3
Rosenberg, David, 149
Rowland, Mary, 112–13
Russell, Jesse, 115
Rutherfoord, John, 46
Rutledge, William, 86

Sanders, Maria, 151
Saville, Joseph, 136
Schafer, Judith Kelleher, 3, 78, 82,
    137
Schiller, Ben, 95
Scott, Rebecca J., 6, 9
Scott, Sally, 133
Scott, William C., 136
Settle, John J., 102
Sexton, John, 113–14, 190n45
sexual exploitation: of black women
    by white men, 22, 129, 130,
    131–32. See also interracial intimate
    relationships
Short family, 86–87, 88
Simms, Edward S., 85–86
single free black women: with
    children, seeking enslavement by

white men, 131–34; "economic"
motherhood, 132–33;
enslavement petitions involving
white southern women, 142–52;
interracial intimate relationships
and motivation for voluntary
enslavement, 123–33; seeking
enslavement to white men,
134–41
Skinner, Capt. Samuel, 140
slave owners: men and women as
potential owners, 151; perspective
of free blacks on choosing in
enslavement, 152; socioeconomic
profiles of potential owners, 76,
84–90; trickery and cajolery in
persuading free blacks to enter
voluntary enslavement, 155–56
slavery: cases of blacks between
freedom and slavery, 71–74; de
facto slavery of free people of
color, 68, 69–70; meaning and
experience of "freedom" and
"slavery" for black southerners,
9, 34, 70–71; paradoxes in the
antebellum South, 10; white
southern rationalization of, 7. See
also enslavement
slaves: speculation in, 73, 183n66
Smalls, Samuel, 113
Smith, Cato, 113
Smith, Edwin, 136, 197n38
Smith, James, 91
Smith, Nicholas, 194n91
Smith, Richard, 100
Smith, Robert, 91
South Carolina: colonization
movement, 70; enslavement and
expulsion laws in the 1850s,
41–42; enslavement petitioners,
176n83; enslavement petitions,
75–76, 93–95, 118–20, 130–31,

169n58; indenture cases, 55–56;
restrictive legislation before the
1850s, 31
southern legal system: enslavement
and expulsion laws in the 1850s,
35–51; enslavement petitions
and, 4, 18; free people of color
and, 4; legal rights abandoned
upon voluntary enslavement, 7–8;
proslavery ideology and the rise
of enslavement and expulsion
laws, 22–26; restrictive legislation
before the 1850s, 27–35; rise of
voluntary enslavement legislation,
25–26
southern newspapers: notions
of white "benevolence" in
descriptions of enslavement
petitions, 100–101; proslavery
coverage of enslavement petitions,
77, 78–79
speculators, 73, 183n66
spousal relationships: Mississippi
laws on enslaved women in,
29; motivation for enslavement
petitions and voluntary
enslavement, 88, 95, 96, 97,
98–99
Sproles, John W., 114–15, 169n58
Spruill, Shepard R., 136, 197n35
Stallin, James, 182n50
Stallin family, 69
Stephens, George, 83, 184n26
Stewart, John, 77
Stone, Amelia (Emilia), 137–38
"stranded" families, 6

Tapley, James, 115
Tennessee: colonization debate
in, 181n41; enslavement and
expulsion laws in the 1850s,
42–43, 45; enslavement petitions,

Tennessee (*cont.*)
77–78, 120–21, 140–41; residency requests, 58
Texas: enslavement and expulsion laws in the 1850s, 43–45; enslavement petitions, 80, 121–22, 134, 141, 162n6; residency requests, 58–60, 64; restrictive legislation before the 1850s, 31–33; Emily West, 179n14
Thomas, Elisha, 60
Thomas, George H., 80
Thomas, Joseph, 89, 90
Thompson, Alvin O., 162n7
Thompson, Robert, 60
Tirrell, David, 127
Todd, Gabriel, 122
Tomich, Dale, 165n23
Trail of Tears, 48
Trial, The (Kafka), 10
Trueblood, Kissiah, 131, 133, 195n18
Truman, James, 112
Tunno, Adam, 132, 196n19
Turner, Nat, 25
Tyler, John H., 91

United States Supreme Court, 25
Urquhart, A. B., 103

Vance, William H., 108, 109
Vaughan, Bolling, 65
Vesey, Denmark, 25, 172–73n35, 187n11
Virginia: cases of blacks between freedom and enslavement, 71–74; colonization debate in, 66–67, 181n41; enslavement and expulsion laws in the 1850s, 45–46; enslavement petitions, 90–92, 97–105, 136–37, 142–43, 169n58; forced enslavement in, 177n106; formalization of voluntary

enslavement, 102; interracial intimate relationships and the expulsion or enslavement of black women, 123–29; monetary value of new voluntary slaves, 90–92; residency requests, 53–54, 64–65, 100; restrictive legislation before the 1850s, 33–34; status of children of free black women, 22
voluntary enslavement: attitudes of white southerners toward, 79; "belonging" as a choice in, 8, 9, 10; depicted in novels, 153–54; differences between men and women, 13; emotional ties across the slave-free divide and, 93–97; historiographical context, 2–4; inherent contradiction in, 4–5, 10; Franz Kafka on, 10; legal rights abandoned upon entering, 7–8; monetary value of new voluntary slaves, 90–92, 113–14, 192n67; motivations for (*see* motivations for enslavement petitions and voluntary enslavement); notions of the right to movement and, 156; opponents of, 163n17; problematic nature of, 4–5; proslavery ideology and, 22, 153–54; seeking to escape legal difficulties, 82–84; socioeconomic profiles of potential slave owners, 76, 84–90; trickery and cajolery in persuading free blacks to enter, 8, 10, 87, 155–56; white southern rationalization of, 7
voluntary enslavement legislation: proslavery ideology and, 22; rise of, 25–26

Wagner, Annie E., 143
Walker, David, 25

Walker, Mary, 134
Wall, Jim, 88–89
Ward, E. W., 116
Ware, H. H., 105
Ware, Inda, 105
Waterhouse, Richard, 121–22
Watson, B. Milam, 121
Watson, Celie, 135
Watson, J. T., 135
Wayland, Nathaniel S., 91
Weatherley, Samuel, 111
Webster, William, 116
Wells, John, 78
West, Edward, 120–21
West, Emily, 179n14
Wetherspoon, Lewis, 106
Whitaker, George W., 134
White, Leah, 134
white southerners: conceptualizations
    of race, 6; framing of residency
    requests on the behalf of free
    people of color, 57–58, 59–64,
    65; interracial liaisons and, 22; as
    potential slave owners, 76, 84–90;
    proslavery ideology and the rise
    of restrictive legislation, 22–26
    (see also proslavery ideology);
    rationalization of slavery and
    voluntary enslavement, 7, 79;
    "traditional" motivations for
    enslavement petitions, 76; trickery
    and cajolery in persuading
    free blacks to enter voluntary
    enslavement, 8, 10, 87, 155–56;
    unease with enslavement petitions
    and free black initiative, 79, 83;
    views of free people of color, 22,
    23
white southern men: coercion of
    black women into voluntary
    enslavement, 155–56; sexual
    exploitation of black women, 22,
    129, 130, 131–32; single free
    black women seeking enslavement
    to, 134–41; single free black
    women with children seeking
    enslavement to, 131–34
white southern women: enslavement
    petitions involving, 141–52
Wilkinson, Henry, 148, 149
Wilkinson, Lewis, 90–91
Williams, Daniel, 89
Williams, John, 106
Williams, Thomas, 105
Williamson, John, 102
Williamson, Lewis, 103
Wilson, Henry, 81–82
Winn, Charleen, 125
Winn, Charlotte, 124–25, 127
Winn, Edward, 126
Winn, James, 126
Winn, John, 124, 125
Winn, John (the elder), 123–24, 125,
    126, 127, 128, 129
Winn, Priscilla, 124, 125
Winn, Sophia A., 125–26, 129, 142
Winn, Susanna, 124, 127
Winn family, 123–29
Witter, Elizabeth, 146, 147, 200n71
Witter, George A., 148
Witter, Henry, 146, 147, 148, 149
Witter family, 146–50
Wolf, Elias, 1, 2
Wong, Edlie L., 8
Wright, Jenetta, 135
Wright, Lucy, 72–73

Yell, Lucy, 110
Yell, Thomas F., 109–10
"Yellow Rose of Texas," 179n14

New Directions in Southern History

Series editors
Michele Gillespie, Wake Forest University
William A. Link, University of Florida

The Lost State of Franklin: America's First Secession
Kevin T. Barksdale

Bluecoats and Tar Heels: Soldiers and Civilians in Reconstruction North Carolina
Mark L. Bradley

Becoming Bourgeois: Merchant Culture in the South, 1820–1865
Frank J. Byrne

Cowboy Conservatism: Texas and the Rise of the Modern Right
Sean P. Cunningham

A Tour of Reconstruction: Travel Letters of 1875
Anna Dickinson (J. Matthew Gallman, ed.)

Raising Racists: The Socialization of White Children in the Jim Crow South
Kristina DuRocher

Lum and Abner: Rural America and the Golden Age of Radio
Randal L. Hall

Mountains on the Market: Industry, the Environment, and the South
Randal L. Hall

The New Southern University: Academic Freedom and Liberalism at UNC
Charles J. Holden

Entangled by White Supremacy: Reform in World War I–era South Carolina
Janet G. Hudson

Cultivating Race: The Expansion of Slavery in Georgia, 1750–1860
Watson W. Jennison

Remembering The Battle of the Crater: War as Murder
Kevin M. Levin

The View from the Ground: Experiences of Civil War Soldiers
edited by Aaron Sheehan-Dean

Reconstructing Appalachia: The Civil War's Aftermath
edited by Andrew L. Slap

Blood in the Hills: A History of Violence in Appalachia
edited by Bruce E. Stewart

Moonshiners and Prohibitionists: The Battle over Alcohol in Southern Appalachia
Bruce E. Stewart

Southern Farmers and Their Stories: Memory and Meaning in Oral History
Melissa Walker

Law and Society in the South: A History of North Carolina Court Cases
John W. Wertheimer

Family or Freedom: People of Color in the Antebellum South
Emily West